HOT FEMINIST

MODERN FEMINISM
WITH STYLE
WITHOUT JUDGEMENT

POLLY VERNON

HODDER

First published in Great Britain in 2015 by
Hodder & Stoughton
An Hachette UK company

First published in paperback in 2016

1

A CIP catalogue record for this title is available from the British Library

Paperback ISBN 978 1 473 61219 8
ebook ISBN 978 1 473 61220 4

Typeset in Biststream Arrus by Hewer Text UK Ltd, Edinburgh

Printed and bound by CPI Group (UK) Ltd, Croydon, CR0 4YY

Hodder & Stoughton policy is to use papers that are natural, renewable
and recyclable products and made from wood grown in sustainable
forests. The logging and manufacturing processes are expected to
conform to the environmental regulations of the country of origin.

Hodder & Stoughton Ltd
Carmelite House
50 Victoria Embankment
London EC4Y 0DZ

www.hodder.co.uk

For my Friends

Polly Vernon has been a features writer, interviewer and columnist for nineteen years. She started as a junior writer on *Minx*, a lecherous, riotous young woman's magazine, which launched in the late '90s. She was picked up as the *Guardian's* youngest ever Comments and Analysis columnist, as a result of her work on the magazine. Since then, she's written for everything from *Vogue* to the *Telegraph*, is a features writer for *The Times* and is a *Grazia* columnist.

Foreword to the Paperback Edition

Bloody hell, this book is causing some bother! There I was thinking: why hasn't someone written a book that broadens the parameters on feminism a bit? That shows feminism can be politically incorrect (cos I am), impure (as above); naughty and sexy and fun. Less angry, less judgey; more honest about how flawed and contradictory and not-necessarily-as-tough-as-we-think-we're-supposed-to-be some feminists (me again) are? Because that's what feminism is to me, yet some of the feminist voices I'm hearing aren't reflecting that, not really, and, surely someone will write all this down in a book, any minute now? Why isn't anyone writing all this down in a book? Come on someone, write down all the things I think about feminists and feminism and publish them and HANG ON! I KNOW! I'LL DO IT! And I'll call it *Hot Feminist* because those words are rarely used in conjunction, and when I Googled them, the number one hit was;

"Why aren't there any hot feminists?" which made me go: "Fuck off, matey boy! There are!"

That was my thought process on this book, which, as you can see, I did ultimately write.

Yep.

I wrote this book. A book intended to make people think, question, laugh. A book I never dreamed anyone would completely agree with – when has anyone ever completely agreed with *anything*? And how odd if we did, given how different we all are! But which, I hoped, might further open up the debate, encourage those who hadn't thought feminism was for them, because they didn't know 'the rules', or felt inferior because they hadn't read any Germaine Greer, or guilty because they sometimes quite liked it when a bloke checked out their arse, to reconsider.

And then I published it. And while I knew it was likely that *Hot Feminist* would cause some controversy – you don't call a book 'Hot Feminist' without at least slightly hoping it will cause some controversy, will make people sit up and take notice – I didn't expect a full throttle, scary, raging river of fury and bile to be unleashed upon me.

I mean: it's a book, and quite a mild-mannered one at that. It's not a crime. Or a sex scandal. Though there were times over the weeks and months following publication, when it felt as if it *was* a crime, or a sex scandal. A full throttle, scary, raging river of fury and bile was what I got. I also got a shed-load of loveliness, I should say; expressions of celebration and congratulation and relief and love. It's just that me being what I am (human), I could only really register the nastiness, the majority of which came from women, all of whom called themselves feminists – like I do.

How dare I say the things I said? asked those people, on Twitter and Facebook, in assorted blogs, and from within the pages of a couple of publications which have employed me in the past (thanks guys!). How stupid I am to write this book, to say the things I have said; how foolish, how wrong!

It was hard to get to the heart of exactly why some people were so angry with *Hot Feminist*. None of them really agreed with each other on the precise nature of my crimes against Being Right; I did get a strong sense that many of them hadn't bothered to read the book before wading in with their individual contribution to the raging rivers of fury and bile. I think some people thought I was suggesting feminists aren't hot, apart from me; when of course I'm not. Others seemed to think they already knew whatever it was that I was saying within this book, so it was pointless for me to say it at all. 'Everyone already knows it's ok to be a feminist and wear lipstick' seemed to be something of a refrain, which, sure, yeah, it *is*; but that's not actually what this book is about. It'd be a much shorter book, if it were.

Others accused me of trivialising something serious; others screamed HOW DARE I SUGGEST THAT MODERN FEMINISM IS ANGRY AND JUDGMENTAL AND EXCLUSIVE AND PO-FACED AND SHOUTY WHEN IT ISN'T. An amusing clutch of white, middle class women accused me of being too white and middle class to have an opinion that counted.

I'd love to tell you I revelled in the furore. I'd love to tell you I lapped it all up as a sign that I had hit a big fat nerve, started a conversation that needed to be had; that I embraced it as proof of the relevance of everything I say within this very book about how dangerously judgmental, narrow and stagnant feminism in particular, and debate in general, can be, how increasingly hard it is to risk an opinion or a perspective that hasn't already been ratified by nine tenths of Twitter, how we all live with FOGIW, (the Fear Of Getting It Wrong). I know some writers – broadcasters, celebs, politcios, whatever – *do* enjoy that level of aggro. They take it as proof of their currency; they stoke the fires of crossness, they shout back! Not me. I responded with quietness and sadness. I ducked off Twitter. I went to ground. Weirdest of all, I felt something I've never really felt before; or certainly not to the extent I felt it then. I felt shame.

I mean every word of this book. It is the most truthful, exposing, heartfelt thing I am capable of writing. There are ideas in here that have been brewing for decades. There are experiences that have been hidden, even from the people closest to me, for longer. When you lay all that out before the world, and some small, but very vocal aspects of the world respond by sneering, scoffing, doing the Twitter equivalent of spitting at you, and finding different ways to tell you you're bad . . . That's just . . . well. Shit. So yeah, I felt shame. Shame for risking things that were precious to me, on people who couldn't be trusted with them.

It took me a while to bounce back. A few months and a couple of Significant Incidences. Seeing a woman reading *Hot Feminist* on the tube, and laughing at it and nodding at it and just looking like she got it. Hearing from people who said they don't agree with some of my ideas, but they love that I'm demonstrating how big and broad feminism should be. The 2015 Henley Literary Festival, during which one audience member took the mic and told me she'd been raped and had an abortion, and that reading about my experiences of sexual violence and abortion in this book, made her feel braver about it. That all helped. Thank you, those women.

Hot Feminist is a demand that feminism be inclusive and including. Interested and curious about new ideas, new perspectives and possibilities. Capable of saying to someone: 'No, actually, I think you're wrong about that...' without *then* saying: 'and also stupid and ugly and bad and ridiculous and OMG we need to destroy this person who said something I don't entirely understand but feel threatened by!'

Hot Feminist asks that we be bigger and better than the raging rivers of fury and bile.

And it's also got fashion tips.

But you're about to find that out.

PART ONE

NON-JUDGEMENT DAY

Hot Feminist

Definition:

> One who cares greatly about the way she looks and greatly about the rights of women, feels that neither concern is compromised by the other – would indeed go as far as to say each reinforces the other; so don't go telling her it doesn't work like that, unless you're up for a fight.

> Are you up for a fight?

> Are you?

> Her legs are probably shaved, her lips are probably by Mac, her wardrobe is on point, her wit is never diminished. She views her own intrinsic sexiness not as an impediment to her feminist politics – but, rather, as its rocket fuel.

Example:

> She who routinely wears leather trousers to work, because she knows their overtly sexy vibe freaks out her male colleagues, rendering them vulnerable.

Introduction
Yeah, but am I a feminist REALLY?

I ain't gonna lie. I think about the way I look. Like: *a lot.*

I think about my fringe and my skin and my lipstick and the proportions and placement of my arse. I think about my coats and my jewels and the origins of my slight ambivalence towards the clothes that go on my top, versus my full-blown, all out obsession with jeans (which, my friend Isa says is a sure sign of a woman who prizes her bottom over her boobs, which would in turn make some sense of the proportion-and-placement of my arse fixation).

And regarding bottoms and boobs: I think about my body – my shape and my structure, my upper arms and my belly – and I think about my body hair (which is everywhere – or it would be, if I didn't spend a good 5 per cent of my waking life getting shot of it).

I think about accessories, which someone (possibly Gok Wan) once called 'fashion's orgasm'; and I think whoever (was it you, Gok? Anyone?) had a damn good point. (Belts and socks, though! BELTS AND SOCKS!)

I think about my eyebrows and my shoes; I think about how and why I'm aging and how much it shows and whether to lie to others about the years I've already clocked up, loitering on this planet. I think about the impact of food – and booze and sleep – on my physical appearance. I think about nail varnish and Spanx, Botox (no!) and semi-permanent root touch up product (yes!), the way a certain style of headphone can affect a mini-facelift and advancements in liquid eyeliner technologies.

I think about serums.

A lot.

What does this mean?

Nothing. Everything.

Does it make me vain, shallow, vacuous, silly?

Oh, maybe, a bit. (But aren't we all, just a little; just a touch vain, shallow, vacuous, et cetera, in some way, at some times? I do hope so!)

Does it make me human? Entirely!

Does it make me a feminist?

Well, I'll tell you what: at the very, very least – it doesn't get in the way.

I know this isn't strictly in the rules.

Classic feminism is a bit 'whoa' about all of the above. A bit 'bleurgh', and 'nah' and 'tut' and 'srsly?', about looks-oriented thinking, about the fringe and the lips and the belts and the socks (*socks*!) and the weight and the product and the strategic framing of the cleavage for ultimate impact (which I may not have mentioned up until this very moment, but which does, without question, feature in the Many Ways I Think About How I Look). Classic feminism is, broadly speaking, rather more 'throw aside the tyranny of all that crap, grow defiantly fatter and greyer and wrinklier and hairier, and run wild and fierce and free, deliciously unhampered by high heels and tight frocks and fashion trends and restrictive dietary require-ments and all that other useless, progress-denying baggage!' than me.

Classic feminism has its reasons. It takes its cue from second-wave feminism, a movement born in the 1960s, designed to take gender equality on from the hard-won business of women's votes towards more complex, nuanced debates about purpose, roles and sex. And it was *brilliant*. A heady whirl of rage and hope, light and defiance, to which I owe everything. Everything I think, do, say and feel; every experience I have of being alive and female in the twen-ty-first century, is better because of those feminists. In some cases: is just bloody *bearable*, because of them. I work, write, screw and swear because they made damn sure I could, and with impunity. To say I am grateful for that, is a bit like saying: 'It's ever so nice there's breathable oxygen on the Earth, don't you think?'

Those feminists railed against the idea that women should bother with their looks. Those feminists considered it an ultimate imposition; absolutely, intrinsically part n parcel of the whole fucking problem, because a woman who concerned herself with being pretty was a woman who aspired to please men, rather than herself. She was a woman who thought the full extent of her worth was intertwined with her capacity to physically beguile men, who believed its full potential was ultimately tested by whether she could get one to marry her; land an actual real life husband to validate her emotionally and support her financially (because she wasn't so good at doing those things on her own)!

That was the dawning of modern feminism's beef with looks.

And I get it. I really do.

More recent incarnations of feminism rage against the modern idea that girls and women must conform to a series of impossibly demanding, increasingly prevalent ideas on physical perfection before they can consider even leaving the house; the endless, non-stop objectification of the ladies, which diminishes us and disorientates us and even puts us in danger

I get that, too.

But.

But.

I think there's another way to look at it. To look at Looks – our own and those of others – to re-evaluate what they could mean to women in general, and feminism in particular.

Because I really am one big, fat,[1] raging and rampant, looks-obsessed feminist.

How did I get here?

As a somewhat self-serving full time inhabitant of a female body type, I was born keen that my basic rights to live and thrive and get paid for work, and not be raped, should equal those of anyone sharing the planet with me, regardless of whether or not they're in possession of a penis. I grew up in Devon in the seventies and eighties, in an environment you'd probably describe as provincial and the teensiest bit insular, and certainly not as a hotbed of feminist activity. It wasn't a hotbed of anything much, unless you count auto-erotic asphyxiation, which was all the rage down that way, in those days. Or so I was always told.

Still, I certainly had feminist instincts and inclinations from very early on. Big ones. I was influenced by a mother who wasn't wild about housework of any description (though I suspect that was a consequence of a fundamental lack of interest, rather than burning politicised idealism) and a father who, when he caught me watching the 1979 broadcast of the bikini section of the Miss World competition, told me to 'turn that sexist crap off', which was about

---

1 By which I mean skinny.

as much as he'd ever said to me up until that point. Or indeed, afterwards. He's a taciturn type. Bearded. Likes wood.

And by their friend Dee, who had a poster up in her sitting room which showed a fish riding a bicycle, the caption on which read:

'A woman needs a man like a fish needs a bicycle.'

'A fish doesn't need a bicycle,' I told Dee. I was all of seven.

'No,' she said. 'No, it doesn't.'

And also by Madonna; a figure who appealed to young me's burgeoning passion for pop and fashion intermingled with sexy empowerment. I dug her flouncy rah-rah skirts and her lapsed-Catholic bejewelment, and her absolute absence of apology and shame. And Margaret Thatcher; the prime minister who presided over Britain from before I knew what government was until I hit my late teens, and whose politics I opposed completely, but whose entitled ascendance to power taught me a thing or two about a woman's natural place in society.

All of that lot made me a feminist. Assuming I wasn't just born one.

I certainly had no epiphany, no revelation; I just grew up believing I was as self-evidently good as any man, and so were all the chicks I knew. Good – with an option on better. It wasn't about an intellectual position, so much as what was just *true*.

I was recently somewhat surprised to find out I

subscribe to a similar school of feminism as the great Richard Madeley – man, husband of Judy Finnegan, former star of daytime TV, dropper of gaffes and card-carrying national treasure. I was interviewing him for a newspaper, and I asked him if he was a feminist. I often ask interviewees this question; it's incredible how varied their responses are.

Anyway, this is what Madeley said:

'Of course I'm a feminist! Yes, I'm a feminist! Why wouldn't I be? Not being feminist is like being racist. It's not that it's wrong. It's that it's thick.'

At exactly the same time, running in tandem with all these fundamental and instinctive feminist beliefs, was a burgeoning fascination with how I presented myself to the world, physically. How it saw me, and the conclusions it drew about me; whether it fancied me and if it 'got' me. How I could impact and direct all that, manipulate and engage with it. Did it understand, for example, how ineffably cool my hair was? Did it appreciate that I'd chosen to tuck my T-shirt in at the back, while leaving it loose and casual at the front? Did it understand the semiotics of this logo, of that slogan, the juxtapositioning of that jacket against those pants?

And so it was that one (possibly-probably) natural born feminist launched her quest for a truly excellent look.

You find me still very much on that flex.

I know this doesn't make me a classic feminist. I know this, because I know about second wavers' rejection of 'pretty, beguiling wife material' as any kind of feminist end goal. On top of which, I've had enough people ask me – in real life, and in the letters that have winged their way to the different publications on which I've worked as a journalist for the last nineteen years, in the online comments sections of those publications; more recently in 140 Twittery characters or less, and usually in not especially flattering terms – how the hell it makes me any kind of feminist at all?

Me! With my hair and my lipstick and my et cetera, and so on! How dare a woman like me call herself a feminist?

I have thought about it. Because it seems to come up a lot. Because it bothers me. I have wondered whether everything I think and feel about my face and body and wardrobe can coexist with everything I hope and want for my gender.

'Yeah but: am I feminist *really*?' I've asked me.

The answer has always been: YEAH YOU ARE!

You are because caring about your looks has never stopped you caring about the bigger feminist picture. Because it doesn't obscure or inhibit your enduring desire that women should get a better deal than we already are; should feel more valued, more powerful, stronger and safer. Because it doesn't get in the way of you recognising how hard it is *still* to be female; how diminished many of us feel, much of the time, how out and out threatened, endangered, in fear of our bloody lives, others of us are. Because it's never shoved you in the Mean Girl camp of excluding and diminishing those women who don't care as much about the way they look; or who choose to look differently to you.

Because you just are.

What kind of feminist does this make me? The shavey leggy, fashion-fixated, wrinkle-averse, weight-conscious kind of feminist. The kind who likes hot pink and boys; oh, I like boys! I like boys so much, I think of myself as 'boy crazy'; such an old-fashioned, charming turn of phrase. I like Topshop Oxford Circus first thing in the morning when it's virtually silent, all the clothes dangle neatly in mounting sizing order, and the staff aren't going half-crazy trying to crowd control a million multinational teenage tourists; and I like to scream unbridled fury about the sky high incidence of rape. I like messing about with new hairstyles, and fighting for equal pay. I like painting my nails different colours, wondering what Kate Moss is doing RIGHT NOW and demonstrating blatant favouritism towards female job candidates whenever I'm in a position to do so because, let's face it, almost everyone else is doing that for the men.

I am the sort of feminist who has forcibly nabbed some ownership over the way she looks. Who shapes and moulds it for power over the situations in which she finds herself. Who applauds good looks – and cool looks and interesting looks and sharp looks and witty looks and fierce, brave, bold looks – in everyone else. The sort who worries we're in danger of ending up banjaxed by a double whammy of shame about

our looks, if we're not careful, Hit One coming as a consequence of the profound and enduring suspicion that we don't
look good enough according to some extraordinary societal
standard, Hit Two coming because: 'Aaargh! Why do I care
what I look like, anyway? I'm such a crap feminist!'

I am the sort of feminist who would like to put a stop to
that sort of nonsense right now.

I suppose you could call me a Stiletto Feminist. Not
literally: I am not a feminist in stilettos; I don't really 'do'
terribly high heels. I don't have the arches for them, plus
I'm totally feeling two-and-a-half inches of Cuban or
cowboy chunk on an ankle boot right now. I think it gives a
more modern silhouette. Stiletto Feminism is metaphorical.
By Stiletto Feminism, I mean feminism which sees absolutely no conflict between the certainty that to be anything
other than feminist is absurd and 'thick' – and an ongoing
interest in the way we, as women, look, the way we present
ourselves to the world.

Stiletto Feminism – more of a vibe than a description,
you see? The Stiletto thing works because it's such a complicated and potent denoter of femininity: on the one hand,
it obstructs women, stops us moving about with ease; on
the other, it lifts us up, puts us on a physical level with men,
who in turn imbue the stiletto with power: the power to
make them weak with lust. Some of them like being walked
over in them, in a sexy situation (or so I've heard).

(As a side note, did you know that during times of economic hardship, of recession and depression, trends in

women's heel heights always go upwards? As if in an act of fashionable defiance almost: teetering, design-over-practicality showiness in the face of dour, depleted distress? It's true.)

A Stiletto Feminist . . .

Is that what I am?

I tried that out a bit, asked people what they thought. My friend E said: 'Yeah! It works! Like Lipstick Lesbian and Yummy Mummy!' Then my friend Other E said: 'I'm not sure about stiletto, Pol; because the stiletto's outdated. I don't think it's right. It's a bit early 2000s, a bit *Sex and the City*, a bit clack clack and a Cosmopolitan, and we've moved on. How about The Feminist In Skinny Jeans, because skinnies *are* modern, and you always wear skinny jeans [which I do], and "skinny" is such a potent word . . .' And I was like: 'Yeah, yeah, maybe . . .' But inside I thought, no, too specific, too *skinny*.

Then I thought: Hot Feminism! As in: Hot Feminist!

'Hot like: hot yoga, and hot topic, and also "hot" as in "sexy hot", obviously,' I told my favourite, longest term editor, N. 'Hot as in "potato", and "dangerous", and "relevant" and "ouch". Hot Feminist!'

'Sounds porny,' N said.

'I think that's why I like it,' I said.

'It's why I don't,' said N.

'Don't call it Hot Feminism,' said my friend M, 'because all that will happen is loads of people on Twitter will say you're not hot, and you'll cry.'

'I won't!' I said. 'And, anyway, it's not all about *that* kind of hot.' I run through the 'potato, topic, yoga' spiel I'd given N. Then: 'Oh,' I say, 'and it's *really* not all about me.'

'*I* know,' she said, 'but other people might not.'

Which is true.

I thought about The Champagne Feminist, but concluded that was too derivative (see Socialism for further deets); on top of which, I found out Kate Moss's left boob has been used as the mould for a special champagne glass destined to service the fizz requirements of all denizens of a particularly posh metropolitan restaurant group, which muddles the matter for me. I can't work out if allowing your left boob to serve as a coupe is feminist or not. Please get back to me on this point.

And I thought about The Bad Feminist, where Bad actually denotes Good (ref Michael Jackson. Or actually: don't), but simultaneously denotes straightforward bad; but then someone else (the writer Roxane Gay) got there first.

I thought about Front Row Feminism, because I am a fashion writer, which means I've done some hard time on the front rows of the world's fashion weeks (also in the middle-to-back rows, let's be honest; with a couple of rounds in the Standing Room Only fash pleb areas, too). And then I thought Fashion Feminism might be just the ticket, because it alliterates (always a plus), and because the word 'fashion' itself is about clothes – as I am – but not *just* about clothes – and neither am I. Fashion is also about moments and movements and expressions of culture and a monitoring of the way things change and evolve and flow, and how we think and feel about that, and ourselves, and our world. That's fashion too.

Fashion Feminism. Fashion Feminist.

But then my gut intervened.

'Nah mate,' goes my gut. 'Rewind. You were right the, erm, third-or-so time. Hot Feminist.'

'Hot Feminist?' I go.

My gut: 'Hundred per cent.'

Me: 'What about it being porny?'

My gut: 'That's why I like it.'

Me: 'That's what I told N!'

My gut: 'No. That's what *I* told N.'

Me: 'I see.'

PAUSE

Me: 'What about Twitter people saying I'm not hot?'

My gut: 'Screw 'em.'

Me: 'Sure?'

My gut: 'Sure sure.'

Hot Feminist it is.

Of course, I should probably say at this juncture that I have absolutely no idea how *you* should be a feminist. None. I don't know, and I wouldn't begin to try to tell you. I wouldn't *dare* tell you, indeed, and nor should anyone else, for the basic reason that you are YOU, which makes you a very different kettle of feminist fish from ME, or indeed THEM. There are as many ways to be feminist as there are people who think of themselves as feminists – as many ways to be feminist, then, as there are women; though also, increasingly and cheeringly, men.[2]

You choose how and why you engage with feminism, you define your own personal customised brand of feminism, because it'll be informed by the life you lead and the issues you confront and the things that matter to you. You will not get it right all the time, maybe not even half of the time. Heaven knows, I don't. But you think about it, you work it out; you act in accordance with your own convictions and your own moral standards and as a consequence of your own experiences, and see what's what.

What I'm offering you here are my principles. The Basic Principles of Hot Feminism. I offer them up so that you can fillet them for anything useful, or reject them out of hand, or use them as a jumping off point, or absolutely comply with every last word, in which case, I may form a cult, if that's cool?

Hot Feminist is a manual, memoir, manifesto (man-mem-ifesto, does that work? Possibly not); it's about how I am feminist and why I am feminist, about the experiences

---

2 Take Richard Madeley; take Jay, a beautiful young boy friend, who most unexpectedly (given that he's a wanton womaniser) came out to me as a feminist the other day. I was so charmed, I slept with him. Well, I didn't. But I considered it.

and fuck ups that shaped and informed my feminism, about the stuff I care about as a feminist-cum-bird and the stuff I just don't care about, even though, according to more trad and longstanding notions of feminism, I really should. It's about celebrating and empowering, it's not about negating and criticising. It's about how brilliant the experience of being a woman can be and should be. It's about how much I like men.

Oh. And it's got fashion tips.

What I Mean when I talk about 'Hot'
(in hard stats and with cute graphics)

*

PIE CHART OF ULTIMATE
AND ENDURING HOTNESS

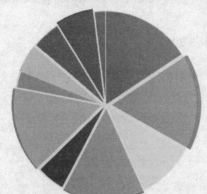

■ 16% Physical allure (Subdivision of which 5% = great hair)

■ 17% Funny

■ 10% Bright/Smart/Sharp

■ 15% Kind

■ 5% Quite silly, underneath it all

■ 15% Undefinable sexiness quotient

■ 3% Excellent use of the vernacular

■ 5% Good at breakdancing

■ 5% Curious

■ 7% Nice shoes

■ 2% Well hydrated

ULTIMATE AND ENDURING HOTNESS

as Expressed Via the Form of the Telecom Tower
(for no other reason other than it's my personal favourite
element of the London skyline)

Physical allure

Fascinated by
other people

Liked by most animals

Heightened capacity to
get slightly obsessed
by surprising
outside interests

Doesn't take self
entirely seriously

Looks good in hats

Inner chill

Can mix three different
varieties of cocktail well

Confidence levels high
enough to kiss the
exterior walls of 'arrogance'
without ever transgressing
wholly into that territory

Accepting of alternative
views of the world

Reliable in an
emergency

Hard worker

PYRAMID OF ULTIMATE AND ENDURING HOTNESS

Physical allure

In possession of one of the sexy accents[3]

Likes sport, but is never boring about it

Has a capacity for unknowable naughtiness that somehow never quite slips into the toxic arena of self-destructive hedonism

IQ/EQ in harmonious balance

Charming when drunk; in possession of excellent table manners

Outrageously passionate about at least one thing that has nothing to do with their capacity to earn money

Has bare skills

Dignified in the acts of both winning and losing

Non-whingey, when ill

[3] French, Lancastrian, Scottish

1

Feminist Fatigue, Fit Shame and FOGIW

No. No no no no no. Oh no. Nope. Sorry.[1] Just, y'know, very much: no. It was *not* supposed to go this way. Definitely not. I mean, I don't know much. I don't. I am a journalist by trade, which means my core skill set goes: 1) charming slaggy secrets from the psyches of debauched celebrities, 2) rustling up a sketchy, half-baked opinion or twelve on any given news event, and 3) Microsoft Word. But that's it. I can't even do shorthand. All I have to bring to this particular party is some decades of hard toil at the coalface of Being Alive And Also A Woman . . . Which, now I come to think about it, is qualification enough. Which is why I am confident when I say this:

---

1 Sorry deployed here very much in the passive aggressive un-sorry sense of the word. A semantic idiosyncrasy of which I disapprove wholeheartedly. Unless, apparently, it's me dishing out the not-sorry-sorries. In which case, it's fine.

Feminism's gone a bit weird.

Way: lost. Point: diverted. End game: diffused to the point of being extremely confusing. Vibe: corrupted and mutated into something joyless and dour and tail-chasey and nowhere-going. Argument: disrupted. End result: counterproductive.

Why do I think this? How do I know?

I know because of Liv. Liv works in the offices of *Grazia*, the glossy women's mag where I base activities twice a week, which is fun. *Grazia* is a pretty magazine produced in hilariously non-glam conditions. The office is strip lit and the electrics in it hum like tinnitus at moments; the *Grazia* office looks and sounds like the office in *The Office*, which confuses interested outsiders, who expect it to look as shiny and sharp as the high-rise suite inhabited by fictional magazine *Runway* in the 2007 film *The Devil Wears Prada*. It doesn't, mainly because it's real and *Runway* isn't, and it's much easier to keep fictional organisations looking amazaloid than it is the real ones, inhabited by real humans, because real humans are messy. Half-hoarder, half-tramp, most of us; with stationery fetishes which grow more intense, as ever-evolving technology reduces the need for notebooks and hole punches and pretty coloured pens. (Has anyone done any research into that, incidentally? It's quite as if all our heftily supprressed interior Luddites are rebelling against the march towards paper-free work environments, by going regularly crazy in the aisles of Paperchase. It would also explain the country's collective Moleskine fetish. The curious allure of the overpriced notepad, eh?)

On the plus side, *Grazia* smells of Tom Ford Black Orchid perfume and rice cakes, and it runs on Flat Whites and hot gossip, and there are glorious shoe mountains beneath every desk; and you only have to walk into it and inhale deeply, like, three times, to acquire a decent knowledge of the only incoming fashion trends you need bother yourself with. It's good value in that respect.

Liv sits behind me. Or I sit behind Liv, depending on your perspective. Given that this is my book, my perspective wins.

Liv would probably argue that point.

Anyway.

Liv is excellent. She is twenty-six and blonde, with emo undertones, and sexy and fun. She spends much of her life attempting to navigate the treacherous waters of romance in the age of Tinder (which she refuses to use, 'Problem is, everyone else does,' she says); I calculate she spends two-thirds of her day on Facebook and Twitter, and that she checks in with her iPhone on a twelve-minute basis. All this, and a full-time job. How the young can multitask! She is loud and proud and verbal: and an entitled, accomplished, determined force to be reckoned with. But Liv does not call herself as a feminist. Increasingly, she shuns what she sees as the feminist movement.

'I am so bored of it,' she says. 'I am sick of the word "Feminist". I am tired of people saying, This is sexist and

That is misogynistic; and you're not a feminist if you give blow jobs or wear the wrong kind of, I dunno, *tights*; and that having an opinion regarding the trajectory of Kim Kardashian's bottom is tantamount to a betrayal of your vagina. I am bored of reading the word and hearing the word. I am bored of every second blogger predicating every third post on some perceived slight on her right to wear crop tops, or her right to slate other women for wearing crop tops when they shouldn't be wearing crop tops BECAUSE CROP TOPS ARE SO SEXIST, and I am bored. Bored bored bored.'

Liv has Feminist Fatigue. Her primary experience of the modern face of feminism comes via the social networks, predominantly Twitter, where un-nuanced black-and-white opinions, and notions of goodies and baddies and heroes and villains, have gained enormous traction on account of Twitter's 140 character count not really allowing for anything more complicated. Twitter's version of feminism is, by necessity, simplistic and shouty, riled and riling, constructed for maximum impact, and deeply aggro. Twitter Feminism is more concerned with amassing Favourites and Retweets than it is moving the argument forward, or making constructive change, or making chicks feel better about themselves; the ultimate consequence of which is Liv does *not* feel better about herself. Liv feels slapped down, suppressed and excluded and overexposed: 'bored' by it. Textbook Feminist Fatigue.

Bea has Feminist Fatigue too; she's thirty-eight and a

mate of a mate. She asked me why I call myself a feminist once, over casual Christmas cocktails; and I asked her why she *didn't*. 'Because it used to be men who tried to tell me what to do,' Bea replied. 'Now it's other women, calling themselves "feminists".'

Bam. Yet another case of Feminist Fatigue, right there.

Michelle meanwhile, doesn't have Feminist Fatigue. Like Liv, Michelle is a writer; like Liv, she's twenty-six; tall and willowy and lovely, thoughtful and circumspect, almost to the point of being earnest. Unlike Liv and Bea, Michelle does call herself a feminist. 'But I worry, all the time, that I'm not feminist enough,' she says. 'I worry that I'm doing it wrong, getting it wrong. I worry that I'm constantly on the verge of saying the wrong thing, or tweeting the wrong thing or retweeting the wrong thing, or tweeting the right thing but in the wrong way, because what if everyone misunderstands and hates me? I feel like there are certain women who know what it means to be a feminist, who know the rules and the form, and there are certain women who don't, who didn't get the memo. And I should know, but I don't, and it's too late to ask and they'd laugh at me if I did.'

Michelle has FOGIW, the Fear Of Getting It Wrong, a social anxiety which is nanoseconds away from inheriting FOMO's – the Fear Of Missing Out's – crown as most prevalent communal social anxiety of our time. Where FOMO propagates the idea that everyone you know is 100 per cent having a better time than you – hanging out with a cooler crowd, wearing better clothes at better clubs, drinking better coffee and watching better TV dramas – FOGIW poleaxes us with the certainty that we're wrong, and bad, and stupid. That our instincts and ideas, thoughts and convictions, politics and passions, are without merit, or wrong-end-of-the-sticky, or simplistic, or derivative; and that we certainly can't risk sharing them or airing them, because then we'll be exposed as utter fools, or charlatans, or bad people.

Then there's my friend Fran, who is beautiful (really. The first time I met her, I just thought she *was* Keira Knightley), but ashamed about it, because she thinks it means she has less integrity: 'That I'm "playing up to the patriarchy", that I don't even know what an easy ride I get in life because people constantly do me favours and I don't even realise it because I'm so used to it, that I need to constantly check my privilege, ensure I'm not trading on my looks, prove myself beyond it.'

(I had to get her drunk before she'd say any of this BTW; the following day she denied it all on the basis that she's 'not all that'.)

Fran thinks the natural configuration of her head makes her less of a feminist. She attempts to hide her charms with big thick jumpers and never wearing any make-up, though they're luminous enough to work their way through these impediments, much to her chagrin. ('You've got Fit Shame,' I tell Fran, when she's still drunk, 'you're ashamed because you're fit.')

Then there's my friend E, who tells me she experiences

feminist guilt every time she books a bikini wax 'because I'm taking my beauty cues straight from porn!'; Hannah, who is bisexual and says she struggles whenever 'I find myself leching over images of models in magazines, because how can I be enjoying the blatant sexual objectification of my own gender?'; Other E, who curses her own lack of height because it means she has a minor crisis every time she hoicks herself up into a pair of high heels 'but if I don't, my legs look like little trotty stubs; and then I hate myself for worrying that my legs look like little trotty stubs . . .'; Jo who worries about 'ordering salad, because feminists don't eat salad, feminists eat anything they want!'; Ang, who worries 'because I just really want to be fancied'; Kelly, who says: 'I know how to sort out my car, but I'd always rather pay a man to do it, because I like watching while they do; does that make me unfeminist, or just a feminist sleaze?'

Katie, who says she's afraid to admit she doesn't want It All: 'even though I don't really know what It actually is, I just know enough to think Having It All sounds exhausting, and that I only want the nice bits please, only how can a feminist say: "I'll just take the nice bits, if that's OK?"'

Having exhausted all my flesh friends and colleagues for their feminist concerns, I turn to Twitter – in all its simplistic, shouty glory – to see how it's feeling. Has it got FOGIW, Feminist Fatigue, Fit Shame?

(I've got a lot of followers on Twitter. I mean, not Obama/ Kendall Jenner/Bieber quantities, but more than I think I deserve. I have no idea why, or really what to do with them. I do periodically think about asking them all for a small amount of money. Just to see.)

'Do you ever feel like you're failing at feminism?' I tweet.

And:

'Do you worry that some aspect of your character, or your lifestyle, or whatever, makes you less feminist?'

'Yes,' says Twitter. Yes, yes, a thousand times yes!

Anna says: Not learning to drive.

Sara says: Getting man in to replace halogen bulbs. Though I'd get a bulb-changing woman in, if I could find one.

Jude says: Using Mrs [husband surname]. Worrying about my weight.

Amelia says: Feeling safer with my husband; finding short men unappealing.

Helen says: Not going out without mascara on.

Keira says: Maintaining an interest in Kim Kardashian.[2]

Elsie says: Paying someone minimum wage to do my pedi, allowing men to carry my suitcase up stairs.

Jo says: Stopping my career to care for my daughters, thereby worrying I'm fulfilling a stereotype for them.

---

2 How that woman recurs when discussing the condition of modern feminism! Or indeed, modern anything at all . . .

Dani says: Lying by omission about being feminist when I'm on dates.

Helen says: Wanting to be fancied by my boyfriend. Changing clothes because I think he'll like them more.

Em says: Not being able to swap contacts when I get a new iPhone, asking man to do it.

Paulie says: Letting my boyfriend deal with joint finances EVEN THOUGH I EARN MOST.

Sarah says: Being good in bed. (I suspect she was joking, but still. Sex. The battle feminism's probably destined to lose.)

And on and on and bloody on.

Feminism has been engulfed in a heady swirl of anxiety and doubt and self-doubt and women talking shit about other women because their ideas of what is and isn't feminist don't match; and, in the case of Liv and Bea at least, ennui, though my suspicion is the Feminist Fatigue is the end consequence of FOGIW, the point you get to when you just can't bear risking it any more. Feminism has been derailed by doubt.

The heart of the matter is this: feminism's been hijacked by the dark forces of judginess, by our communally created fear that our every deed, word, thought, joke and Tweet is being monitored for fuck ups. Feminism is increasingly defined by a sense of what you can't do, shouldn't say.

Then again: what isn't? We've entered a spectacularly

critical, witch hunty, finger pointy episode in the history of humanity. It's all gone a bit Live And Let No One Else Do Anything At All Without Letting Them Know We're Watching Them And We Think They're Probably Doing It Wrong. A bit destroyed in an online review, booed off *Strictly*, or out of the early rounds of *The X Factor* audition process; a bit ridiculed for trying a different kind of look out on the red carpet. This slap 'em down, shout 'em down, tell 'em what a twat they've been approach – an In The Flesh version of that old phone game Whack-A-Mole – seems to be the prevailing attitude *de nos jours*, which would be awful in itself, if it weren't for the fact that it's inevitably accompanied by a sense that They are judging Us quite as hard as we're judging them. Which they are. That's how an all-encompassing culture of judginess works.

I blame the internet. I blame the internet for many things: for the hideous over-deployment of the non-word LOL (IT IS NOT A WORD); for our inability to fully move on from defunct relationships, on account of the tiresome interconnectivity of the social networks never quite allowing us to pretend our ex is dead for however long it takes us to stop wishing they were, in fact, dead; and I blame the internet for the cult of what it calls 'sharing', and I call 'showing off'.

I certainly blame it for making mutual, non-stop, 24/7 rolling judginess a reality. The internet, whose prime purpose appears to be giving us a window into each other's lives, hopes, fears and thoughts, so that we might then slag each other off because of them. The internet, which encourages us to have an opinion about absolutely everything, all the time, only it turns out that the easiest opinion to maintain is that everything everyone else has said before is absolute bollocks. Judging, criticising, trolling and diminishing: so much easier than risking our own ideas. So much handier than having to formulate an opinion, or create a perspective, or stand for something – *anything* – other than: 'Everyone else is stupid!'

We judge each other so harshly and so repeatedly, and on the grounds of our: hopes, dreams, desires, views, interior design concepts, hairstyles, approach to motherhood, choice of partner, choice of smartphone, taste in literature, taste in music; whether we're PC or Mac, how big our flat screen TV is, where we go on holiday and where we send our kids (the ones with the names people are judging on the grounds they're completely chavvy, or too horrifically middle class to be believed) to school. We judge because of class and money and profession; recycling proficiency and who got onto the hot new TV drama box set first and how much milk we take in our coffee and how unutterably shit does she look, while sunbathing on that beach, or waiting at the school gates, or on her way to yoga? OMG I can't believe she even left the house like that!

We hate-read and we troll, we sneer and we disapprove, every time the opportunity presents itself; and so inevitably, feminism has become caught up in this same toxic swirl.

Like I say, it's been hijacked by the dark forces of

judginess, redefined by a sense that there are ALL THESE THINGS you can't do, or think, or feel, or wax, or wear – for FOGIW. That long, long, ever-lengthening list of No! and OMG THAT'S SO BAD, and Oh No She Di'nt!; which we constantly compile and revise via the medium of our collective, growing anxieties, and distribute over the social networks, a rolling ticker tape of updated: Stop Right There Missy, You Just Fucked Up!, so that we've arrived at a point where it feels like every last one of us is monitoring every other last one of us for mistakes . . . Which is a terrifying, exhausting and unhelpful way to live.

What I would like to propose is an end to all that judgement. Right here. Right now. Let's call today, Non-Judgement Day. The dawning of a brave new era of accepting that not everyone feels the same way you do about stuff, but that's fine. Of objecting to the things others say (assuming you find them objectionable), without feeling duty bound to destroy the people they *are* at the same time. Especially if they're women. There's enough woman-destroying going on already, without us pitching in.

Above all, stop judging yourselves! Because you're women, which means self-judgement is a profoundly unfeminist act. As for self-judgement on the grounds that you might not be being adequately feminist? That's just bonkers.

2

No Offence

A barista apologised to me for using the word 'chick'. 'It's a contextual thing!' he said, hastily, frothing my milk. 'Huh?' I said, for I had been too busy surreptitiously eying up the lay of his abs beneath his T-shirt to focus on his chat. He is young and shaggy-hairedly cute, and he wants to be a video director one day, unless that's the other one? It might be the other one. This one might be the poet. Well. He is definitely one of my top ten baristas, a mental chart I carry around and reconfigure regularly in my head, which rates all my favourite coffee boys in accordance with their physical charm, their chat and their ability to make my Flat White just perfectly, bonus points if I don't even have to remind them what my order is. I am a terminal lech. I consider fancying people to be a feminist act.

'She calls herself "chick" – but I *think* with irony – so I was thinking of that when I said it, but then actually, as a feminist, I do really hate the word myself, so . . .'

'Do you?' I said. 'I couldn't give a monkeys. Call me

35

chick any time.' Then I took my coffee from his hand, winked at him and playfully smacked his arse.

No. I didn't, really.

In my head, I did.

But I did tell him 'chick' doesn't bother me.

Because it doesn't. As a feminist, I reserve the right to not be offended by the word 'chick'. Or by almost *everything*, mainly because being offended requires vast quantities of energy, and I have little left over, what with all the lusting after baristas I do.

Here's some other things which don't offend me, not one jot. Being called 'love' by some bloke, or 'darling', or 'lady', or 'girl'. (Although I do think that last one is pushing it on a trade description level, increasingly.) I don't *love* being called 'madam', but that's a question of vanity muddled up with an instinctive repulsion at the unique combination of snottiness and toadying the word suggests; it's got nowt to do with gender politics. I don't like being referred to as 'a female' admittedly, don't entirely enjoy being reduced to my biological function.

But I'm fine with 'babe'.

'OK, but say a male boss calls you "babe",' says Original E. 'Surely that's not OK? Surely that suggests an inappropriate level of intimacy, or a tendency to patronise, or at the very least that he doesn't take you entirely seriously?'

'I don't have any male bosses,' I say, which is true. I've tried them in the past; they didn't suit me, I got shot. All my bosses are women.

E sighs, because I'm 'so literal'.

'What if you *did* have a male boss, and he called you "babe"?' she goes on.

'It'd very much depend on my relationship with him, his intentions, the subtext of the situation, whether or not he was gay, whether or not I liked him and felt that he liked me. I've been called "babe" with affection, even respect. And I've been spoken to, by men, in ways which would technically tick every box on the 'respectful engagement with a woman' checklist, but which dripped with quiet contempt or basic dislike.'

'Yeah. Well. I still think "babe" is dicey, as a rule,' says E.

'Oh, you and your rules, E!' I say.

Other things which don't offend me: I don't mind being wolf-whistled, if I consider the wolf whistle to have been delivered with profound reverence, that the whistler whistles in the vein of one dreaming of something he'll never have. I don't much like it when they[1] direct the kind of noises at you they might also make trying to attract the attention of a recalcitrant cat (I am not a cat), and I *did* mind it that time one of them pulled up alongside me at some traffic lights, looked over, and said, quite as if he were asking the time:

'Excuse me. I was wondering. Do you take it up the arse?'

---

1 You know *them*. The Men.

I got offended the time I thought the cute guy and I were eyeing each other up in a mutual flurry of casual midday fancying, only then he accused me of looking at him 'funny' because he was black; at which point I stuttered: 'I'm not racist! I'm lecherous!' Which didn't help.

But if they're pausing briefly to express some form of admiration with whole words/a whistle: honestly? It doesn't appal me.

I do not get remotely offended if a man holds a door open for me, or offers me his seat on public transport. Does any woman, ever, actually mind that? Soft sexism,[2] I believe it's been rebranded, because it's imbued with the suggestion that women are meek, weak and weary creatures, who can neither open their own doors, nor stand up for half an hour while their tube rockets round the underground system like a demented mole. Me? I've always viewed that sort of offer as the acknowledgment that I am either too obviously hungover to remain upright, what with the remnants of last night's dry white having saturated my inner ear and screwed up my capacity to balance; or too obviously overburdened to have a hope in hell of opening my own doors. My capacity to collect baggage – canvas tote bags, Sainsbury's carriers; laptops, tablets, iPhones and Kindles I somehow failed to put away properly when the opportunity presented itself; paperback

---

2 I think they've missed a trick there, I'd have gone with Sexism Lite. Snappier, more European.

books (even though I've got the Kindle); six-packs of Coke Zero; and a spare pair of shoes in their very own draw-string pouch – is stunning. It's nothing to do with my being a woman, everything to do with me being over-ambitious and, also, freelance: when you're not tied to an office, you have to carry all office requirements around with you, like an urban nomad. As a consequence, I have oddly strong fingers, and a semi-permanent need for someone else to open doors for me.

But no, I've never met any woman who does mind the door-opening seat-offering routine, although I have met a few men who say they're far too wary of sparking a feminist meltdown to dare offer any chick (see? I use it myself) such services; reading between the lines, I think what they actually mean is: they can't be bothered and they love having that seat too much to give it away.

I do not get offended by the widespread practice of photo-shopping commercial and editorial images of beautiful women; in which the already-minimal flaws on the faces and bodies of models hired to prance and pose and show off clothes or handbags or just themselves, on the covers of magazines, are digitally eradicated. I think I'm supposed to be offended. A lot of people say they are horrifically affronted by photoshopping. Losing sleep and waging cold, cultural wars against it. There's a feeling that Photoshop is destroying women's self-confidence, landscaping our world with images of physical perfection we can't hope to live up to, not least because not even the women in the pictures look like that, not in real life.

The phenomenally influential blog Jezebel.com describes itself as offering 'Celebrity, sex, fashion for women. Without airbrushing', 'airbrushing' being a charmingly retro word for the practice of Photoshop, although knowing the speed at which technology moves, 'Photoshop' will be a charmingly retro word for Photoshop, by the time this gets printed. One of Jezebel's many schticks is to identify incidences of Photoshop in advertisements or on the printed pages of magazines which it considers especially dangerous, or remiss, or deceptive. Jezebel is in the habit of posting Before and After Photoshop images, pinpointing the varied ways in which the pics have been tinkered with; because Jezebel does not approve of Photoshop! Nor do some politicians. Periodically, I hear rumours that someone or other's thinking seriously about anti-Photoshop legislation. The Liberal Democrats are all over it – Junior Minister for Women and Equalities Jo Swinson has very much made it her Thing; in the US, an organisation called Off Our Chests launched a movement called the Self-Esteem Act, which campaigns for clarification on Photoshopped images, for stickers alerting all those who encounter Photoshopped images to the fact that they've been Photoshopped.

But I don't care about Photoshop! Not a bit! If anything, I'm offended by the idea that I'd be offended by Photoshop. First, because I know it happens, what with me not being completely bloody stupid. Anyone who ever whacked a filter on their own Instagram shot knows digital trickery happens, knows that the truth behind every photo is a lot less pretty than it first seems. Anyone who ever went to see a Spielberg film knows that! Second, because I already know models and film stars are better looking than me! Like: *loads*! Younger and firmer and fresher and thinner, with vast eyes and rosebud lips and silken, silken hair! Even without Photoshop, they'd be a lot better looking than me. Being better looking than me is their job! And I don't mind! My self-esteem is not impacted one way or the other by a passing glimpse of Gisele Bündchen's honeyed thighs, or Cara Delevingne's immaculate cheekbones, or Miranda Kerr's spectacularly perky bottom! Not a jot! And yes, I understand that the concern is for eyes and minds younger than mine; but let's give teenage girls an option on not feeling like victims, eh? Let's suppose some of them – maybe even lots of them – aren't destroyed by those images, aren't deflated or diminished. Let's certainly accept they know more than we ever will about the digital altering of media, because that's what happens when you and Facebook were born at roughly the same time.

I am not offended by the amount of women who aren't on TV panel shows, because I can't stand TV panel shows (too dull! Have you seen them? I mean – really! How could I be offended by my gender not being integrated into a format which is outdated and ruefully lacking in imagination? I am grateful, if anything); nor am I offended by crowd shots of sporting events which focus on the hot girlfriends of competing athletes. Or by, I dunno, the semiotics of twerking. Or *Game of Thrones*, HBO's blockbuster TV adaptation of George R.R. Martin's novels about a fantasy power struggle in a fantasy land which is not unlike medieval England in a lot of respects, give or take the zombies. Obsessed, yes! Totally, utterly, joyfully obsessed! But not offended. 'What about all the gratuitous nudity, what about the sky-high tit count?' asked my friend Ross (a boy feminist), anxiously. 'I know! It's excellent, isn't it?' I said. 'And also: the wolves!'

I didn't get offended that time *Cosmopolitan* magazine ran a series of sex tips for lesbians, and I didn't get offended when the *Daily Mail* featured commentary on the clothing choices of some newly appointed female Tory MPs. 'But when a newspaper does something like that, it reinforces the idea that women's first purpose will only ever be decorative,' rages E, who is losing patience with me fast; but then, she often does. 'Only if you think a woman can't simultaneously be well-dressed and potentially really good at her job,' I say. 'Only if you assume she's peaked at coordinating her skirt and her tights. I don't. I'd go as far as to say it suggests a level of base competence which hints at a wider-reaching potential for competence, one which could well include running the country, not least because they presumably knew the paps would be there that day, and correctly anticipated that.'

'But no one ever talks about what the male politicians are wearing,' she countered.

'No, and they bloody should! It's a disgrace. I don't think female politicians should care less about their physical appearance, I think the male ones should care more. Much, much more! Dudes! People can see you!' (The whole episode reminded me of the time I took a woman lawyer friend shopping in advance of her making a high-profile court appearance, one she knew would result in her being photographed on her way into the courtrooms. In a move that was definitely Hot Feminist in nature, she told me that she'd taken the time to badly advise a clueless and arrogant male colleague on what he should be wearing to undertake the equivalent walk into court, thus ensuring that he looked awful in all resulting newspaper coverage. 'It's not my fault he didn't realise the suit I told him he should totally buy and wear was a fucking revolting colour,' she said.)

I don't rage against the continued existence of the *Sun*'s Page Three. I mean, I'm surprised anyone wants to look at those daily updated, full-page shots of a 23-year-old's boobs, what with the internet flushing free, moving porn direct to everyone's smartphone. Page Three seems archaic and a bit infantile, and if I were the *Sun* I'd ditch it from a journalistic perspective, rather than a feminist one. It's been done and overdone, and bums are much more of the moment anyway. But I don't rage against it. My friend L is furious about Page Three, hugely involved with the campaign to eradicate it. She has the T-shirt, she celebrated in January 2015, when it looked like the *Sun* had dropped the feature, once and for all . . . Then she wept with frustration when it turned out it hadn't, after all. L thinks I should be furious, like her. '*WHY* aren't you offended?' L says. 'Because I'm just not,' I say. 'I can't fake offence if I don't feel it, can I?'

'But you care about the incidences of rape in this country!' L tuts, which indeed – I really do. More on this shortly. 'Rape, Page Three; it's all part of the same thing, a culture which objectifies and dehumanises women. You can't care about one, but not the other. You just can't.'

'OK, well, I think I can,' I say. 'Maybe rape and Page Three are interconnected, but I don't honestly think we'll end rape by ending Page Three. I think we'll end rape by focussing specifically on ending rape, and that Page Three will die its own tired little death in its own time.'

'So why can't we fight to end both?' asks L.

'Because it's knackering and I haven't got the energy,' I say. 'Also, I don't feel Page-Three-related offence in my gut.'

'Well, I do,' L says.

'Then fight on, my friend,' I say; which of course, she will.

Here's where the Hot Feminist stands on being offended by stuff: we keep our fury focused, pure and sincere. We do this for a couple of reasons. We do it because we know that if we fake offence about the things we don't really feel offended by – the things which kinda vaguely irritate us, or seem a bit odd or a little off, but don't make our blood boil

44

and our head hurt and our fingers itch with the sheer injust-ice of it all – but which other feminists insist we really *should* care about . . . If we fake offence in those circs, we're being dishonest, which never helped anything in the long run; and we are diluting the full impact of our rage when we need to unleash it at a later date, at a point when it *is* honest. A feminist who doesn't get offended by A, B, C or indeed D will be taken pretty bloody seriously when she kicks off about Y.

We also keep our fury focused, pure and sincere because to get angry about all the things, all the time – about every last transgression against womanhood, as perceived by all other women – is just not feasible. It'll confuse you and distract you and overwhelm you with a sense that this is an unwinnable war of epic proportions.

I would never tell another feminist which battles they should fight, what should and shouldn't offend them. If you, like L, loathe Page Three, if you view it as ground zero on a culture which continues to value youth and beauty in women over their ability to change or rule the world, then fight that recurring newspaper feature with every last breath in your body.

But I also defend my absolute right to not really be offended by a lot of things. It frees me up to care enor-mously about the things which do offend me. The things which do leave me genuinely, sincerely enraged; apoplectic, head-spinny, bile-spitting and incredibly sweary – even by my own, fundamentally foul-mouthed, standards.

Here are my top three.

Thing One is the gender pay gap. The persistent and growing discrepancy between how much more money we pay men to do a job than we pay women to do the same, or a similar, job; which, according to most recent figures, means that women are paid an average of 81p to every male pound[3], and which, at current rates, will take another sixty years to correct, by which time I shall be dead. This is annoying. I'd like to see it sorted out.

When women work full time, we earn an average of £5,000 less than our male equivalents. Unless, apparently, we work – as I do – in the field of culture, media and sport, when we earn an average of 27.5 per cent, or £10,000 a year, less. Yay, culture, media and sport! Oh, but hang on . . . It's worse if we work as health professionals, and *loads* worse if we're working part time, when we earn an average of 35 per cent less per hour. Oddly, the precise same deficit applies if you're a full time, all guns blazing female *boss*.[4] Thirty-five per cent less bucks to *that* woman than the guy running the next office along, please!

I call it the Penis Upkeep Grant. I mean, that's what it's about, right? That's why all our bosses just keep on doling

---

3 According to figures released by the Fawcett Society.
4 According to figures published in the 2014 National Management Survey, which showed that male company directors take home an average of £21,084 more than female colleagues in the 46–60 age bracket.

out more money to men than they do women? On and on, year in, year out, fixing the winning turns on the company's One Armed Bonus Bandit machine so that it pays out for the chaps, while the ladies . . . the ladies just keep on missing out. It's so they can look after their penises properly. Good penis care costs big bucks. I get hazy on the details of what penises require, that accounts for 5 whole k annually. Pants, I suppose. Trousers. Jockstraps, that could be some of it. Tape measures? Special unctions? Erm. Those devices you see advertised on email spam that offer to increase the size of your manhood? They must cost a bit. And, oh! Viagra! Of course. Talc? Men seem to like talcing their knobs. Or is it their balls, with the talc? It is, isn't it? Side note: are balls included in the Penis Upkeep Grant scheme? I expect so.

If it isn't Penis Upkeep which accounts for the big – and terrifyingly increasing, according to latest figures – shortfall in women's pay, then it's . . . what? The instinctive and unshakable belief that men are just worth more money than women? That their Y chromosome and their extra testos-terone is equivalent to Mulberry branding on a handbag: it imbues intrinsic, unarguable value? That can't be right. Can it? I mean, I know it isn't uniquely a consequence of the money women lose when – if – they take time away from their jobs to have children, because although that is a con-tributing factor in the pay gap (it shouldn't be. But it is), figures from the Office of National Statistics show that the pay gap between men and women in their (often childless) twenties has doubled since 2010; also, new stats from the US testify to the gender pay gap setting in one tiny, tiny year after employees graduate from universities.

So you see: it *must* be Penis Upkeep.

I am profoundly anti Penis Upkeep Grants, deeply and truly offended by them, on two counts. One: I like money, same as the next man; I need it, for buying stuff and doing stuff. My experience of working for or near or indeed, *above*, men, has taught me that I definitely should be paid in step with them. Rarely[5] have I ever encountered one who I thought was better than me at doing what I do. Two, I don't think the maths add up. I don't think penises *do* cost all that much; and, also, I don't think whoever's doing those particular accounts has given adequate thought to how much it costs women to keep our bodies on the road. I mean, you would be hard pushed to get change from a fifty on a decent bra, these days, and don't even talk to me about the exorbitant cost of periods!

I am contemplating launching an anti-Penis Upkeep Grant lobby. I'll coordinate demonstrations, we will march on Parliament. We shall hold banners aloft which read:

DOWN WITH
PENIS
Upkeep Grants

---

5 I say rarely, I mean never.

And our emblem will be a pug. As in P.U.G. Do you see?

I do wish the politicians would talk more about that, and less about Photoshopping on adverts. It's almost like they're trying to bedazzle us with the small stuff – the stuff which isn't all that consequential, and which, as an added bonus, they don't really have to do anything much about – to distract us from the big, sticky, tricky stuff, stuff they *could* do something about.

In the meantime, I thoroughly encourage you to discuss your pay, openly and without embarrassment, in the name of encouraging all others to discuss theirs, which will in time bring about greater transparency in pay gaps; and then to swing by your line manager's desk and ask for a meaningful pay increase, beyond anything inflation linked. You may not get it, but you should get used to asking for it. If it makes you uncomfortable (and heaven knows, women are not hardwired to ask for things), tell them I sent you. Tell them it's a feminist act.

Thing Two, is this:

The amount of women and girls who are getting raped and sexually assaulted.

All the time. All over the shop. By all sorts of people. 85,000 of us are raped on average every year in England and Wales, according to figures released in January 2013 jointly by the Ministry of Justice, the Office of National Statistics and the Home Office; over 400,000 women are sexually assaulted every year, and one in five women aged

16–59 has experienced some form of sexual violence. According to Rape Crisis, only 15 per cent of those women and girls who experience sexual violence report it to the police. Fewer still get their cases to court; far fewer get convictions.

This is so staggeringly not OK it blows my tiny lady brain, and yet it's also somehow not that shocking, is it? Because we *know* it's happening. It's either happened to us, or to someone we know, or we've just heard those figures, over and over, and become inured to them, almost bored by them. Rape is such an everyday crime, statistically speaking, it is so very boringly common, that it's become almost unremarkable. That offends me. On top of the raping itself. That pisses me off. The idea that rape is so prevalent, so damn ordinary, we've got almost rape-blind. Only really ghastly rapes capture our imaginations now. We expect something really fancy from rape, if we're to pay it any mind. Like the horrific grooming, rape and violent sexual abuse of underage girls in Rotherham and Oxfordshire; or when a gang rape gets videoed for posterity, and the film goes viral; or when a convicted rapist footballer gets released from prison, and Twitter tries to work out whether he deserves to play professionally again. We need something truly awful before we get interested.

Oddly, we seem to get jolly excited by the malicious false reporting of rape, which, according to Crown Prosecution figures, could account for less than 1 per cent of reported cases. Other studies suggest it hovers around the 4 per cent mark, in line with the figure for false reporting of any crime. But fake rape garners big headlines, incommensurate media coverage. Maybe it's because the false reporting of rape is so rare. It's the Man Bites Dog approach to news, it's only worth it when it's weird. Or maybe it's because we sort of really don't want to think rape happens as often as it does, so we cling to the faux rape cases with passion. Magnify their significance, make them look bigger than the actual problem, so that the actual problem will appear to shrink.

Only of course, it doesn't work like that. The actual problem – non-fake rape, non-fake sexual assault – is getting if anything bigger, more common. Which, on this scale, will make it more ignorable yet.

Now, I don't believe you have to experience something to be wholly fucking offended by it. I don't think you have to have been subject to rape or sexual violence to understand how shit that might be, any more than you have to be gay to know that homophobia's hideous, or non-Caucasian to think racism is, in the words of Richard Madeley (who I promise I'll stop quoting soon), 'thick'. However, as it happens, and I guess this shouldn't be all that surprising, given the stats, I *was* sexually assaulted, by a stranger, on a canal path, when I was eighteen. Mine was one of the mundane, everyday ones; one of the ones no one's that arsed about. Let's bookmark it. I'm not in the mood just yet, and it feels a little early in proceedings for such darkness. I'll come back to it.

But yeah. I am one of your one-in-five.

Well.

There was a 20 per cent chance I would be, wasn't there?

And Thing Three is the gentle and not-so-gentle and definitely persistent attempts to limit our right to access legal and safe abortion. They come in waves and mutterings, they come from across the Atlantic Ocean, in the US, where abortion is now restricted to the point of being illegal in nine different states. They come in the form of groups of British MPs sporadically campaigning to limit the powers of UK abortion providers like Marie Stopes and the British Pregnancy Advisory Service; or to reduce the cut-off point on abortions, which currently stands at twenty-four weeks; or ban abortion on the grounds of sex selection. (Anyone who says they 'only' want to reduce any of the grounds on legal abortion doesn't 'only' do anything. What they *really* want is to make abortion illegal; quibbling over questions of weekly limits is an attempt at kicking off a war of attrition.)

I've had three abortions.

Yeah, you read right. Three. I am railing against the thought that I have to explain that 'three' away, I mean, with any line other than: 'Because shit happens.' Because shit *does* happen, and because no one ever asked a man to explain the part he played in an unwanted pregnancy (or three).

Yet I feel as if I do have to explain, because I can see that three abortions seems like a lot of abortions.

So. Wearily. Here we go: I couldn't ever take the pill

(makes me sad and a bit sick) so I stopped trying; had a medium-sized fling with a man who one night (while I was too tipsy to adequately monitor the situation) claimed he'd used a condom when he hadn't (abortion one!); had a toxic relationship with a controlling and manipulative individual[6] who expressed his contempt for women in general and me in particular by refusing to wear condoms, and I was too vulnerable and enthralled to protest (abortion two!); and then just messed up with someone completely lovely, because that happens too (abortion three!). Three messy, icky, silly scenarios; but then, messy, icky, silly scenarios are often all that lies behind unwanted pregnancies.

Here's what I learned about abortions. They are *fine*. Mine were fine. Not particularly harrowing or traumatic or painful. The hardest part of my abortions by far was the fear I experienced before the first – a direct consequence of my having been convinced by a lifetime's consuming of soap opera storylines, the stern warnings of people I mistook for authority figures and the prevailing wisdom that I'd endure awful consequences from a termination, that my mental health would suffer, or there would be awful unforeseen life repercussions; that, at the very least, I'd be poleaxed by guilt and regret.

When I wasn't poleaxed by either guilt or regret, I was virtually ecstatic.

---

6 Sadly, being a feminist doesn't entirely protect you from taking up with bad lovers.

'You mustn't feel guilty. Do you feel guilty?' a friend asked me, the day after abortion one.

'Nope!' I said, because I didn't.

'Good!' She paused. 'Do you feel guilty about not feeling guilty? I've read that's quite common.'

'Um . . . nope!' I said, because I didn't.

'Right. Um . . . Guilty about not feeling guilty about not feeling guilty?' she persisted.

'Not guilty on any counts. Mostly, just glad not to feel sick all the time,' I said.

I accept, of course, that everyone's experience of abortion is different. I know some people suffer horribly. But I also feel that this perspective – the regret-laden, guilt-addled, consequence-engendering, depression-activating perspective – on abortion is already well represented. It's out there, isn't it? Widespread and pervasive enough to fill me with what proved to be unnecessary anxiety in the build-up to mine. Which is why I need to make it clear that mine did not hurt, physically or emotionally, that I have not one shred of regret, and that this is definitely an option on how to feel after having an abortion.

I also want to make it clear that it must always and for-ever be up to the owner-operator of the womb in question to decide whether or not a pregnancy is allowed to proceed. There are people who believe otherwise. There are people who believe that life begins at conception, and who equate abortion with murder. They call themselves Pro-Lifers – though other people call them Anti-Choicers and *I* call them Ovary-Botherers; which is not terribly grown up of me, but I can get puerile when riled. They are driven by passion and rage equivalent to mine, which I should respect; except that I can't, because I simply do not believe that my internal organs – and their contents – are anyone's business but mine.

So there you are. Three of the things that really, truly offend me, in no particular order. Pay, rape, abortion rights: three of the things I shout about and keep informed on and watch and worry about. It's specialised offence, if you like. It stops me getting overwhelmed with ill-directed rage; it also stops me sweating the small stuff, the stuff that could otherwise clog up my feminist fury ducts, overload and confuse me.

Some things simply are much more of an affront to women's struggle for equality than others, and it does not behove us to get cross about all of it. So female genital mutilation is a much more important and pressing feminist issue than 'man-slamming', the recently identified but in-no-way-new phenomenon of men bashing their way impatiently forward through crowded streets. It is only seemly that we minimise the offence we express over man-slamming in the interest of saving it up for the FGM.

Of course, it may well be that the smaller things and the bigger things are interconnected, that the things that don't offend me feed into the things that *do*; but there will always be feminists whose offence focus differs to mine (see L and Page Three, above), catching the offence balls I'm choosing to drop. And I still argue that the really effective way to deal with the shit that drives you crazy is to deal with the shit that drives you crazy, while not getting too stressed about the shit that doesn't – but might be related.

It makes our outrage more convincing, gives it more momentum, means we don't spend most of our waking life in the unenviable position of feeling cross all the time.

Save your offence for the times you really feel it.

PART TWO

THE FASHIONABLE FEMINIST

3

Wear the Good Clothes

Everyone cares about the way they look. Everyone. Male and female and young and old, clever and not-so, shallow and deep. The ones who say they don't care are probably lying. The ones who try to *look* like they don't care are *really* lying, because they care enough to make it look like they don't care at all; a double whammy of deceit, self-deceit and effort. Technically, they care more than those of us who happily admit that we do care, that: oh! We care very much indeed! The only people who truly don't care, who've lost even the faintest sense of what their physical appearance means and why tending to it matters, are the ones mired in such emotional or physical distress that even this really quite basic impulse has fallen off their radar. It's one of the last things to go.

As for absolutely everyone else: from the very moment you brush your teeth and your hair, and go to even minimal lengths to ensure that today's jeans are not too obviously stained with the remnants of yesterday's latte – congratulations, my friend, you are in the game!

And good for you. There is absolutely nothing wrong with caring about the way you look. We are human beings and there are really quite a lot of us; 90 per cent[1] of the interaction we enjoy with one another will amount to nothing more than the fleeting glimpses, the sketchy and speedy impressions we acquire as we zip past each other on the street. This means that most of what we tell most of the world about ourselves will be reported via the medium of our physical appearance. Our hair, our facial expression . . . and our clothes. Our clothes, which chatter away constantly on our behalf, expressing and exhorting and explaining and asserting; mitigating, demanding, defending and dramatising.

Like with that woman over there, who wears hard, bright rings on every finger of both hands, because she thinks of them as sexy armour, and sexy armour is precisely what she requires today, for reasons you may speculate over briefly, before moving on.

The guy who is risking the pink tailored shorts *finally*, because he woke up and thought: fuck it! I just really like them! And why not?

The girl with the long hair and the princess demeanour who likes to play it off against some fiercesome androgyny in the form of her extensive blazer collection. The other girl with the long hair and the princess demeanour who likes to edge it up with a biker jacket and tattoos. The guy with the

---

1 A blatant guesstimate. Go with it.

socks, the guy with the sunglasses, the guy with the hat, the guy with the mint green hoodie ... The woman with the vintage print sundress, the Nike swoosh running vest so intriguingly juxtaposed against that heavy costume jewellery, the heels, the flats, the trainers, those boots! (Did you *see* those boots?)

We're all at it, all the time, tipping each other off, telling our stories with our T-shirts and our piercings, our hairdos and our hosiery. Communicating our hopes and our aspirations, our fantasy notions of ourselves along with some dollops of truth about our backstory and our struggles and any grief/jollity/wild abandon we anticipate encountering before the end of the day and our grateful ceremonial switchover into no bra, trackie bottoms, stretched out jersey shirt and face cream. It's one of the best things about us, how eager we are to give a good account of ourselves to all those people we'll never speak to, never even meet.

And also, there's this: every time we get dressed we play a part in dictating the environment of everyone else. We define their landscape, their view. We are moving architecture; flouncing, swishing, strutting, shambling, running and breathing wallpaper. We're in this together: we should literally show each other a good time with our outfits. To care about what you look like, to try and direct how others perceive you, to try and influence what they see for the best – or the most surprising, or the most dramatic, or the coolest – isn't stupid. It isn't superficial or intellectually suspect or morally questionable. It's just human.

Which is why I've never seen one iota of conflict between being a feminist and caring desperately about clothes.

I do know that this isn't a common view. Fashion and feminism have a chequered history; feminist academics aren't keen, by and large. The mighty, magnificent Germaine Greer isn't. In her 1991 book *The Change*, she writes: 'if a woman never lets herself go, how will she ever know how far she might have got? If she never takes off her high-heeled shoes, how will she ever know how far she could walk or how fast she could run?'

Mary Wollstonecraft, the eighteenth-century writer, philosopher and women's rights advocate, said: 'An air of fashion, which is but a badge of slavery, and proves that the soul has not a strong individual character.' Joanne Finkelstein, author of 1991's *The Fashioned Self*, an examination of the way our obsession with physical appearance has impacted our identity, made these points: 'Fashion has been seen as a device for confining women to an inferior social order, largely because it demands an unequal expenditure of time and money by women on activities which do not attract the professional attention and efforts of men. Fashion works to intensify self-absorption and thereby reduce the social, cultural and intellectual horizons of women.' Also, my friend Josi told me her mother got spat at while attending a feminist rally in the mid-seventies, by another female protester, 'because she was wearing a skirt'.

On top of which, almost every time I've written any kind of fashion article – interviewed a designer, expressed any sort of interest in a certain catwalk show, offered a check point system of guidance for anyone interested in indulging the formerly hot trend in Ugg boots or the initially painful transition from bootcut to skinny jeans or lookie-likie high street variations on Marc Jacobs' sell out army jacket of the summer of 2002 – for any kind of newspaper – I have invariably attracted reader comment of the: 'Oh do fuck off, you stupid woman; do you not realise wars are being waged and famine is raging in this world?'

And I get this. I hear it. It all makes sense . . . *if*. If you assume women dress to impress and ensnare and arouse and beguile men. To catch a husband, and then keep him interested. If you subscribe to the idea that fashion serves a singular purpose, and it is to prettify the ladies, so that chaps have something lovely on which they might rest their eyes while they take brief pauses from the business of running the world. *If* you assume that women have brains too small to simultaneously entertain an interest in fashion and world politics, and/or their career progression, and/or the horror of rape in war, and/or the issue of quotas for female CEOs on FTSE 100 boards . . . And it makes sense if you deny clothes power: the power to make the world sit up and notice you and offer you respect because you've nailed an outfit, and by extension, you can probably do other things rather well.

But what if you don't make these assumptions? What if you don't subscribe to this view? What if you, for example, question the basic notion that women dress to attract men?

What if you know for a fact that it's infinitely more complex than that: that women dress for a million different reasons and to a million different ends?

I'm a woman, and here's why I dress the way I dress:

Sometimes, I do it not to impress men, but to terrify them. To confuse and challenge and alarm and destabilise them. And sometimes, I *do* do it to impress men – it's just that the specific man I'm seeking to impress is gay with an aesthetic so evolved I gasp every time he enters the room; I know his entry level requirements on a well-constructed outfit are considerably higher than those maintained by your average heterosexual male (whose base requirements are, indeed, often just pretty base) making him a much tougher crowd, meaning his approval is particularly gratifying when – if! – secured. Sometimes I dress because I've awoken and been overwhelmed by the certainty that today's the day I'll bump into an ex, and though I am, without question, entirely over it, I still need him to experience a bittersweet pang of regret over the woman he's destined to spend eternity without. And sometimes I dress because I've awoken and been overwhelmed by the certainty that today is the day my path will collide with that of a professional nemesis, and I need her to fall to her knees and quake in the face of my superior fashion vibe.

Sometimes I dress because I want to fit in, or stand out, or dominate, or intimidate, or amuse, or surprise, or subvert. Because I want to rule over a meeting, or perk up a funeral congregation, or own a reunion, or spark some tension at – I dunno – M&S, a corporate box at the O2, on a tube carriage. Sometimes I dress to compete with other women – but rarely, if ever, will I be competing with them for the attention of men. Sometimes I dress in a way that I know men won't get, won't appreciate, won't understand, won't enjoy . . . but women will, and that's the point, that dual purpose conversation: chicks getting it, men not. And sometimes, I *do* dress to seduce. To all out, no excuses, no two ways about it, Pull.

'Sometimes, I dress to impress my nieces,' says Other E. 'Especially the three-year-old. I know she only likes me in a skirt.'

'I dress for my shrink,' says Original E, 'because I want her to like me. We're working on that, though.'

How much attention do you pay to the way other women dress? I ask them both. We are Sunday morning brunching.

'Loads!' they say.

'I check women out constantly for fashion,' says Original E, 'more than I check out men for sexy reasons, honestly. What works, what'd work on me; how they're dealing with the rain, the snow; assorted new trends, blah blah . . .'

Do you compete with other women in a fashion sense?

'Oh fuck, yeah!' says Other E. 'Not because I want them to feel shit. Because I want to make sure I keep upping my game.'

Have you ever felt crap about your own clothes, in comparison to the clothes of another woman, I ask.

'Of course,' says Original E.

'Inevitable, innit,' says Other E. 'But I've also felt really kinda, I dunno . . . *supported* by another woman dressing well.'

'Eh?' says Original.

'It was you, as it happens,' says Other to Original.

'Eh?' says Original, again.

'OK, it was a couple of years ago, when I was having a shit time at work. You remember. Hated my boss, hated his boss, felt like there might be a little bit of constructive dismissal on the cards for me. Dreaded going in, et cetera. So I had to go to a colleague's leaving do, and I really didn't want to. It felt like going into a vipers' nest, when the vipers were drinking cheap vodka. And you said you'd come along for backup, even though you didn't know anyone, and I was so grateful. You turned up looking outrageously hot – new boots, new hair, obscenely short skirt – and everyone was impressed and totally intimidated by you, and we hung out and looked impervious and ignored the bad people, and I felt strong because I was hanging out with a friend who looked amazing.'

'Oh yeah!' goes Original. 'I remember. That was cool. Awww.'

'Actual power dressing,' says Other E.

These are just a selection of reasons why Hot Feminists get dressed, and why their fashion obsession does not derail their political agenda.

Oh, but wait! There's one other reason Hot Feminists get dressed, and it's the most important one, the one which stays the same regardless of all other circumstances and intentions, the one which scotches all other rationale, the one which means we'll take pains over the getting-dressed process for the rest of our lives. It's this.

Because we *like* doing it.

Because we are good at it.

Because there's an art to it and an end to it, in itself. Because it's inherently creative, because we all learn a little bit more every time we do it. Because we make mistakes and correct the mistakes and get better still at it; and that's as rewarding as the acquiring of and improving on any knowledge or talent or craft, no different to learning how to play the piano or cook great meals or paint pictures or French. Getting dressed is a life skill.

4

A Fashion Education

How did I come to think and feel about clothes as I do? How did I wind up conflating the concept of a 'fashion statement' with the concept of a 'feminist statement'?

Ah, you know: trial, error, time and a few awful aesthetic incidences.

My first conscious attempt at a fashion moment struck when I was eleven, and a founder member of a four-piece electro punk girl band called Pink Ice. Oh shush. It was the eighties, I was at primary school; it seemed like an excellent idea at the time.

We were appalling, I'm pretty sure. I can't sing now – not a note in tune, tone deaf – presumably I wasn't any better then. If Justine B, Sally A and Heather M – my bandmates – were any more talented, it never showed. Tellingly, Pink Ice weren't invited to perform at any end of term recitals or Christmas talent shows or local gatherings. More tellingly – in a town too small and too far from London to be overwhelmed by a pool of untapped talent, or even a puddle of untapped talent, or even a damp patch of untapped talent – no one tried to tap us.

This didn't concern us. Under the influence of the 1980s classic TV series *Fame* (an adaptation of a book based on the experiences of students at New York's School for Performing Arts, all of whom were given to expertly choreographed yet entirely spontaneous musical turns performed on the table tops of the college canteen of a casual lunchtime; do track it down and watch it if you haven't already, it's spectacular), we put on our own shows in the playground at playtime; running through our extensive repertoire of two songs for anyone who showed any interest, or was even just walking past, en route to the water fountain.

I was Pink Ice's lyricist, the Gary Barlow of our situation; my finest work came in the form of a sort of introductory theme song, the chorus of which ran:

> *Pink Ice, Pink Ice,*
> *Pink Ice is so nice*
> *Aruba*
> *Aruba*
> *A cha cha cha*

I'm so glad I can remember that, so very vividly.

The other song was a ballad.

Oh, but it's all very well having a band and two whole songs and two separate, tightly synchronised dance routines (which we did. Of course we did). No band is truly a band until it has formulated an associated fashion statement, right? Morrissey had his cardigans and his gladioli, and Adam Ant had his cheekbones and his antique military garb and Bucks Fizz had their removable skirts.

Pink Ice needed a Look.

A combination of very limited funds and a timely screening of a seminal ep of *Top Of The Pops* – featuring a number one performance by the not dissimilar girl group Toto Coelo, whose one-hit-wonder 'I Eat Cannibals' was doing swift business in HMVs across the UK at that juncture – led us to decide that belted bin liners were the way forward for us. That's what Toto Coelo (a sort of British precursor to the Pussycat Dolls for the uninitiated; who really needn't become initiated, although I have just discovered during intensive Wikipedia-ing of the group that one of its members – Ros Holness – was the daughter of *Blockbusters* presenter Bob Holness, a fact I'm enjoying hugely) did, you see.

Were provocatively ripped, strategically Sellotaped, tightly belted bin liners, and absolutely nothing else, appropriate attire for a bunch of skinny, Devon-accented eleven-year-olds in a wannabe bitch band? Probably not, but no one stopped us. Or maybe they just didn't notice. We were subtle-ish – we left home in our school clothes (the quasi-formal attire which wasn't yet an actual uniform; we didn't get those till secondary school), and changed into the bin liners at the beginning of each break and lunchtime, and back out of them before returning to class. So we persevered with the Look (not sure who among us acquired the bin liners in the first instance, my money's on Justine B; she was in the unique position of being both organised and marginally more advanced developmentally than the rest of us; also her mother was well-stocked domestically, as I recall, the most likely of all our mothers to have bin liners at all in the first instance, and enough of them to not notice or mind if a few of them went AWOL) and we wore it whenever we could for an entire term, up until the group combusted following an inevitable fandango over creative differences.

This, then, was my first conscious brush with the transforming, liberating, expressive, provocative, inventive and prematurely slaggy forces of fashion.

And it felt sticky.

Tribal.

Rather more grown up than I was.

It felt promising.

I wasn't an especially happy kid. I was anxious and awkward and I felt perennially Other, because ... oh, who knows why? I wasn't born in small town Devon, I arrived there from Brighton as a toddler; maybe that was all it took to convince me I wasn't entirely in the right place. To make me feel as if I just didn't really belong.

I very much wanted to belong.

Clothes are, hugely, about belonging. About allying

yourself very obviously and blatantly with a group, by acquiring the group's unofficial uniform. Clothes are about being emo because you aren't sportswear, or wearing bin liners because you can't afford or don't know or don't understand the major fashion trends of the moment, but you hope to look like you're trying. Pink Ice wasn't an In Crowd by any stretch of the imagination – we were mid-to-low ranking in the prevailing popularity hierarchy, at best – but it was still A Crowd. A crowd to which I belonged, more than partly because I was dressed for belonging.

Like I said, I very much wanted to belong.

Things – fashion things – kicked and spluttered into being from that point onwards. Now, as a sometime style writer, I find myself moving among a professional caste inhabited by women who dedicated their youth to educating themselves in fashion. Women who started collecting back issues of *Vogue* aged twelve, who'd play dress up in their grand-mothers' furs and mothballed couture and help their mothers get ready for nights out at Annabel's or Tramp, dreaming of a time they, too, might wear Diane von Furstenberg wrap dresses and diamonds and go to night-clubs. They knew that Boy George was a Blitz Kid, a leading light in the New Romantic Covent Garden-based fashion and club scene of the late seventies and early eighties. They knew that Jean Paul Gaultier designed Madonna's Blond Ambition tour bustier in 1990; they knew that Marc Jacobs put grunge on the runway in '92.

Me: I had no idea. No interest in or awareness of the existence of *Vogue* (*Smash Hits*: now you're talking!), no grandmother with furs or vintage couture stuffed all higgledy-piggledy in a forgotten closet in the west wing of the house, and a mother who had never heard of Tramp or DvF, and didn't care to either.

I blundered my way forward into early teenage, sporadically guided by bossier friends with bigger ambitions inherited from older siblings. So it was that at thirteen I ended up pretending that my mate Tracy N and I had dressed as Madonna in the 'Like A Virgin' video (tulle frothy skirts over cycling-short-length leggings, top cropped to the midriff, fingerless lace gloves, et cetera) because we were taking part in an annual local Town Fair fancy dress parade. In fact we were trialling a real life style statement, one we'd stick with long after the fair had passed on, and despite the fact that many of our contemporaries pointed and laughed openly at us. At fifteen, I went white-stiletto and neon-knit casual, a déclassé look widely condemned as 'Sharon-ish', cheap and tarty and obvious, named after a scathing stereotype of a downmarket girl. But I liked it, for the same reason I liked the bin liner period; because it signified belonging. I mixed with other Sharons; we hung about aimlessly yet cheerily on bus stop benches, not really smoking and not really drinking, but looking like we could if we wanted to; revelling somewhat in our trashy reputations. If Sharons weren't considered classy, we were considered sexy and hard. I wasn't either, not really; though

73

– one artfully bored bus stop bench day – I did allow a Sharon (who really was called Sharon) to pierce my left earlobe for a second time, using a silver stud she'd previously disinfected in the flame of a lighter, just for something to do. That was a *bit* hard, no?

The major downer to my Sharon stretch, as I recall, was that Lycra technology had yet to reach Devon, and therefore the leggings I wore constantly were in the habit of bagging out at the knee if you sat down in them for more than a few minutes at a time. This meant I spent a great deal of my fifteenth year standing up.

At sixteen, I attempted to carry Sharon style forward into a new life at a self-consciously trendy sixth form college, but found it an untenable aesthetic position to maintain in the face of mass mid-teenie pretensions towards bohemianism and angst and terrible poetry realised in a palate of sludge green and shit brown. So I cashed Sharon in for a new kind of belonging: one which incorporated the *jolie laide* fake-vintage posturing of the late eighties indie kid. This involved such a dramatic, non-gradual and knowing aesthetic transformation that I realised for the first time what I was doing with my clothes had as much to do with 'fitting in' as it did 'belonging', with rejecting the crowd I'd previously allied myself with – the Sharons – as it did expressing affiliation with the new lot, the Indies; and that this could be considered something of a compromise, never mind somewhat disloyal.

I did it anyway. Not least because the boy I suddenly

found myself unrequitedly adoring – a beanpole tall, bru-
nette student union activist with loooooong lashes, who
smelled of tea tree oil (for the zits), and who faked a
Manchester accent (a tribute to Morrissey) – was doing it
too.

Like all decent young person's fashion statements with
traction, Late Eighties Indie Kid worked because it was
really cheap: second-hand granddad knits, crap jeans and/or
woollen tights under moth-eaten miniskirts were your basic
components. Pull the overlong sleeves of your woolly cardi
far down over your wrists and grip them with your fingers,
in a practised and utterly insincere gesture of self-conscious
unease, dance alone and in small circles on the outskirts of
the dance floor at the one club in town which plays The
Smiths, with your head bowed so your bowl cut fringe
covers your face (quite as if you can't bear to catch the eye
of anyone, only in fact you're hoping, very hard, that *everyone's* watching you), and you're basically there. Late Eighties
Indie Kid's biggest financial outlay was for the Doc Martens.
I can't remember how or where I acquired mine. I was
working Saturday jobs by this point, mainly serving as an
ineffectual waitress in a coffee shop in the Harlequins
arcade in Exeter's city centre – so presumably, I earned the
money. I do remember that, in keeping with micro-trends,
my DMs were shoes, not the classic boot, and that they
were matte black in finish. I also remember quietly congratu-
lating myself on the fact that they allowed me to wear my
moth-eaten miniskirt particularly short, their dowdy heft

counterbalancing the large expanse of thigh I'd routinely display.

Aged eighteen, I left home to study French at university, blundering unawares into the belly of an academic institution which was nothing if not incredibly cool. Oxford and Cambridge might be for the clever kids, but *my* one, Sussex – red-brick, park-encompassed, totally chillax re the amount of time anyone was supposed to spend studying – was for the cool ones.

It didn't advertise its coolness – preferring, presumably, to be regarded first and foremost as some kind of seat of learning. But cool was undoubtedly its central MO. It was – and I suspect, remains – the UK's premier hipster university.

My fashion horizons were expanded exponentially by it and a student body which was almost uniquely London in origin. They washed down from the gleaming metropolis towards the sea, pitching up in Hipster Uni almost as if by accident, a bunch of swishy urbanites who knew much, much more about life and clothes than I did (or at least, pretended to with such conviction that I believed it). They went to clubs and wore Nike Air Max trainers rather than DM shoes, because they'd ditched Late Eighties Indie Kid for the earliest incarnation of 1990s Dance Kid, like, *ages* ago. The boys had grown their hair into long bobs which brushed their shoulders becomingly (getting a boyfriend with a bob became my prime objective on first landing at Hipster Uni), the girls' hair was longer yet, and divided into a hippyish centre parting. Fresher term started in October, and that cool London crowd talked wistfully about how they'd whiled away the just-departed summer of '89, which they referred to as The Second Summer of Love.

Others inhabited a fashion zone I now recognise as YHC: Young, Hot and Chelsea; they were cool in the Sloaney sense, moneyed in the traditional sense. That lot talked of the abject desirability of a man called 'Joseph'. It took me a few months of blagging to glean that Joseph was not a man, but a brand (well, he *was* a man too; a man *with* a brand), an expensive, unremittingly French celebration of minimalist chic, where trousers (black and tailored) cost over a hundred pounds a pop (the very idea!), and the cashmere was more than my term's rent. 'I'm always surprised that people from the provinces know how to get to Joseph,' remarked one of my newly acquired sophisticated metropolitan cohorts, 'but they always do!' I nodded sagely, half terrified she'd find out that I was a) from the provinces myself, and yet b) had no idea how to get to a Joseph; half flattered she'd mistaken me for one of her lot.

I assimilated these various style influences just as quickly and as furiously as time and my significant financial restrictions would allow. I borrowed richer friends' Joseph and I bought second-hand Levis 501 jeans, knowing (suddenly!) that if I belted them in, high around my waist, so that the bottom and thighs ballooned out before tapering into a slimmer knee- and calf-line, I was achieving absolutely the right leg silhouette.

Then I got a boyfriend who not only had a bob, he had a place on the sculpture course at the nearest art college, an academic environment which was, if anything, hipper than the Hipster Uni itself. Bob (not his real name) loved clothes; he loved dressing himself and he loved dressing me, we went shopping in second-hand stores and Sunday markets, and what started as an attempt to maintain his interest by pleasing him with my wardrobe, ended up with me understanding – for the first time in my life – exactly how I wanted to look at any given moment – and then, miracle of miracles: *looking* like that!

This involved: fake fur coats and Adidas shell toe trainers, vibes culled from the artwork of De La Soul album covers and also the Stone Roses. I layered men's blazers over denim jackets, I wore false eyelashes and Marcel heated-rollered my hair. When the horrific bleached, baggy, mega-flared Joe Bloggs jean trend of '92 hit, I knew enough, and was confident enough, to refuse it as a dud, which – in retrospect – is definitely was. By the time Bob and I split up (two good, happy, sexy years after we met), I was better dressed than he was.

And after university, I spent a year and a half working six nights a week in a cocktail bar in Covent Garden – a flashy, trashy, neon lit, B-list celebrity luring joint called Rumours – wearing a catsuit and a Wonderbra, because the punters loved it.

This episode, it's fair to say, was not a great example of

the empowering potential of fashion.

I thought I loved it at the time; prancing around in a scoop-necked knee-cropped bodysuit which just about encased the absurd proportions faked up by the Wonderbra. It wasn't just me, you understand: every other female staff member had a Wonderbra too (Rumours was also known as the Wonderbar, for precisely this reason), along with every other young or youngish woman in the country. It seems like such a bonkers trend in retrospect, the comedic, preposterous overemphasising of our tits; the Eva Herzigová Hello Boys campaign, the billboard version of which was supposed to have so distracted men they crashed their cars, although they probably didn't. It was sold as empowering, but it wasn't, really; inviting one part of your anatomy to dominate everything else isn't power, and nor is it aesthetically pleasing, on top of which, that bra was *not* a comfortable wear. It dug in everywhere – at the back, around the cups – and the shoulder straps pressed deep ridges into your flesh, because how else would they maintain the tension necessary to keep those mighty cups aloft?

But I did wear it. We all did.

Men – the bankers and footballers and soap stars and orchestras of the Andrew Lloyd Webber musicals which played out in the theatres around us, all of whom frequented Rumours – used to jibber and giggle and blush when they saw me (or rather, my bra), and tip me heartily. I was broke, in debt from university, scraping by, with no real idea how I'd progress professionally, or financially, or anyway-at-all-really. I needed dosh. And there I was, doubling my earnings by virtue of my underwear.

Around me and my daftly enhanced knockers, the early stages of Ladette consciousness stirred. Ladette culture, you'll recall – though perhaps not if you're disgustingly young – encouraged young women to be brazen and drunken and sweary and sexually predatory, to not brush their hair or consider the consequences of their actions. It encouraged an abandonment of traditional ideas of femininity; and in some ways there really was empowerment to be had there.

My friends and I were reconfiguring the terms according to which we had sex: sleeping with men we kind of thought were OK, because we'd somehow ended up back at theirs, and it was a case of have sex or pay for a cab, and we were broke; sleeping with men we thought were sexy but thick; sleeping with not quite the men we'd intended to sleep with, because they'd somehow got mixed up in the minicab queue; sleeping with men who told us they were going for cigs at five in the morning, but who then never came back; sleeping with a man and then discovering, in the cold light of day, 'that he had a *really* substantial collection of cowboy boots, so I asked if there were any possibility of rescinding the shag' (Laura, a Rumours compatriot, did this, concluding: 'fanny is a harsh mistress, Polly'); . . . and never feeling bad about it, never feeling anything other than: 'this will make a *hilarious* story for the flatmates!' about it. The kind of thing you can't get away with any more, in case someone, somewhere gets all sanctimonious about it on Facebook; but which truly did feel liberating at that time.

The Wonderbra was an early icon of the Ladette movement, but it wasn't its finest, or its most fun, contribution. The Ladette rationale on the Wonderbra ran: there's power in turning men into lustful slush by confronting them with their most adolescent cartoonish fantasy of what tits look like; Ladettes wielded their tits like weapons or trophies or both.

Only I rather think the Wonderbra misfired.

I loved my Rumours colleagues, half of whom were drifting recent graduates of the Hipster University, the other half of whom were young Serbs and Croatians, on the run from the first war in the Balkans. We called them the Yugos – because they were still, at this point, Yugoslavians, none of whom seemed particularly attached to the distinct racial identities which were tearing their home country apart. They taught us how to swear in Serbo-Croat; we taught them cockney rhyming slang. They were all in the UK on tenuous, overstretched student visas; one of our favourite gags was to tell Jovan, or Stasha, or Alex, or Voya that they were wanted on the phone.

'Who is it?'

'Home Office.'

Periodically, one of them would get married for green card purposes. All my early experiences of weddings – the ritual and pomp and dress up and discos – were green card-driven.

The Yugo girls did not wear Wonderbras.

The bouncers were sweet to us, and management was reasonable. These were the days before zero-hours contracts; if the pay was minimum wage (which it was), and if there was no question of sick pay or holiday pay (and there wasn't), my Wonderbra and I would, at least, always make the rent.

It might have been a good job, except that any job predicated on the alignment of your boobs will ultimately make you sad. So it was that, in the end, my Wonderbra job made me sad. Depleted, diminished, disrespected. I was a good barmaid. I made excellent Martinis, and I could dribble the three individual liqueur components of a B52 shot into the glass so competently they'd float on top of each other, like alcoholic art. I was quick and I was sharp and I was particularly good at the mental arithmetic required to calculate bar bills. There's companionship in working so intently and intensely to service the hedonism of others; plus the other women bar staff and me knew we were on the front line of gender politics, managing the increasingly tricksy legions of boozed-up men who'd get more verbal and take more liberties as any given night progressed. We'd back each other to the hilt with the losers and the lechers and, the worst of the lot, those whose lechery had turned to bile because they'd been rebuffed, and too often.

But gradually, shift by shift, I stopped feeling like I was good for anything much. Nothing that I had to offer – the Martinis, the wit, the mental maths – could compete with the significance of the artificially enhanced upper segment of my torso, where that gig was concerned. Although I was too young to realise my tits would ever be anything less than perky-peachy-perfect, I did know the impression they were giving was fake. That's Wonderbras for you.

Maybe I wouldn't have felt any of this if I hadn't been so broke, so dependent on the literal, nightly, cashing in on my breasts. Maybe if I'd had a job which felt like it might be going somewhere, and a bank balance that didn't make me want to puke every time I walked past a branch of The Midland (the institution which would, in time, become the HSBC, within which my menacing debts skulked like an uninvestigated possible cancer). Maybe if I'd been marginally more secure – spiritually, professionally, financially, domestically – then the Wonderbra would have represented the sexy liberated joyous subversive style eruption I pretended I thought it did. But as it was, it represented compromise wrought in upholstered cotton with stretchy inserts and substantial padding. It represented an excuse for hundreds of men to look me straight in the tits, rather than the eyes, because, presumably, that's why I'd bought the thing in the first place. To draw attention away from my face.

I stropped out of Rumours eighteen months into my tenure, shortly after a Premier League footballer offered me £2,000 for a one-on-one look at what lay beneath my Wonderbra. It wasn't that which broke me. Honestly? I considered his offer. Two grand for a look only – 'no touching, no touching!' – seemed distinctly possible (verging on sensible) to someone who'd been seriously contemplating green card marrying one of the Yugos for a similar sum. Plus the footballer didn't seem menacing. Actually, he seemed lost and terminally messy; mournful. I turned him down in the end because of the mournfulness. It didn't seem right to take two grand off someone who was trying so hard to make himself feel better by doing absolutely all the wrong things, one after another. I said no, and watched him shuffle off into night-time Covent Garden in a terrible-but-expensive trench coat. He looked bleak – but he'd looked bleak when he came in. (He went into rehab for drug and alcohol addiction not long afterwards, where – as far as I can tell – he got permanently better. So that's nice.)

But no, that wasn't why I stropped out of Rumours. I stropped out of Rumours because a year and a half of being mistaken for the hazy impression of a backdrop for your own tits is long enough; also because I thought I'd got a job at the Atlantic cocktail bar off Piccadilly Circus.

The Atlantic was without question the most screamingly fashionable joint in town, it was buzzed about and gossiped over and you could not get a table in the restaurant for love nor money; nowhere was hotter, nowhere was more oversubscribed. It was done out like the ballroom of an ocean-going liner with chandeliers and sweeping stairways and cigarette girls and gilt edges everywhere. Its clientele was beautiful or famous or powerful or all three; its bar staff were required to wear high-buttoned shirts and waistcoats and aprons, in the style of upmarket French garçons. The Wonderbra would be retired out of necessity.

In fact, I didn't have a job at the Atlantic – my contact had got his facts wrong or had been trying to impress me by wielding power he didn't really have – which was a bit of a blow, until (following a week of unemployment) I discovered I had landed what would be both my first office job, and my first job in fashion. Tipped off by my flatmate Jules the Goose,[1] who was doing work experience in the fashion cupboard of a women's magazine, I'd applied and interviewed for a job as a very lowly assistant in the press office of teen fashion emporium Miss Selfridge. Miraculously, and despite the fact that I wore a catsuit and Wonderbra to the interview (I didn't have anything else), I got the job.

I had never intended to work in fashion. I'd never really understood that fashion could even be worked 'in'; never considered the industry and processes and business that backed up the world's wardrobes. But I walked into that office (then located in an obscure back room two floors up the Selfridges Oxford Street building) on my very first day, dressed in – who knows what? Probably something surreptitiously acquired in the bedroom of Jules the Goose, a woman generally (usefully) seven steps ahead of me in the fashion stakes, and only slightly thinner.

So I walked into the office and I surveyed the rails of

---

1 Not her real name.

sample clothes – singular examples of the stock which would shortly adorn the shop floors – all ready and waiting for the attentions of visiting representatives of the fashion press. I began to attune my brain to expressions and vernacular and concepts entirely new to me: 'buyers' and the fashion singular 'a trouser, a jean'; the received form of referring to an individual piece of clothing as 'him' . . . 'Oooh, that's a nice jumper, we like him!' I found myself submerged, completely and utterly, for the very first time, in the culture of fashion.

And I thought: this is *awful!*

I thought: dear God, take me back to the bar.

I hated it. I hated all of it. Well. Almost all of it. I worked for two wonderful women in the press office; one was brusque and posh and no-nonsense and scary in a way that never entirely obscured the fact she had a damn fine heart; the other, cool and fun and big sisterly. But still: I felt excluded and out of my depth and like I was constantly getting stuff wrong. I felt incompetent and green and also really, really tired, because now I had to get out of bed at, like, 7 a.m. (which had most certainly not been the case when I was still at Rumours, and my bar shifts began at 4 p.m., which made rolling out of the sack anytime before midday preposterously premature). I couldn't fax and I'd never phoned for a courier before, we didn't yet have an office computer but we'd get one, at which point I'd enter a whole new zone of pain and inferiority complexes, and

WHAT AM I SUPPOSED TO DO WITH THIS BEAST ONCE I'VE TURNED IT ON WHICH TOOK ME HALF AN HOUR BY THE WAY?

And I hated fashion from this perspective: a corporate churn of entirely unremarkable, cheaply- and mass-produced flotsam, selected by buyers under such pressure to generate sales they existed in a neurotic haze of hyper-caffeinated perma-jitters. I thought it was clever the way a label could take that fabric flotsam, paint a gloss of band identity over the top of it, tell a story about it, which con-sumers would, miraculously, respond to and then, literally and metaphorically, buy into, with their money. But I also thought it was weird. Toto had run off, pulled back the cur-tain, and the Wizard of Oz was not up to snuff.

Still. I got better at getting dressed as a consequence of that job. This was partly because I suddenly had access to a shedload of clothes. A shopload of clothes, in fact. Whenever any clothing sample became defunct because the collection it was part of was no longer available to buy in store, I got first dibs on it, as the lowliest and lowest-paid member of press office staff. This meant my personal wardrobe would soon rival that of Jules the Goose in terms of size, if not quality. Jules the Goose had by this point secured herself a staff job on the fashion magazine, which meant she had similar access to clothing samples, only her clothing sam-ples came from multiple sources.

But it was mostly because, for the first time in my life, I was introduced to the extraordinary art of styling. I got this from the assorted fashion editors who'd take my samples away to shoot, mixing and matching and tweaking and pinning and folding and fluffing them, in tune with other samples, acquired from other stores. And I got this from Miss Selfridge's band of visual merchandisers, the window dressers, the company's cool kids, whose aesthetic operated on such a heightened level to that of the rest of us, whose visual frame of reference was so extensive, so honed, and so evolved and so erudite, they could transform a basic grey marl ribbed vest, as soon as look at it, into something extraordinary, usually by entwining it with a necklace they'd reimagined as a belt. Or by layering it over a shirt. Or by hitching it up or tucking it in, just so.

Styling is the heart of good dressing. Not shopping. Not being up on your trends, or your names. Not having the new thing, first. Styling. Knowing how to wear something – how to tuck it in or let it hang, fold it up or belt it round, drape it over or button it high, allow a flash of contrasting colour sock to protrude while ensuring that the exact right amount of shirt cuff peeps from below the jacket . . . That's where the magic happens. That's where the joy is. That's where fashion stops having any power over you, and you get power over it; which is the precise point at which it becomes a vital tool for any Hot Feminist.

I left Miss Selfridge after two years, when I got my first job in journalism: as a trainee writer on *Minx* magazine, a short-lived young women's title aimed squarely at the Ladette demographic, which may have moved on from its Wonderbra fixation by this point, but was still flourishing.

I was being paid to write, paid to see my byline in print, paid to talk about myself and interview celebrities and fake printable correspondence with which to fill the readers' letters page and – on more than one occasion – do the horoscopes.

In addition to which, I somehow managed to develop a reputation as a fashion writer, despite the fact that – honestly? – I have never really properly engaged with that particular discipline. I was never a stylist, never charged with arranging fashion shoots; sourcing, ironing and transporting the clothes. I have never dressed a model or a celebrity, I never assisted a fashion editor, never even ran for her coffee; I never corresponded with photographers or booked lighting or secured anyone higher up the food chain than me (fashion is extremely food chainy) a parking spot. I did not pay my fashion journalist dues; and you're really, really expected to.

I *did* do a brief stint at *Vogue* (terrifying!) and I've sat through fashion weeks (which I've never really enjoyed; they're so oppressively hierarchical that even when you're flying high in that particular caste system, front row at the important shows, recipient of all the best freebies, getting hustled backstage to meet the designers and air kiss the celebrities, you're sickly giddy with social vertigo, with knowing you'll slip slide way back down the rungs, any day now, to the lesser seats and the uninspiring gifts, because that's just the nature of this beast . . .).

I've attended label launches: Banana Republic, J.Crew, and (my particular fave for, um, some peculiar reason) David Beckham and his H&M pants. I've interviewed Vivienne and Roland, Cavalli and Stella; Kate Moss, David Gandy, Georgia Jagger, Jerry Hall.

But I've never really done it, or been it, or got it. I've never felt fully immersed, like I'm quite penetrating the scene; never completely (or even slightly) accepted, or embraced, or allowed. I'll never understand its rules, its semiotics; I'll always feel a little bit anxious at its bashes, scrutinised and ultimately found lacking, while languishing in the audience of its catwalk shows.

Mind you, I sometimes suspect everyone else feels this way too. Even those who've followed protocol and climbed the ladder and secured the car parking slots.

I've asked about, but my enquiries have generally been met with quizzical, uncomprehending stares – though, of course, that could just be some indication that I've broken the code of silence no one told me I'd entered into, upon attending my first LFW.[2] It'd make sense though; an industry which thrives on the sense that you're almost, but not quite, good enough for it, but if you'd only pre-order next season's collection right now, well then . . . you'll be in with a chance! Only of course, you won't. Because there'll always be a next, next season . . . That sort of a culture would encourage all who submit to its

---

2 London Fashion Week.

rules to behave like they're part of one, giant, girls school of mean.

Yet, very occasionally, I've encountered a kindred fash spirit.

A couple of years ago, I attended the annual British Fashion Awards shindig in London. For various reasons I had to go alone. I turned up in the lobby of the Savoy Hotel and got snubbed by a succession of four women I knew quite well, all of whom seemed hell bent on talking to someone infinitely more important, or better dressed – or, perhaps, just not being seen talking to me. My dress was two-season-old-Preen, might that be why? Or was it that my freelance status meant I was a fashion writer without an entirely clear portfolio at that point, and that it therefore wasn't entirely obvious how useful I was to anyone? Combination of the both, in all probability. Or maybe they'd just spontaneously decided they didn't like me. As I shrivelled and buckled under the weight of so much unspoken disapproval, I stumbled over Gigi, a major fashion PR who I imagined would be thriving in such circumstances. Gigi's stock was high, her label was newly successful following an elegant takeover by a big name CEO, her advertising budget was large (which meant magazine editors were duty bound to blow smoke up her arse, in the hope of securing some of it for their titles), her dress was unquestionably next season. Maybe even the one after that.

But Gigi was shrivelling and buckling too.

'I hate this,' she said, through clenched teeth. 'Four women just blanked me. Four!'

'ME TOO!' I said.

Gigi scanned the room. 'It's not going to get any better,' she said. She was growing wild eyed. 'Let's evacuate the area.'

We scampered off round the corner, and found a hotel bar filled with the exclusively male, middle aged and predominantly lecherous delegates of a shipping magnate conference, who were winding down for the day. They plied us with V&Ts and tried to get us to come to a strip bar with them. They were awful. But they were better than what we'd left behind.

'Why is it like that?' I asked Gigi, who is more entrenched in fashion than I ever have been, who qualifies as 'proper fash', in a way that I don't. 'This business is run by women and for women, it employs women, it values women, because it has to! We're its customer base! Why isn't it nicer to us when we all get together? Why can't we all just be warmer, sweeter, more supportive?'

'I dunno,' said Gigi. 'Maybe that's just what happens this far up any ladder. I guess you'd never wonder why a bunch of powerful, back-stabbingly ambitious male businessmen weren't nicer to each other socially, would you?'

'No,' I said, 'no, I wouldn't,' and let another shipping magnate buy us another drink.

That, then, is my life in fashion so far. Clothes have made me feel like I belonged, and then like I had to fit in. They have made me feel complete and right and So Very Me (at Hipster Uni), and then compromised and ripe for exploitation (ref the Wonderbra years). Fashion has presented itself as an acquirable and incredibly useful art form (at Miss Selfridge, via the stylists), and it has flat-out ignored me at an industry social event, or seven.

Fashion: it's complicated.

How's a Hot Feminist to proceed?

By winning fashion. By owning it, rather than allowing it to own you. By understanding its power, while denying it power over you. By using it as a medium for self-expression, for asserting the self, for claiming your spot on the planet, for declaring yourself well worth looking at, actually . . . and never using it as a disguise or an apology.

A Hot Feminist understands that, basically, fashion is her bitch.

5

And Fashion Really Is Your Bitch

There are two ways to think about fashion.

The first way is as a big bad sneering damning You Can't Sit With Us sort of a malicious Medusa monster, the kind I've encountered in the fashion weeks and at the events, the kind which only wants to make you feel inadequate. Which wants to rule your life, with a view to ruining your life. Which wants to make you feel perpetually two steps behind, a little panicked, a little out of the loop.

Which wants to sap you of cash and self-esteem.

Which wants to sweep you up in a giddy, cocaine-y flurry of lunchtime solo missions to the high street in advance of a significant night out, lure you in with the whiff of possibility, the promise of transformation, the never-ending suspicion that the dress (or jeans or jacket or top) that'll change *everything* hangs on the next rail along . . . Before dropping you on your arse because every single thing you try looks a bit crap.

Which only really answers to scurrilous big buck

businessmen, cashing in on cheap labour and prime property deals and the fluid and evolving vulnerabilities of women who never think they look quite good enough; the ones who hide their tax assets in offshore bank accounts so the government can't get at them; who homogenise the formerly eclectic centres of our towns; dealing in the questionable ethics of quickly produced, cheaply sold designer rip offs.

Which perpetuates the morally dubious antics of the modelling industry, snorting up the hopes and fantasies of tall, skinny compromised young vulnerables whose dreams of being the next Kate Moss never pan out, because no one ever will be. (I wouldn't go as far as to say that Kate Moss, being Kate Moss, has made damn sure of that somehow – but nor would I entirely put it past her.)

Which batters you with eternally fluctuating ideas of trends, which makes you jump through flaming hoops marked COLOUR BLOCK and MIDI IS THE NEW MINI and NO ONE DOES BUCKET BAGS ANY MORE, SO AWKS!, just to make you prove you still love it, even though, heaven knows, it doesn't love you back.

Which tells tales of a far distant, glittering land, inhabited by Donatella and Roberto and Dolce&Gabbana, David Gandy on a yacht and Anna Wintour in a penthouse suite; a land which is more fabulous than you can ever imagine – into which you will never be allowed access.

Which uses the word 'fabulous' to abstraction, and to the point where it sounds like a bad thing. (The expectation that you'll over-deploy hyperbole is one of the most tedious aspects of being involved with fashion professionally. I've had to leave fashion weeks early simply because I ran out of adjectives, when the risk of saying: 'yeah, that's quite good I suppose, if you like that kind of thing' had become very real.)

Whose representatives on earth are shop assistants so sneering and haughty and superior you don't even dare venture into their lair, never mind touch their wares.

Which casually dispenses ghastly clichéd vernacular like 'must-have!' and 'season essential!' and 'hero piece!' and 'game changer!', all designed to make you feel like you're missing a memo or seven, like you permanently teeter on the edge of making some monstrous style error no one will ever let you live down.

Which is just one giant, demanding, malcontented and ultimately very cruel mistress.

The other way to think about fashion, is this:

Fashion is your bitch.

Your Baldrick.

Your loyal and grateful servant.

Seriously.

It serves you.

You own its arse.

Fashion's sole purpose is to help you look good. By which I mean: precisely the way you want to look. That is its *raison d'etre*. Its vocation. It's why it gets out of bed in the morning.

It's the last thing it thinks about at night. It's all it wants. All it's ever wanted.

To make you look good.

That's why it keeps on trying, coming up with the new ideas, the new colours, the shapes and the fabrics, the new vibes, the newly revisited old ideas.

Because it thinks you might like them.

Donatella? Dolce&Gabbana? Miuccia Prada, Michael Kors, Stella McCartney and Victoria Beckham? They work for your look. Alexander Wang and Isabel Marant, Christopher Kane and Roksanda Ilincic? Them too. Sir Philip Green at Topshop, Belinda Earl at M&S, Jane Shepherdson at Whistles, Jenna Lyons at J.Crew? Oh yeah! And them.

Fashion doesn't run you. Fashion runs *for* you.

Fashion is nothing without you.

The Hot Feminist goes with option two.

6

The Taming of the Clothes

B ut hold on just a minute.

It's all very well telling you how unremittingly fab fashion can be. Issuing grand proclamations about fashion being your 'bitch', an empowering force for good which can and should turbo-drive your feminism; spouting the brave rhetoric about 'belonging' and 'self-actualising' and 'claiming your space on the planet' . . .

Unless I actually tell you *how*, unless I actually give you some specifics – what good is that to you?

Right?

Right.

I will, then.

I'm not a stylist, mind you. I've learned how to style myself, I am a person who loves getting dressed every day, who relishes it, who thinks about clothes a great deal – but that's quite distinct from being a Gok Wan-y, Trinny and Susannah-y, 'take one look at you and know how best to accentuate your clavicle bones with a certain kind of neck-line' type of a professional. I am not one of them. I can't tell you exactly how you in particular should dress, because I can't actually see you (books eh? Limited technology!); although also because even if I could, that wouldn't help you. Fashion works as a tool of Hot Feminism precisely because the individual Hot Feminist has worked out for herself how to do it herself – not because some other joker has made free with some tips and a waist-cinching belt.

What I can give you is principles. Overarching philosophies. Stuff to try for yourself. And I am going to do this partly because if I keep it all locked up in my brain – where it's been accumulating slowly and steadily over the last two decades – I may have some sort of fashion aneurism, and partly because I rage against the idea that a woman would ever jealously guard her fashion secrets in the interest of not helping other women look as good as they possibly can. A Hot Feminist shares that shit.

DO frankly and honestly appraise your base look, the residual sense of *something* – the something you were *born* with, or inherited, or was implanted in you during the course of your upbringing in an indelible, undeniable way – which you can't shake, assuming you want to. Which you probably do. I think that stuff is often interconnected with any pain you felt as a kid. Anyway: is it preppy, is it gothy, is it girlie, is it butch? Is it undercover policewoman, is it Can Somehow Make Anything Look A Bit Like Sportswear, is it princessy, is it corporate? Is it Ballerina in her civvies (if so: I long to swap with you!), is it Cabin

Crew, is it 1980s children's TV presenter, is it matron? I could go on.

This is your jumping off point. It needn't define your style, but it will inevitably be of some influence. You may choose to embrace it wholesale, or you may choose to play against it. Take me. My base look is middle-class boho hippy girl. Not in the cool festival-bound party chick sense, sadly; more in the 'throws pots at Dartington Hall, has written a small and unpublished volume of her own verse, pretends to be vegan, isn't really' sense. I can't say precisely why; it's something about the way my hair sprouts and the angle my head meets my neck and a sort of perennial glaze over my features. I'm not keen, mainly because it's an inaccurate reflection of my soul. Well, apart from the poetry bit, which hasn't happened yet, but I wouldn't entirely put it past me. So I play against it. I avoid: cheesecloth, embroidery, floaty flowy stuff; maxi skirts, turbans, kaftans, bejewelled sandals, flounce, musical instruments worn as accessories. Instead, I veer toward stern androgyny (blazers and overcoats and shirts done all the way to the top), and a lot of bad girl leather (trousers, biker jackets, attention-seeking boots) and as much pseudo-French sexiness as I can muster (black bra visible through white tee, et cetera). I also like studding. My base look dread is also, I suspect, a deciding factor in my long-term aversion towards tights. I do not believe in tights. I think they slow up an outfit, I think they obstruct the impact; I think they are the point at which practical considerations totally outshine aesthetics (which should never be allowed. We strive for balance here). Consequently, I do not do skirts or dresses through winter, unless the winter happens to be spectacularly mild and bare legs are an option.

So yeah. Work out what you're dealing with in terms of core look, naked aesthetic; then decide to what extent you want to indulge/avoid it, with the subsequent decorations.

DON'T indulge a single vibe from head to toe. This is how you venture into the fancy dress danger zone. Rather, operate on a 70/30 ratio of vibes. 70 per cent smart to 30 per cent casual (trouser suit with Birkenstock sandals, faux fur jacket with trainers and/or statement headphones). Or 70 dressy to 30 not (grey marl T-shirt with leather trouser; high heels with jogging bottoms . . . Except that's 70 casual to 30 not, which is also fine). Or 70 punk to 30 prim (distressed skinny jean with a leather jacket with a blouse), or 70 sex kitten to 30 sporty girl (LBD with trainers, LBD with oversized Adidas track jacket thrown casually over it). Or 70 andro to 30 sex kitten (tuxedo suit with nothing but a sliver of lace underneath it? Always an option). Or 70 girlie girl to 30 goth (sundress with multiple piercings). And so on.

DO work out your silhouette. I don't mean your flesh and bone silhouette, I mean the one you create with clothing, the one you think suits you best. This is the algorithm according to which all your outfits must comply, in the name of you truly defining your signature look. Silhouette is balance: it's how skinny you like your lower half versus how voluminous your top, how pronounced your waist, how defined your bum; how elongated, how cinched, how prematurely cropped, how broad-shouldered, how hip-minimising, how full, how flat. This will, inevitably, be in part defined by your body shape; although heaven knows, that's a) probably not what you've convinced yourself it is through aeons of profoundly self-critical appraisal, so do have another look, and imagine, for a brief instant, that you *really* like yourself, and b) there's nothing you can't redefine dramatically with clever dressing, anyway. Silhouettes are defined by layers, by the way you allow a T-shirt to peep from the bottom of a jumper which nestles below a blazer which reaches to your mid-thigh, ideally synchronising with the end point on your skirt. Silhouette is also determined by heel height: by whether you choose to prop your whole up, on something vertiginous and spiky, or truncate it by a neat flat, or bolster it with chunky booty foundations, and so on. And it's *also* determined by hemlines. On which:

DON'T do anything until you've sorted your hemlines. I *know*! Who'd have thought that something so meh, so absurdly unexotic as hems, could be so crucial. Oh, but hems are! Hems change everything. For example, roll the hem up inside your jeans, so that it flashes an inch of ankle – even a quarter-inch of sock, then three quarter-inches of ankle – above the top of your boot, and see what a difference it makes. Not just to the jeans – to your entire silhouette. Now: check out how rolling the same hem outwards will create a different effect to tucking it up and invisibly inward; or how a deep outward roll (an actual turn-up) will create a different end result to a single small fold-up, which will, in turn, create an entirely different overall effect to no turn-up at all. Every single one of these variations will work better in relation to different types of footwear. Try them all until you hit hemline interplay gold.

DO send out some slightly contradictory messages about your sexuality with your clothing choices. Keep everyone on their toes.

DON'T buy the thing that looks like the thing you already have – the thing you love, the thing you wear over and over, only not quite as good. You'll never like it as much as the original Thing. Every time you wear it, you'll resent it for not being the original Thing.

DO buy the Thing, which, when you try it on, looks somehow like you've owned it for years. Even though you haven't. The thing you can't believe you didn't buy ages ago. On confronting your image in the changing room mirror, ask yourself: 'Do I look like I already own this?' If the answer is 'yes' – that's the definition of something suiting you.

DON'T spend a lot of money on evening wear, which you just won't get the chance to take out and show off to the wider world that often, unless you're, like, an It girl or something, paid to attend parties. In which case: I know damn well you're getting kitted out for free, anyway. And even if you're *not*, even if you're a sociable kind of non-It normo who's also big on parties: parties happen after nightfall, in the sexy gloam of clubs and fairy-lit houses, where booze will be spilled and sweat will be sweated and cheaper clothes will Pass.

And while we're on the subject of life-appropriate wardrobes:

DO be realistic about your lifestyle, about how and where and when you'll wear things. Live in the UK? Invest time, energy and the medium-to-big bucks in coats, not sandals, sunhats, shorts. It's cold more often than it's knees-out-toes-out weather. Spend more, and more frequently, on flats or mid-height shoes than you do on vertiginous heels of ridiculous proportions, because – unless you have a driver on hand twenty-four hours a day, and assuming your life is somewhat reliant on your being able to shift yourself from one place to another quickly and with minimal pain – you will wear the lower-heeled shoes much, much more often. You just will. You'll *think* you're going to wear the high ones. You'll be so sure of it! But then you'll eye them up, in all their ritzy erect proud glory, and all you'll really see will be pain and hobbling about and frequent stop-offs at Boots for emergency blister pad purchases. I do a hundred quid a year on a single new pair of high heels, maximum; and even that's too much. Having said which:

DON'T get too hung up on the feminist ifs and buts and semiotics and Should I, *Really* . . .? of high heels. Yes, they are contentious. Yes, they could be viewed as a way to prevent women's trajectory through society, on both a literal and metaphorical level; as fashion's attempt to hobble ladies. One of their earliest purposes was as a device to prevent the mistresses of rich men from wandering off to sleep with *other* men: heels were presumed to be enough of a physical impediment, and to offer a noisy enough alert in their clacking, to serve as a chastity belt in footwear form. But we aren't there any more. We've been through some stuff, high heels and us: that time when they were associated uniquely with the upper classes (because only those who didn't work in muddy fields, and wanted to draw attention to their own arrival, could afford to indulge such fripperies; both men and women, at this point), that time when they were associated uniquely with prostitutes; as we've seen they've shown themselves to be a barometer of a wider economic situation (the higher the heels, the deeper the financial depression, traditionally . . .).

But now? Four hundred years after their creation, a decade after *Sex and the City* fetishised the Manolo and the WAG brigade claimed ownership of the red-soled Louboutin? They're just shoes, aren't they? Another weapon in the Strong Look arsenal, another option in the silhouette adjustment process?

Personally, I opt for sturdier heel forms when seeking additional height; a wedge, or a straight up-n-down blocky heeled affair – nothing too spindly. But that's just me . . . (as anyone who ever proffers an opinion which they definitely think is whip-smart is inclined to say, in the name of faking humility). Oh, and one other thing: the notion that high heels offer their female wearers equality with men, by raising them up physically so we're on eye-level with the blokes, doesn't really fly. As Elizabeth Semmelhack, senior curator of the Bata Shoe Museum in Toronto, once pointed out to me: 'If high heels were about power, men would wear them too. We know how much they like power.'

DO be mindful of your mood, and how it affects the way you feel about the things you wear. You know how, one day, you walk out in this outfit, and it feels stupendous and perfectly judged and everything you've ever wanted from your clothes? And then, ten days later, you try it again, and it feels lacklustre and flat and not at all hot? That's your heart, not your frock. Be gentle with yourself.

DON'T go shopping with an established notion of an entirely new outfit in mind. A good look evolves on a gradual, piece-by-piece basis; a new jeans' wash notion here, a new neckline there, a different kind of jacket, a lower heel-height . . . Baby steps, people.

DO acquire your jewellery in antique shops and pawnshops. Jewels should be imbued with history and personality and meaning and edge. When they're old, they have that built in. And you get to add to it.

DON'T always wear everything exactly as it is supposed to be worn. A French fashion editor once told me that the easiest way to look French (which I do, so very much!) is to 'shoulder robe' your jacket or coat: to balance it on both shoulders without placing your arms through the relevant holes (which you may also know as 'sleeves'). I don't know why this works so well, but it does. It's sort of careless and yet grand, a bit: I'm too busy and important to bother with tedious things like arm-to-sleeve insertion. Also, it adds flourish, drama and swoosh to your jacket, which will now move more like a cape. *Also* it's good if you happen to be a bit sweaty – which I am – because it aerates one's pits. (The same French fashion editor told me that another good way to look French is to make sure your outfit is immaculate, then smear your make-up a bit, and/or muss up your hair a lot. She also told me that only the truly French can get away with a navy and white matelot stripe, though I'm not sure she's right about that.)

DO wear any expensive stuff you own like it's cheap as chips. Carelessly. Freely. And above all: often. Wear it during the day, wear it to work and to the pub, under no circumstances reserve it for special occasions.

Wear it with trainers, under a camo army jacket. Give it a casual, cheap, chilled out juxtaposition against which to cause havoc. Treat it mean, wear it with insouciance, and it will serve you well. Treat it like it's a princess and it'll dominate your vibe; it'll also mean you don't ever get your money's worth out of it. The only concession you should make to it is in its upkeep. Dry clean it, if that's what it requires. Hand wash it. Though equally:

DON'T dry clean too often. An inside-out overnight airing, plus a precautionary squirt of Febreze, will often suffice. This, fresh(ish) from the Middle Class Sluts' Guide To Good Housekeeping.

DO find your own ethical code with fashion; and then live, shop and dress according to it. Feel your way forward on designer fakes, on catwalk knock offs, on fast fashion – the stunningly quick turnover of styles sold cheap in high street stores, which has become a byword for large corporations cashing in on the cheap labour available in developing countries. Do you like your clothes to be disposable – a minimal style commitment, a bit of fun – or do you worry about them becoming landfill, worry about what that means for the environment?

How *much* do you care? Which bits do you care particularly about? Are you OK with leather, but not fur; or vintage fur, but not new fur? Or are you fine with fur – just not with cotton, the production of which can involve pesticides and irrigation practices which, according to some, poses a major environmental risk?

DON'T go down in a whirlpool of want. If you have to get on a waiting list for anything, or queue outside for anything, or wait up to midnight when a new and over-publicised range goes online for the first time, or buy it on eBay for three times its original cost – just don't. I speak as a woman who's done all of the above when I say: it's never worth it.

DO spend shitloads on jeans. Certainly more than you 'should', whatever should means. Jeans are the hardest working, most flexible, most obliging, most perennially chic, easiest bit of cloth you'll ever own. They're hot, they're cool, they're casual, they're sexy as sin. Ergo they are worth the money. They go with the whole bloody world, they're machine washable, they'll pass at smart parties (when worn with either a slinky top *or* tuxedo-ish jacket *or* heels; at a push, any two of those items simultaneously – all three is overkill). Dedicate time and effort to tracking down your very first amazing pair (assuming you haven't already); the pair which make you feel better about everything, every time you wear them. That'll be the pair on which all future pairs will be based, all future pairs will echo to some extent. Frequent department stores to this end; all the decent ones have a dedicated jeans section now. Once you're there: try on any jeans that seem even vaguely intriguing, or amusing;

the developing fabric technologies, the things those jeans people know about cut – about how to shape the flow of the jean thigh into the jean knee, where you place the back pockets, where the waist hits, when a crop works – would blow your mind, and it evolves, constantly and continually and miraculously, the end consequence of which is you can never tell what's going to work on you just by looking at it. You have to try. You'll need a minimum of four pairs constantly on tap: a razor-sharp black pair (the LBD of the daytime), an only-marginally-less-razor-sharp indigo pair (in either cigarette fit, or a skinny fit, possibly with a higher waist, if you enjoy a higher waist – and do try it, won't you?), a grey pair (sexy night-time vibes) and a distressed pair (for all other eventualities).

DON'T ignore the details. Obsess over the details! The details will elevate every last item of clothing to a whole new level of wowsers, if you give them half a chance, and you really should. Think: are the buttons lovely? Is there something spectacularly satisfying about the lining on this jacket, which – given that it's almost always appropriate to roll the sleeves on any jacket up a couple of inches above the wrist – will end up at least somewhat on display (although even if it doesn't, just knowing the inside of your jacket is a bewitching shade of navy, or slate, or deep purple, will add something to your overall swagger)? Does the heel on the court shoe descend in a straight line, or does it curve inwards slightly, and which of these options do you like best?[1] Is there something quietly amazing about the minimal pointiness on the collar of that white shirt, about the way in which the buttons are hidden beneath a specially constructed extra hem, about the stitching on the yoke? Does the hard wear on the eyelets of those brogues make your heart beat a little faster? Brilliant. Oh, and also:

DO pay more attention to yet other details – specifically, the ones which only become apparent during the act of wearing clothes. Do the buckles on the biker jacket jangle like spurs, in a really delicious manner? Does the overlong zip pull on the boots flick about pleasingly, like one, long, flirty eyelash, or a horse's mane? Does the washed-out jersey on the T-shirt mean that it clings to your body in a supreme gesture of stealth sexiness? Does the contrast-colour cord surrounding the rim of that hoodie swing about, adding rhythm to your walk? Does the bag nestle into your waist like a small animal?

DON'T underestimate grey marl jersey. Ever ever ever. It's the defining modern neutral *de nos jours*, it's your counterpoint to pretty much everything else. In whatever form (T-shirt, vest top, sweatshirt – even jogging pant), it has the capacity to calm down the highly glam, chill out the mega formal, soften the extreme, clash elegantly against a

---

1 I've always thought straight down looks classier. Couldn't tell you why.

neckful of costume jewellery . . . Also: don't make the mistake of thinking there is only one shade of grey marl. There are, like, *fifty* shades of grey marl. Which may be the title of my next book. There's the darker, more charcoal inclined, and the pinkishly lilac heather tinged, there's the blue-leaning and the moss-green-reaching, and there is one, precise shade that'll suit you best of all. Seek it out.

DO go shopping for new clothes while wearing clothes you already like. Buy nothing that doesn't look at least 10 per cent better than the clothes you came in.

DON'T go shopping when you're in a bad mood. Or a sad mood. Or a lost mood. Or a frantic mood or an angsty moody or heartbroken or vengeful or nervy or neurotic or menstrual or hungover, or so on and so forth. You won't make good purchases like that, because you're shopping to shift that mood, to distract yourself from some deeper grief, in a misguided attempt to escape yourself by transforming it physically. It won't work, and you'll spend money on stuff you aren't sure about, which at best will only serve to remind you of that day you felt so shit you went shopping forever after, and which at worst will be a horribly overpriced error destined to lurk in your wardrobe, eternally unworn, price tags intact, making you feel slightly ghastly every time you encounter it. When you feel any of those things: go for a walk. Call a mate. Smoke a little weed. Shopping should be reserved for the days when you're happy, when you're calm, when you're into yourself. The days when you know yourself and like yourself and want to honour that with some sane- and well-chosen adornment. Having said which:

DO shop while a little drunk, from time to time. Takes the edge off your retail inhibitions.

DON'T buy anything in the sales, unless you wanted it (like LOTS) when it was full price.

DO operate a one-in-one-out policy on new purchases. Know, even as you stand at the till, Visa card aloft, new thing clutched eagerly, proprietorially to your breast, which of the pieces you already own will be leaving your wardrobe to accommodate the new thing. What's going on eBay, what's headed for Oxfam, what's finally going to the friend or sibling who's coveted it, so obviously, so vocally, for so long. Ideally, you'll do this on a like-for-like basis: old boot leaves as new boot arrives and so on; if you feel this is unworkable, I'll accept a two-old-non-similar-things-for-one-new-thing approach. I promise you, this is the only way to keep a wardrobe alive, to stop it stagnating under the weight of unworn, unliked, untended clothing. Let stuff go freely and easily. You won't miss it. You won't even remember it.

DON'T be afraid to return stuff if it isn't working. Get it home post-purchase, try it in the mix with a succession of classic You looks; if it doesn't work in conjunction with at least a third of them, take it back. Or send it back, if it was an online buy. I know, I know. It's a hassle. But: just do it.

DO be charming to shop staff, while you're returning stuff. Even if they rebuff you on the grounds that you've overstayed the welcome on your receipt, or because they suspect you've already worn this piece out and decided, halfway through the wearing out, that – in fact – it wasn't for you. Generally, be charming to shop staff. Don't treat them like servants. Be considerate of their time: rehang garments which slip from hangers if you brush up against them, replace unwanted items on the rails where you found them. It's only polite.

DON'T follow trends blindly. Trends serve a purpose, without question. They keep things busy, keep them moving forward, they propel, they enliven, they keep us on our toes. But they are notions, ideas – they aren't *rules*. I speak as a style journalist when I tell you: half the time, we're just popping ideas out there, see if they fly. We think: wouldn't it be cool if golf visors/digi-printed leggings/thigh high wader boots/fishnet socks were a Thing? Then we try our luck with an article or three, see if anyone else is game. Which is not to say we're doing this in the spirit of bored, petulant, mean-spirited Greek gods: in the name of dicking about with the hearts and minds and purses of those who think we may – just possibly – know what we're talking about. We're just trying to stir this party up a bit. As for the idea that there are trends which descend directly from the catwalk: yeah, but there are so many of them, you could just carry on doing what you're doing in the absolute confidence that some designer, somewhere, has sent something just like it tripping down a catwalk.

Adopt a new trend if it works for you; if it's a colour which just happens to flatter you, if it's a leg length or a fabric or a strap configuration which, you've discovered, melds with your established style. Otherwise, JOMO[2] on them. Be frugal with trends. Don't indulge more than one a season. Buy the cheapest incarnation available, then graduate up to something more expensive, if – following a series of wears – you find you're really getting into it. Otherwise: don't stress about it. It's a trend; by definition, it'll be gone in a few weeks – months at the most – quite as if it never happened. If it hasn't, if it's instead reached tipping point, stopped being a trend and started melding with a more pervasive, more general sense of Established Things We Just Wear These Days, then pay it a different kind of attention, because it's telling you something about the way women live and think about themselves now. On which:

---

2 JOMO = the Joy Of Missing Out; observing the arrival of a new cultural quantity, before deciding it's nothing you have the time or energy to engage with, thanks all the same.

DO think about fashion trends in terms of what they tell you about the way women live and move and how they think about themselves now; what we want, and need and expect. Which they do. Any truly important trend, any trend which has traction, which hangs about for longer than two seasons, does so because it's offering us something we can't let go of. Skinny jeans have endured for over a decade – much to everyone's amazement – because they are just really easy; they give a clean, sharp, neat, chic line, they can be worn with flats and heels, they bend, they flex, their hems don't drag in puddles . . . They make sense.

When clothes get more voluminous – as they have lately – when jumpers get bulkier and jackets get bolder and broader and coats get oversized, it's an indication that women are giving up on their obsession with looking as thin as they possibly can, which means we're beginning to think about our bodies in different ways. The constant ebb and flow of power between mega-heeled flagrantly sexy court shoes and trainers, neatly delineates the ongoing tug of war women experience between the desire to look sexy but like we're about to fall over, and the desire to look cool, if a little casual, a little race-y, as opposed to racy.

Those incredibly short denim cut-off shorts, the falling in and out of fashion of cleavage, tiny handbags worn in conjunction with the 'overflow' canvas tote (designed to hold the ebooks and gym kit that will not fit into the tiny handbag) . . . All of this is coded insight into the way women view themselves, the things we want and need.

DON'T buy anything you won't be able to wear within the next fortnight for climate reasons. It's almost impossible to predict what you'll really want to wear when the weather changes and the light alters. Wait until it's happened.

DO hats. Nothing quite like a bright-coloured woollen beanie to enliven an otherwise monochrome winter look. Colour round the face: never a bad thing.

DON'T buy something on the grounds that 'it's an investment'. There's no such thing. Not literally: give or take Hermès' insanely priced, extremely unavailable Birkin handbags, no single fashion piece gains value over time. They only lose – hand over fist, at that. Nor is there any such thing as an emotional investment purchase: it's incredibly rare that anyone ever wants to wear the same thing, over and over, year in, year out, for decades, before passing it onto their daughters and granddaughters, and yeah yeah, I know some people claim they do – that such-and-such frock has been *such* a loyal friend to generations, et cetera – but I don't believe them. So. Buy because you want to, and you think you'll enjoy wearing it over the medium term. If you can envisage a two-year lifespan on something: bingo! Don't reach for any other justifications: you're kidding yourself. Oh, but hang on:

DO ignore the above if we're talking leather. Leather can last you five years. Maybe even ten.

DON'T limit your fashion education resources to catwalks and mags and – gosh – me, actually. Definitely don't rely too heavily on the style influence of celebrities, many of whom have no idea what they're doing really, they're wholly dependent on the guidance and shopping acumen of stylists whom they pay handsomely for the privilege, which means by and large: celebs don't really know what *they* want to look like, never mind what *you* should look like.

Instead: look further, look harder. My biggest ever style influences are, in order: Hans Solo in the second of the original *Star Wars* films (skinny leg, belted jerkin, flat boot, option on a cape), the Child Catcher in *Chitty Chitty Bang Bang* (skinny leg, *again*, pointed shoe tip, blazer), and Shane McCutcheon, a character in the 2004 TV series *The L Word*, a fantastically accomplished, staggeringly beautiful, hyper-glossy fictional lesbian who favoured trousers with criss-cross ties up the side, and bandanas.

DO aspire toward looking cool. Possibly above and beyond all else. Cool holds sway over everyone, all ages, all genders, all situations. Cool is very active, very potent. Cool demonstrates a working knowledge of the cultural moment, and of past cultural moments. Cool asks questions of whoever beholds it. It's acquired via minimal acts of fashion subversion – of making things look less perfect, and more curious – and through the constant effort to abandon prettiness in favour of edge. It's doing your own thing with absolute assurance and minimal concern for the opinion of others. Contrary to popular belief, cool does categorically not involve the sneering at, dismissing of and disregarding of other people's taste. Cool embraces, it doesn't deny. Cool is not ironic, or arch, cool doesn't pretend it's doing what it's doing as a bit of a joke. Cool does not go around thinking it's better than everyone else. That's not being cool. That's being a cunt.

DON'T subscribe to the myth of effortless cool. There is no such thing. No one's born with it. No one just *is* cool. Cool is acquired through work; joyful, revealing, pleasant work . . . But still. Work.

DO think about the relationship between your hair and your outfit. Does it need to go up into a ponytail, with that high neckline, to expose a sexy little flash of nape . . . Or will that just tip you into austere and Amish territory? In combination with the sleeveless vest top, is your fringe overkill on the Chrissie Hynde tribute level or is it bang(s) on? Hair: clothes you wear all the time.

DON'T overspend on knitwear. It rarely washes well. I've found that regardless of how much they cost, few jumpers make it through an entire winter without winding up on the wrong side of bedraggled and shapeless.

DO check out everyone around you for ideas. All the time. The old geezer with the tailored shorts, the loafers and the double-breasted jacket. The immaculately chic middle-aged woman in head-to-toe Chanel, with a surprise tattoo on her wrist. The front of house with the kimono over her jeans. The gap yah boy with the topknot. The Japanese tourist with the excellent headphones. Pick n mix from all genders, all age groups, all cultural and pop cultural influences.

DON'T get embarrassed, if you're caught out during the checking out process. Instead, smile. Communicate with pleasant demeanour that you're appreciating that person's look. It's my dream to construct an internationally recognised hand signal for: there's something about your style which I really like.

DO meld any style ideas you've gleaned from others to your pre-existing look. Never copy head to toe. You're working towards an expression of self; cuckooing other people's expression of self is not going to help. *Au contraire*: it's going to represent a major derailment. Be especially careful with this when taking inspiration from friends. Partly because the temptation to imitate the style of someone you also really like can confuse the matter hugely. Partly because:

DON'T believe a friend or colleague who says she doesn't mind if you buy the exact same thing she just bought. She almost certainly does. Plus, you're looking at, what? At least one season's worth of: who gets to wear it here, and there, and then? *Plus*, you will never love it, as much as you love it when she wears it. You just won't.

DO compliment all people, freely and sincerely, on their clothing choices. Do it the very moment you feel a positive remark bubbling up inside you. Everyone wants to hear that stuff. Everyone. Ensure that the compliment is fulsome and without qualification, mind. Ensure your agenda in offering it up is solid and well-meaning. And also:

DON'T ever make anyone else feel bad about their clothes. Ever ever ever. However well-intentioned you think you're being. However 'helpful'. If your advice/ opinion is being directly solicited, consider the circumstances before proceeding. Are you in the midst of a social gathering, with there being no hope of adjusting or changing the outfit in question? Then tell the person doing the asking that they look magnificent, that – quite possibly – they've never looked better, regardless of what you really think. I couldn't give a damn what you really think. Are you in a changing room, where your shopping friend/colleague/sibling is weighing up the pros and cons of a purchase which you think ill-advised? Are they clearly in love with whatever it is, smiling at and flirting with their own reflections? Then tell them they look sensational. Or are they unsure? Tell them you think they can do better, and that, furthermore, they *will* do better; tell them it's not good enough for them.

Never offer an unsolicited criticism. Why would you? Never tell anyone they're 'brave' to attempt a particular outfit (the unsaid judgement in making free with notions of bravery . . .) Never tell anyone they look anything short of a kerjillion bucks when they're in a vulnerable situation: feet away from encountering the new girlfriend of an old flame, for example. And never, ever start a sentence: 'Not that you asked, but . . .' or end a sentence: '. . . I'm just being honest.' Neither of these expressions ever conjoin with anything other than pure nastiness.

DO be wary if another woman offers an unsolicited opinion of *your* look. If it's anything short of a rave review, tell them where to stick it. Or reply: gosh. I wasn't aware I'd asked for your input! Or tell them I said you looked hot, and my opinion dramatically outranks theirs. Then walk away in the knowledge that her agenda is as suspect as sin. Which it is: why else would she be attempting to take you down a notch?

DON'T wait for other people to applaud your clothes. They won't always. Sometimes because they're too busy worrying what you think of theirs. Sometimes because they don't care. Sometimes because they think you hear it all the time, anyway. Sometimes because they want to, but they're embarrassed, most probably on account of being terminally English. Do you look the way you want to look today? Then that will do, my friend. That will do.

DO wear pink with abandon. Well, y'know: assuming it suits you. I don't subscribe to the traditional feminist objection towards pink. I don't even understand its origins. Pink can't be offensive in itself, to those who strive for gender equality, can it? It's a colour, not a law or a cultural convention.

I see that dishing it out habitually to very young girls might send out messages about their being different to very young boys, about their roles and their expectations being distinct – though I don't quite see how pink property might limit a girl's sense of her own potential; on top of which, the main young girl influence in my life (the godchild) was drawn ineluctably toward pink aged three, before rejecting it as passé at five. Re: the adult woman's relationship with pink, I think feminism has entered a post-pink era. One in which no one in their right mind would think pink signifies anything other than a colour which isn't red, or blue, or lilac; which plays well against chocolate brown and monochromes and suntans, and which looks mighty fine on men. Give or take razor blades marketed at women (which you shouldn't buy incidentally, they're no different in design to the man ones, and they're often more expensive), no one considers pink to be a female-skewing marketing ploy, do they?

DON'T do irony. Ironic dressing is a fundamental lack of confidence passed off as a giggle and a sneer.

DO be as theatrical, as outré, as – I hate to use the word, but – *wacky* as you dare, with your sunglasses. They are so easily take-off and put-onable, a lack of commitment which lends itself to the trialling of more challenging accessorising.

DON'T mourn when you lose those sunglasses, which you inevitably will. That's the nature of sunglasses. You take 'em out, you take 'em off, you put 'em down, and you forget about 'em. Be Zen in the letting go, and think of it as an opportunity to be more daring still when purchasing the next pair.

DO ensure a degree of relevance in your choice of logo T-shirt. Do you even like the band referenced in your faux vintage tour shirt, for example? You better . . .

DON'T underestimate the importance of umbrellas or belts. There's no reason to walk about with the black, flappy nylon equivalent of doom hovering eight inches above your head, especially not when it's raining and life's beyond bleak already; and a spectacular belt is like an exclamation point holding up your pants.

DO think of technology as a fashion statement.
The single most successful accessory I've bought in the last
three years is a £2.50 iPhone case shaped like a knuckle-
duster. I get congratulated on it by an average of four
complete strangers a day; I've peaked at twelve. In London,
by the way, where no one can bear to speak to anyone they
don't know for fear of being branded horrifically weird.
Young people scream: 'Lady! Your iPhone cover is sick!' An
Italian grandmother had to get her grandson to translate,
while I told her how and where it was acquired (China via
Amazon, following a Google search). A Polish guy sidled up
to me, extracted his fag from between his lips, nodded at
the case and said, 'Is chic . . .' before sidling off. IPhone
covers are like dogs, they give strangers license to chat with
you. (See also: cool headphones.)

DON'T worry if you get it all horribly wrong. If it's
not working out today, no matter how hard you try, no
matter how many times you tweak, and change individual
components, and give it all up and start again. It never matters all that much. Not least because: tomorrow is another
day/opportunity to do it all again, differently.

PART THREE

BEAUTY AND THE FEMINIST

7

The Urge

―――――――――

Can a feminist stress about her weight? Can a feminist order skinny milk for her latte, maintain a rigorous skincare regime, contemplate Botox, try and get herself hooked on kale because she's heard it's a powerful ally in the great battle against the aging process, although who knows if that's actually true or just some fleetingly popular but ultimately spurious notion peddled by the pro-kale lobby?

Can a feminist collect mascaras, perfect her liquid eye-liner flick, curl her lashes, play with her hair? Can a feminist work out and diet, face mask and zit-evade, entertain lengthy interior monologues about whether – when the time comes, and age and gravity demand that she prioritise – she will choose to preserve her arse over her face (with dieting and exercise and the kind of stuff which might tone the bum, while diminishing the cheeks) or vice versa (ignore the downward descent of the arse cheeks, in favour of maintaining the peachy plump quality of the face cheeks)?

Can a feminist know damn well that she should be

resisting the infernal pressure to tweak and colour and primp and groom and wrinkle-proof herself into some arbitrary and socially-approved notion of physical beauty, only she's given up fighting it actually, because she's too bloody knackered to not try and comply? At which point, should a feminist renounce her right to call herself a feminist?

Well now: isn't *that* the question?

So I'm hoping very much that I've made a case for fashion and feminism coexisting in blissful-ish harmony, one which hinges on us understanding that fashion's central purpose just *isn't* the bewitching of men. Which it isn't.

Really.

It. Just. Isn't.

But feminism's relationship with beauty – with the elements of self-presentation which aren't about clothes, but are about the hair, the skin, the make-up and the body – is tricksier. This is because beauty's central purpose very much *is* the drive towards being beautiful. You can tell that, by its name. And the drive to be beautiful is sort of irrefutably about courting the approval of others. And some of those others will be male.

So here's me, right: primped, shaved, threaded, facialised and body-conscious to the max . . . And less comfortable, feministically speaking, with my beauty stresses . . .

I blame The Urge.

Oh, the Urge! THE URGE! The Urge, I tell you! The Urge: to look good, to look pretty, to look sexy, to look fit;

to look buff and hot and gorge and I Totally Would! The Urge is a cruel mistress, a dominant force; a troubling and conniving and persistent fucker, which holds more of a sway over most of our lives than any one of us would ever care to admit.

Who doesn't get The Urge? Who doesn't, periodically (or considerably more often than that, let's be honest: sometimes it feels like a continual state of being, like The Urge is the single greatest subtext on our every conscious moment), submit to it, flounder in it, answer its constant demands to think about how other people see us, and wonder if it's good?

I bet the Queen gets The Urge. I bet Angela Merkel and Dame Judi Dench and Hillary Clinton and Lorraine Kelly and Hu Shuli and Gisele Bündchen and Beyoncé and Sheryl Sandberg and the city superwoman with nine kids and a squillion pound annual bonus and Tracey Emin and anyone who ever won the Booker or Baileys Prize . . . I bet they get The Urge.

The Urge is strong within woman, as Yoda never said.

The Urge finds its form and seeps out into our consciousness – and often out into the world, via our actual mouths – in the form of four teeny tiny little words. Whisper them with me:

'Do I look OK?'

Such a brief, succinct turn of phrase; which encapsulates such boiling, roiling issues, such angst, such deep-rooted sadness. Because The Urge is built on a foundation of fear, the fear of never being desired, wanted, and by extension, never being loved.

That's The Urge.

Our relationship with The Urge is intense and complex. We resent it, because it takes up so much of our time and energy. We pretend we don't submit to it, because we think that if we do, we are weak willed, vain and not very feminist. Then we beat ourselves up a little bit more, because The Urge comes and gets us anyway, and it feels like there's nothing we can do to stop it. Double whammy of self-doubt and self-loathing, The Urge, and then Oh God, I've Got The Urge.

We shiver and shudder when The Urge envelops us, takes us down to our very lowest ebb, which The Urge is wont to do in times of trouble, in times of being dumped, or failing to get a job we really wanted, or falling out with a friend.

We dance the Dance of the Deflected, Rebuffed and Rebounded Compliment with each other, loads, because otherwise, what would people think? That we've tamed The Urge? Never! The sheer hubris of acting like you've tamed The Urge! The very idea!

So we have conversations like this:

FRIEND: You look different.
YOU: Fat?
FRIEND: No.

You: Old?

Friend: No! *Good* different.

You: Because I normally look like crap?

Friend: You normally look great! You just look like . . . I dunno. You've done something new. Your top?

You: I've had this top for so long. You've seen this top so many times before I'm surprised your eyes aren't bored of it. I literally hate this top.

Friend: Your hair?

You: I literally hate my hair.

Friend: It looks good.

You: It looks fat.

Friend: I look fat.

You: You don't.

Friend: I do. Fat and old.

You: You don't. *I* do.

Friend: You don't. *I* do.

You: I do.

Repeat to fade.

Entire economies are built on The Urge. Business models and industries and scientific research projects. Rapidly developing mascara technologies? The Urge did that! Improbable devices to discourage cellulite? The Urge loves them! The Urge makes a lot of people very rich.

What's to be done about The Urge?

Well, we can stop saying it doesn't matter, for starters. It does. The origins of The Urge are undoubtedly ancient and patriarchal and rooted in the expectation that girls and women serve as easy-on-the-eye baby-vessels, and not much more.

I must say at this juncture that I am immensely fond of men. Truly! I've met, like, *loads*, and some of them – lots of them! – are fab: tip top, first class humans. Some of my favourite people are men. I liked one enough to take him home and keep him in my flat. He's still there, to this very day, happy as Larry, or at least, not in any noticeable distress. But I do also think, in the case of The Urge, men probably started it. Oh, The Urge has got men written all over it, hasn't it? Mainly because men fear attractiveness in women: it's the first way that they accepted we had power over them – and it's (sadly, tediously) probably still the most significant way in which they accept we have power over them. They see our potential to enslave them sexually as our most significant power.

They've recognised it and feared it for millennia. It's got historical precedent. Foxy-chick-destroys-king (empire, government, sports hero, mild-mannered civil servant, the bloke next door, your dad) is an ancient and frequently recurring trope. See Cleopatra, Katie Price orchestrating the downfall of Gareth Gates (among others), Christine Keeler, Wallis Simpson, all the footballers who lost merchandising deals after some kiss and tell sensation destroyed their public rep, and anyone they ever burned as a witch, for further details.

The Urge is a way of tempering that power. Of ensuring

no woman ever thinks she's quite hot enough, no woman ever dares assert her own hotness, but rather waits for someone else (ideally, a bloke) to recognise it; and all women live in the sure and certain knowledge they're being compared unfavourably against each other, by Men, the only and ultimate judges.

Which worked for ages, until the unforeseen happened, and men got The Urge too.

This is part of the reason we can, just maybe, make some peace with The Urge: because in a modern context, it's equal opportunities.

I bet Barack Obama, Warren Buffett, Alan Bennett and Justin Bieber get The Urge, too; and Harry Styles and Simon Cowell and Vladimir Putin and Jon Snow. The Urge's gender bias is falling by the wayside as our society becomes increasingly visual, increasingly selfie/YouTube/Facebook-profile-shot oriented, and men become increasingly aware of being looked at, just as they look.

I bet God gets The Urge. I bet God looks at all those myriad depictions of Himself – stained glass windows, covers of prayer books, Michelangelo's frescoes, et cetera – and goes: does my nose *really* look like that in all their collective consciousness? Oh God (God's a terrible blasphemer), it *does*, doesn't it? Should I get it fixed?

And there is no point in pretending The Urge doesn't matter, in beating ourselves up for complying with its diktats, hating ourselves while simultaneously buying the new light-reflecting tinted moisturiser.

The Urge is bigger than that.

I do think – just maybe – The Urge can be reimagined as something a little more jolly. I think The Urge can be befriended, diffused, better understood.

Mainly: I think it's OK to want to be fancied. It might not be feminist, strictly speaking. In a feminist dream of an existence, one would go about one's business without giving a single hoot about who was or wasn't drooling after you in your wake, because you understood on a fundamental level that you have more to bring to this party than how fit you may or may not be considered by other people. Yet at the same time: the desire to be fancied isn't Not feminist. This is in great part because, while our looks have a place in the greater scheme of our being fanciable, they are in no way the limit of it. I'm not sure if they're even a jumping off point. They're just in the mix, somewhere, jostling up against the chemicals we put out and the high note we hit when we laugh and our passions and our accents and our goodnesses.

Maybe we give our looks – and the maintenance of our looks – precedence over those other factors because we're told we absolutely categorically *must*, by the commercial interests I mentioned earlier. Or maybe it's just an easy, obvious place for us to rest our deeper fear that we're all fundamentally unlovable.

But as concerns go, I think we can work towards

tolerating it better, in ourselves and in other people. We can forgive our own desires to be considered a bit beautiful. We can and we must.

Because the desire to be fancied is also charming. It is a uniting, universal vulnerability. It's also *fun*. Fancying people is one of my top three all-out fave ever human idiosyncrasies. I do it often and with wild abandon. I encourage others to do it often and with wild abandon. Why limit yourself to fancying those who fall into the demarcations established by your sexuality? Make free with the fancying! Fancy pretty ladies and hot men alike; fancy with no expectation of anything other than the unadulterated pleasure of the momentary fancy. A little interlude of casual daily fancying is like a fag break for the hormones. Plus the act of fancying is so closely intertwined with liking and admiring and approving, the world can surely only be improved, if we do more of it?

As for being fancied back? That is one of the purest pleasures known to mankind. Life is worth living – all the pain and the trauma and the tragedy and the uncertainty and all of it – is worth enduring for the possibility that at some point along the way, you'll discover that the person you fancy most on the planet, totally fancies you back.

PS: If we can minimise the Deflected, Rebuffed and Rebounded Compliment conversations, that would definitely be another step in the right direction.

8

How to Be Fancied

I've spent the last three decades trying to be fancied a bit more than I already am. I fully expect to spend the next three doing the same thing. In some ways, it's my life's work. So sue me.

I kicked off proceedings, aged eight, in response to my first full viewing of the film *Grease*. I watched it, and resolved on the spot to grow up into a person of gorgeousness. What other conclusion can one reasonably draw, following a debut screening of *Grease*? Olivia Newton-John ensnared John Travolta via a lengthy makeover process which culminated in her dancing provocatively on a low-tech shaky platformed fairground ride in very shiny disco pants, the Pink Ladies were exotic and poised, AND CALLED THE PINK LADIES, FOR HEAVEN'S SAKE! My life's work was set out for me in the course of those 110 minutes. I knew what I wanted to be, and what I wanted to be was fanciable.

Like I say, I was eight, so this was perhaps a bit premature. It was certainly ill-advised to share my newly identified ambition with my mother ('Mum! I want to be sexy!'), who is not at all discreet and who wasted little time in telling her friends. They laughed about it a lot, and within my earshot, as well they might. Still, as it turned out, I got the last laugh in that I started actively pursuing sexiness on the spot.

I haven't stopped since.

What is perhaps rather amazing about all this, is that I was not a pretty child. Not even vaguely. I was not cooed over, not rolled out to bedazzle the relatives; not fancied at primary school. Never cast as Mary in a nativity, a role traditionally reserved for pretty little class princesses. (I was always the narrator. I once did a poll on Twitter and discovered that all the working journalists in town were also once the narrators in their respective nativities. This means something. No idea what.) I never took receipt of an endearingly cute prepubescent Valentine's card. Never got hounded during kiss chase. Never got asked to dance at end-of-term school discos.

I wasn't ugly, exactly, just odd-looking. Bad hair, cut badly, by a local hairdresser, instructed by my maternal grandmother to 'unleash her curls', only I had no curls. Sticky-out front teeth. Big fat lips which I'd like in the fullness of time, but which made no sense at that point. Eyes which tended to rest too long on whoever had caught my attention. I was fascinated by other people, by their faces and their purpose and the way they moved. I was nosy in a way that would eventually make me a half-decent journalist (that sort of curiosity is good in my trade); and which would also mean I'd often get caught out in my gazing, and inspire rage of the: 'What are you staring at?' Or 'Take a fucking photo, it'll last longer!' variety.

I was the eldest of three girls; I got no assistance from a sporadically indulgent older sib with access to London, *Just Seventeen* or Chelsea Girl, who knew a little about skincare and blush. All I had was the *Grease* epiphany, then nothing and no one to back it up. To my chagrin, and despite hoping really hard till later in life than was, strictly speaking, seemly, it transpired that I had no fashion industry-related peripheral/de facto family members available to fly in from a teeming and fashion forward metropolis and give me a makeover of epic proportions. It's no coincidence that I've basically turned into the embodiment of the glamour-fixated, fashion enabled adult influence I longed for as a kid. I am an insanely good godmother/aunt in that respect.

But, it wasn't to be. Basically, I was shapeless, awkward, hampered with far more dungaree variants than could ever be considered good for one child; inept, goofy, starey-eyed and awkward. I was a mess. An unfancied mess, who wanted to be fancied.

I wasn't the least popular girl in my school, but I was definitely low ranking, which might have been a consequence of my slightly-off appearance; but then again, might have been a consequence of my being simultaneously very shy and very opinionated, an almost impossibly contrary position to maintain. Although I managed it. I was vaguely bullied and generally ignored; on a slow day, the boys from my school were not beyond cycling past me in the street, shouting 'Ugly Polly' into their wake; which I thought didn't bother me except I can still remember it very vividly, which would suggest that it did.

I became marginally less weird looking as a teenager. My features settled, my sticky-out teeth were reined in with a brace. My first indication that I'd undergone a minor physical transformation for the better occurred when I was fifteen. My school had, for reasons known best to it, merged for the day with another school, during which time I overheard one unknown other-school-based teenage boy remark to his mates, of me:

'How much does that twat fancy herself?'

It was such an improvement on 'Ugly Polly' that I was pleased; although heaven knows, I didn't fancy myself at all.

But then, hoorah! Huzzah! At eighteen, I went to university, where, as we've seen, I learned many things. The *least* of the things I learned was French. The most of them was how to dress. The second most was the noble art of how to be fancied.

My university, as I've explained, was a hipster university. While it offered no formal training in How To Be Fancied, fancying was integral to its overall vibe: the pretty-yet-modern campus was considered to be of great architectural merit. Its general sensibility and long term rep was bohemian leftie with a taste for the finer things in life, and its geographical location was close enough to Brighton to be almost completely infused with a dirty weekend-ish, gay-glamour-capital-of-the-UK-esque sensibility.

It was intrinsically a bit louche.

That sort of a scene runs on being fancied. On being fancied and fancying back, and the fancying of self.

I got with the programme, pretty quickly.

Here's what I learned:

Swagger. Move like you mean it. Like you're a fucking pop star. Like you know, absolutely, 100 per cent, no question, what you're doing and where you're going. Even if you don't, not really; fact is, no one does, but there is an insanely bolstering quality to be gained from the physical act of walking as if you really *do*. It's in the sway of the hips and the swing of the legs, and the upward tilt of the head, the prime purpose of which is a) seeing where you're going, and b) maximising all opportunities to meet the eyes of passers-by, at whom you smile, because, why wouldn't you? I highly recommend practising your swagger: start at home, extend it to the actual street (swaggering for a deserted block or two at first, then further, in the presence of other humans, then further still, onto high roads and into shopping districts, and even into itsu during an especially busy lunch hour). Swagger into rooms, and swagger out of them. Oh no, sorry, that's wrong . . . Swagger *into* rooms; *swish* out of them.

Expect people to fancy you. Male, female, young, old, whatever. Assume they find you appealing. Not merely on a physical basis. Fancying people is so much more complex and interesting than that; it's chemical and multi-platform and involves a delicious alignment of all manner of factors (smell, the way their brain ticks, that amazing thing which happens to the nape of their neck when they laugh raucously), which is why it's so incredibly cool. And it's not like you're ever going to know, definitively, one way or the other, if the people assembled in any situation *do* all actually fancy you or not. Not unless you ask them all, one by one, which would be an odd move to make. So why not assume they do? As a jumping off point.

Ah . . . actually, scratch that. Do this instead:

Expect people to like you. And expect that you'll like them in return. You'll be right at least some of the time, and the funny thing about assuming people already like you, and that you like them, is: it's a self-fulfilling prophecy.

Revel in the fanciability of others. All of them. Men – and perhaps most importantly, women. Do this and you'll diminish that nagging sense you're in constant competition with other women physically. That feeling that someone, somewhere is comparing all of us physically, all the time; wishing we'd look more like so-and-so and less like us. We often do feel threatened by the hotness of other women, but we shouldn't.

Good looking women are not an admonishment to us; they are not living, walking, beguiling proof of the ways in which we fail, physically. They're just other women. Their hotness in no way diminishes ours; it's just different to ours, so why respond to it with anything other than appreciation?

I know it's not an easy shift to make. We have been conditioned towards physical envy of other women, cos that sort of thing keeps the ladies divided and on our toes. And it's tough to deny it. But we have to. It's all quite logical, if you think about it. Any time you find yourself feeling the sharp prickle of envy over the abject beauty of the supermodel on the billboard, investigate it a little. Ask yourself what you and Cara Delevingne, say, are in competition for. Work? Nah. Men? Unlikely on a number of levels. So why does her beauty serve as an affront to your sense of how attractive you are? It doesn't, does it? You may apply the same rationale to any other attractive woman you ever encounter.

And as for men: fancying is a deliciously two-way street. The more time you spend observing and applauding the fanciability of them, the less time you'll have to contemplate/deconstruct/angst over your own fanciability, which is a sexy way to be.

Listen. Actually, I didn't really learn this at uni. I had inklings, I think. But I truly learned the importance of listening later when I started working as an interviewer. (Interviewing is, without question, the very best bit of being a journalist;

the biggest privilege, the biggest kick. Not because you get to talk to celebrities, but because celebrities are – it transpires – humans, and if you talk to humans properly, and you're very, very lucky, well . . . They might just show you a bit of their soul.) There is nothing more alluring than a person listening to you. Really, truly, properly listening to you. Prompting you to tell your story. Empathising without patronising. If you can listen to people properly, and sincerely, without judgement and with understanding: I promise you, you can make pretty much anyone fall at least a little in love with you. As an added bonus: very few people actually do this, which gives anyone who *does* the major advantage in the Being Fancied stakes. It's the emotional intelligence equivalent of having a massive dick.

And so you see, university was not wasted on me.

(You may also see, if you've been paying attention, that none of these pointers are related to physical beauty.)

Following a year of total, grateful, joyful submersion in my uni's unprogrammed but highly effective How To Be Fancied learning initiative, I came back to Exeter, my home town, for the summer vacation. I'd benefitted from a minor physical transformation during the preceding months: in keeping with the teachings of the glossy urbanites, I'd cashed in the year-before's Indie Kid look for an early nineties preppy acid vibe. It hinged around black Lycra bodysuits worn with white Levis 501s belted tightly in at the waist, and striped Adidas

All Star trainers as a replacement for the clompy DM shoes. My celebrity points of reference for this were: Neneh Cherry, Caron Wheeler (the vocalist on Soul II Soul's 'Back To Life (However Do You Want Me)') and Lady Miss Kier, of Deee-Lite's 'Groove Is In The Heart' fame. My hair was a shoulder-length bob, the ends of which I was in the habit of tonging into an outward flick.

But the beating heart of my makeover was emotional.

I hadn't been back in Devon very long at all when I ran smack into the boys who'd once called me Ugly Polly.

It was the middle of town on a warmish summer day. They were monopolising a patch of pavement, down which I needed to walk.

I saw them, and they saw me: only they didn't really *see* me. What they saw was an unknown quantity who swaggered about in the spirit of one who demanded to be fancied, in the expectation of one who thought she probably would *be fancied* . . . and who they instantaneously started to fancy. Such delicious compliance!

And, oh, they were thrilled! They were instantly transformed into predatory, competitive, jostling wannabe peacocks; a vibe which heightened as I walked closer.

Which I did. I watched them preen and puff and ready themselves for a fleeting interaction with New Chick In Town. I vividly remember one of them – the very worst offender of the Ugly Polly days, no less – turn to check out his hair in the mirrored escalator side of the C&A store window. I got closer. And closer. The tension rose.

And then, Hair Boy got it.

He recognised me.

His eyes widened, he couldn't quite make the transition from lust to disbelief undercut with gobsmacked amazement in the short period of time available to him. But he tried. Failed. Tried again. Failed. Ended up just looking profoundly disturbed. One by one, the others caught on around him, to similar effect. Lust. Disbelief. Doubt. It's her. But it's not her! But it is! But she's fit! Where does this leave us? Et cetera.

By the time I drew level with them on the pavement, they were frozen, a mess and a mass of bemusement.

I turned to face them.

'Oh dear!' I said.

They gaped some more.

I walked on.

Vengeance: a dish best served to those who've just realised they fancy you after all.

So it's in this spirit that I have kept right on trying to be fancied a bit more. Not always effectively, by any bloody means. Mate, I lose it all the time! Completely lose the mojo. I've felt too fat, too thin, too old, too tired, inadequately chic; not cool enough, too bloody cool for my own good: who do I think I am? Too short, too tan, too brash, too timid; too smart-arse, too dim, too common, too daft. But I've managed to dig it up again, re-tap it; or at the very least, fake it to the point that I convince everyone else, and ultimately: myself.

And I strongly encourage you to do it, too. And to certainly not question your desire to be fancied. There is power in feeling fanciable. There is energy and momentum. There is fun and there is something liberating there. And all of these things interconnect with feminism ultimately. They might not chime with it completely. They might occupy a slightly different zone, one which is a little more 'Hot' and a little less 'Feminist'. But there is certainly . . . a sort of mutual reverb.

How to Be Fancied in Handy List Form

- Wear excellent lipstick, have strong ideas. The lipstick draws attention to your mouth, via which you express the ideas, ergo: the lipstick draws attention to the ideas.

- Read good literature. Allow yourself to routinely become so deeply and utterly immersed in a novel, you're oblivious to what's going on around you. Have you ever watched anyone get so consumed by their book on public transport they miss their stop? Have you watched someone stumble over a paving stone because they can't take their eyes off their Kindle? Sexy, no? Also, according to psychologists[1] this sort of engagement with literature

---

1 Raymond A. Mar at York University in Canada and Keith Oatley, professor of cognitive psychology at the University of Toronto, who published studies into the minds of 'deep readers' – those who get completely involved in stories – in 2006 and 2009 respectively.

makes you more capable of empathy, and of entertaining opinions, theories and interests other than your own, which clearly = highly fanciable.

- Maintain good posture, good grammar, heightened integrity.

- Never cancel because you've had a better offer.

- An extra hour's sleep plus two pints of water will do your skin more favours than any anti-wrinkle serum currently on the market.

- Which is not to say you shouldn't moisturise. You should *definitely* moisturise. And SPF. But you know that already.

- Also: facials don't hurt. (Well. They do, if there are extractions. That hurts loads.)

- Be as good at the application of your own make-up as you can be, but never worry about being seen without it. The more often you *are* seen without it, the more latitude you have to enjoy a show-stopper all-guns transformation moment, when you *do* take the time, and energy, and art, to paint it all on.

- Remove that make-up every night before you sleep. Cleansing wipes: there for the drunk times.

- Run with your peculiarities. Never fear appearing a little odd. See it rather as: being rare.

- Find yourself a good eyebrow threader. Eyebrows are the curtains on the windows of the soul. (Or maybe the pelmets?)

- Mean things. Stand for things. Stand *up* for things. Avoid lazy thinking and uncritical adoption of received wisdom like it's herpes. It *is* herpes. Herpes of the soul.

- Be generous: fiscally and spiritually. Never under-tip.

- Pick your lipstick the way you pick your women . . . Sorry, sorry, not *women* . . . Racehorses! The way you pick your racehorse. Go for the ones with the good names.

- Be smart, but never intellectually snobbish. Never deny your capacity to be shallow. There's no emotional or intellectual depth without corresponding shallows, in my experience. And, if you *really* consider yourself to be non-shallow: never sit next to me at a dinner party, thanks.

- Be self-aware, without being self-conscious.

- Concern yourself with your hair, but never bother other people with it. Talking about your hair is like talking about your dreams: literally no one else cares.

- Although a (really good) blow dry can be more effective than a new dress, in terms of bringing men to their knees. They're oddly hair-oriented, that lot.

- Eat avocado, whenever and wherever it's an option. Tastes like heaven, plumps out the epidermis.

- Accept credit when it's earned and due you; never dodge the blame, or steal the accolades of others.

- Take care of your feet, as well as your hands, or they will end up looking like wizened Doritos.

- Demonstrate attitude – which shouldn't be confused with being mean, or bitchy, or showing off.

- Demonstrate poise; although equally: never be afraid to let the façade drop, to let other people know that you are fundamentally a bit of a dick. I am *such* a dick. All the best people are.

- Stop smoking, right this minute.

- Proceed with kindness. Kindness; sexy as sin.

9

Scary Hairy Mary

I begin my daily depilatory campaign bright and early and in the shower, regular as clockwork, ritualised as religion, regimented as the Changing of the Guard. Having shampooed the hair on my head,[1] I scoop up a little left over skull froth, which I smooth along the full extent of my right leg (always the right leg first, no idea why; I'll prop it up on the plinth of the bath side, via a balletic, fluid swinging manoeuvre I've perfected over the years). I slop n slide the second-hand lather over my (yikes!) slightly hairy toes, and I continue, over my foot and my ankle, up the shin and the knee, aaaaaaaaaall the way to the tucky fold where my thigh encounters my arse at the back and my hip at the front. Then, I set about that slippery, soapy limb with a razor: a fully fledged non-disposable man razor, mind you, none of that girlie girlie pink shit for me, those fluttery affairs with the vigorous names and the additional Aloe Vera strips are simply not up to the task of my

---

1 Henceforth with, the 'good' hair.

robust leg stubble. Their safety bars get uselessly clogged if I so much as flash them a glimpse of my pre-shaven shins; they faint away like fairy princesses if I try to actually apply them to my flesh.

Having scraped away diligently and expertly at every square inch of my prickly foot, calf, knee, thigh, and the lower portion of my bottom, having very nearly, or just *actually*, nicked something somewhere; having marvelled over the skill necessary to deal with the rapidly evolving crevasses in my knee caps, I rinse – and then I repeat the whole process on my left leg.

Next: I'll trim at what's left of the lady garden. Formerly, a resplendent and wayward multi-directional, electrified shock of a pubic explosion, which I tamed with semi-regular Brazilian waxes; now – following a six month course of IPL[2] – an old man's bedraggled goatee of what's technically a bush, although I'd doubt you'd describe it as remotely bushy if you were to see it in real life, which you won't. Unless you ask very nicely.

Then: I'll dismount the shower for the purposes of shaving my armpits, which I do in front of the bathroom mirror. You see, my pits are curiously deep and complex, a system of interconnected underarm mini caves rather than a one-off pit, and if I don't get a very good look at what I'm doing, I'll miss bits. (Not that even this level of scrupulous attention will stop my underarms developing the

---

2 Intense Pulsed Light treatment

pit-equivalent of five o'clock shadow in the course of one day – often by 3.30, at that. My armpit hair grows *fast*.)

Finally: I position myself so that my reflection in the mirror catches the light filtering through my bathroom window, illuminating any random overnight sprouters, individual hairs which emerge suddenly, unbidden, and at dramatic angles, from beneath my brows, or my sideburny cheek area, or my top lip, or (most hideously of all, promise you'll tell no one?) my chin. I tweak and tug and ease these out, using one of the three pairs of precision tweezers I've placed strategically around my flat, for the purpose of emergency random sprouter removal. (I have a fourth pair in my handbag, because random sprouters are no respecters of schedules, they can occur at any time and in any location, and will almost certainly come to one's attention in the midst of a tricksy meeting, while you're frantically stress-caressing the contours of your face.)

Et voila! The daily depilatory campaign in step-by-step form; the not-all-that-little and incredibly-often efforts I go to, and which I complement with alternate weekly visits to the threaders for an all-over face job – and those (rarer, but *still*) times I get my nostrils professionally waxed. Because I'm . . . worth it?

Hair removal, hair removal! So much bloody removing of the hair! Am I hairier than most, or just more squeamish about the hair I have, more OCD about its eradication? Is everyone this bad, this dedicated, this devoted, this intense?

Is it a hobby or a compulsion or a chore or a job? Couldn't tell you. I tell some women about my hair removal regime and they are appalled or amused or disbelieving or they conclude I must be one hairy motherfucker. 'Seriously?' says H. 'Every day?' I tell others, and they tell me I'm an amateur compared to them.

I began waging one-woman war on my own follicles aged twelve; attacking my newly pubescently hairy shins with slatherings of eighties wonder cream Immac, secreted away in the depths of a guesthouse in Swanage. I was on summer hols with my mother and two younger sisters, all of whom had gone off in search of seashells and souvenirs, which was a result, because I wanted to Immac in secret, without permission or judgement. It felt like a grown-up thing to attempt, defiant and embarrassing in equal measure. You can't do that stuff with an audience of blood relatives.

I read the instruction sheet three times over, reasonably convinced I was about to squirt the product directly into my own eyes, thus blinding myself with my own vanity. Then I unleashed the Immac, spatula-ing it onto my legs with the plastic device provided. I timed fifteen precise minutes, then I rinsed: hauling one leg after the other up and into the guestroom basin, too terrified of discovery to risk a stiff, sticky-legged jaunt to the shared bathroom along the corridor.

It was a tense, gloopy, smelly, illicit and ultimately satisfying interlude, in the established tradition of all rites of passage. I revelled in how smooth and sheeny clean my legs felt afterwards.

Once was all it took: I was hooked on hair removal.

I did it again, a month later. And again, two weeks after that.

Immac was my gateway depilatory product; within six months, urged on by a daring school mate, I tried a razor. And wow! If the cream had felt adult and verboten, this was a whole new level of thrilling! This had *knives* in it! I shaved and I shaved, first my shins (front side only, because I couldn't see the backs, so who cared?) and then my armpits. And then I ran out of hairy bits.

Well: I thought I had.

When I was sixteen, my boyfriend looked deep into my eyes, brushed his forefinger – so very delicately – over my top lip, and breathed:

'Some girls get a bit of a moustache, don't they?'

Which would have been rude and outrageous and devastating enough to the wobbly esteem of a daft young thing who thought herself truly very deeply in love for the first time, even if he hadn't subsequently dumped me: *so that he could go out with a man.*

But he did.

Convinced, nonetheless, that he was right and I was hairy, I added 'top lip' to the list of things I had to de-hair. And so it was that, before I had even reached my majority, I had launched myself on an epic beauty quest which would only grow in scope and intensity over the forthcoming years and decades, monopolising more and more of my body, time, cash and energies, leaving me hairless in ways I couldn't even dream of.

The waxing! The threading!

I follow developments in depilation lotions and technologies like other people follow the stock markets. I have tried pretty much every hair removal process known to (wo)man, up to and including: creams, machines, something that's supposed to cauterise the roots with sound waves. I've waxed and I've self-waxed, sugared and tweezed; I've done my legs with pumice stones, with bleach, with pulsed light and with something very like sandpaper. I was an early adopter of the Brazilian bikini wax, dispatched in the late nineties to investigate the then newly arrived pube-removal trend for an article. One treatment later, I was a convert; I've barely let my bush settle, ever since. Did it hurt? Yes, it hurt! So much of hair removing hurts! Or at least: it used to. I've become inured to that particular kind of pain. Which is either a mark of how damned hard I am – or an indication that something profound in me has given up the ghost, shrivelled and died.

I am vigilant and scrupulous, I know at all times roughly where I am in any given hair growth cycle; I know what needs to be tended to next, and how.

'Where are you?' friends text, when I've gone temporarily off radar of a Saturday morning. Then: 'Oh don't tell me. You're being plucked.'

*

So now, here comes the part where I tell you that righteous feminists depilate too, right? That there is, in fact, something intrinsically empowering in the very act of hair removal, in the routine and discipline of it, in the pain tolerance required to endure it, in paying another woman handsomely to coat your limbs and your genitals in hot wax, and then rip it from your prone body in one smooth moment, while you sweat and swear and try not to squeal too obviously? That modern feminism is, at its very heart, about choosing for ourselves how we live and what we shave, and therefore our right to depilate is up there with our right to vote! That this is nobody's business but our own!

Well, no, actually. Sorry. I can't do that. No matter how hard I try. There is no way that hair removal can make its peace with feminist leanings. None. I don't buy the 'feminism is all about the right to choose' argument, because I think there are some things that might feel like choices, but are actually slavish adherence to widespread expectations, and I think hair removal is definitely one of them. As for this being no one's business but your own . . . We are almost all of us doing this, aren't we? Virtually every last one of us is complying with the incredibly dominant faux hairless diktats, which means it isn't an individual statement of grooming preference, it's pretty much the opposite.

Oh, there's a couple of factors which might mitigate it slightly. If you look at them in the right light (like I look at my tache). There's the fact that men depilate too these days, more and more; which means society's revulsion at body hair is going both ways. It's like there's an evolving equality in this particular repression.

And then there's the thing which I always say about how strong, fierce and traditional a feminist stand you take with your own body hair – that it is strongly related to how hairy you are. I quietly suspect that those women who decry depilation, who denounce it as a snivelling capitulation to the ridiculous whims of our endlessly demanding male overlords, the ones who say there's something savage and feral and sexy about their own armpit hair – are also not all that hairy. Certainly not Hairy Scary Marys like me.

But still. The removal of body hair takes time and costs money, a literal and metaphorical tax on us for having the audacity to show off our skin in public. It's compliant with an entirely arbitrary, and entirely unnatural, societal idea on how women are supposed to look – one which may have something to do with our equating body hair with the kind of primal and sexual urges nice women are supposed to ignore.

Pubic waxing traditions borrow heavily on the aesthetic of pornography, which is rarely your dream jumping off point. And all forms of lady-hair-stripping are at least partly a consequence of the beauty industry's eternal desire to cash in. Women started shaving their armpits for the first time after the US edition of magazine *Harper's Bazaar* ran an advert, in 1915, showing an image of a young woman in a sleeveless dress, with her arms arched above her head to reveal hairless armpits, and a strapline that said: 'Summer dress and modern dancing combine to make necessary the removal of objectionable hair'; although it equally could have read: 'Razor manufacturers have just worked out that they can double their market share by flogging to women as well as men'.

The UK hair removal market is now estimated to be worth around £300 million a year; during the economic downturn, it proved recession proof.

The truth is that I remove my body hair for one reason and one reason only: because I think that if I didn't, it would scare men. Because men are less and less used to seeing women with hair anywhere but on their heads and above their eyes. It's not fun and it doesn't require much skill; and, unlike getting dressed, applying make-up, making the good hair work with today's neckline, it isn't creative: it's merely a dull, tedious process of getting rid of something which will, inevitably, come back. And possibly bring its mates.

So I do it only because I think that if I left it, men wouldn't like it. It would shock them and appal them and turn them off and make them a little queasy. All of them: the one I keep in my flat, the ones I buy my morning porridge from, the ones I kinda fancy a bit and I'd like it if they fancied me back, the ones with whom I have entirely platonic relationships, and whose opinion of my appearance is of absolutely no consequence or interest whatsoever, the ones I don't know and will never know.

Them. I do it for them.

Yet this is me: and I do almost *nothing* to please men. I don't dress for them (well . . . like, almost ever), I don't moderate my opinions or my foul language in front of them. I happily and lustily shout the odds at men in my professional capacity, all the time. I told Donald Trump off when he curtailed an interview in New York seventeen minutes early on the grounds that 'I'm a busy man', explained I'd come a *very* long way to meet him and that I, as it happens, was a busy woman . . . I made Jon Bon Jovi remove his sunglasses at the start of another interview, told him it was absurd to expect me to hold a conversation with him with his eyes covered. I made David Cameron blush during a drinks reception at Number 10 (I asked him if he was telling me he thinks Michelle Obama is too good for Barack. He'd just returned from a trip to the White House, and was very full of how beautiful Michelle is). I told one of One Direction off (fondly) for calling me a bitch (again, fondly), and there's a prominent member of the Manchester City first team who will, I'm confident, *never* cross me again. I've asked Noel Gallagher, Piers Morgan and Paul Weller if they were any good in bed; and I asked Marilyn Manson – who was, at the time, dating the actress Evan Rachel Wood – if it helped that his girlfriend was half his age. He laughed, and said it probably did.

You see, I do not suffer fools gladly, and by 'fools', I do generally mean 'men'.

*

So here I am: neither a man-pleaser (more of a man-agitator, let's be frank), nor a serious groomer: yet when it comes to this one, literally hairy, issue, I become hyper neurotic and a little bit Jane Austen. I SIMPLY CANNOT RISK A MAN – ANY MAN – SEEING MY BAD HAIRS! Because, my dears! Whatever would they think?

Because men really do not like body hair, do they? While I think it's entirely possible that they are far less judgemental about almost all other aspects of our appearance than we ourselves are – while I think, for example, that a fresh facial impacts a woman's fanciability levels in terms of the confidence it imbues her with, but not because a man gives a flying fuck about professionally maintained pores – I do think men are somewhat body hair phobic. They notice. They see. They shudder.

Why do I care?

Why am I so distressed, when I care so little about the other stuff? What is it about those fine, protruding stalks of almost-nothing, which challenges me so profoundly, which persuades me to go to such lengths? Why body hair, but not my teeth or my toes or my skin tone or my under eye bags?

No bloody clue. None. I've thought about it and thought about it and ultimately come up with nothing, except: oh bloody hell! Have my fingertips encountered the very earliest stages of yet another random sprouter, right there in the midst of a previously non-sprouting plane of my face?

No. I cannot make my body hair hatred coexist

comfortably with the feminism. Because it doesn't. It isn't feminist. It just isn't.

Where does it leave me?

I'll tell ya: It leaves me asserting my big fat feminist right to fuck it the fuck up from time to time . . . And *still* call myself a fucking feminist.

Right here, right now, I proudly and defiantly declare that sometimes I will know exactly what I should be doing – feministically speaking – and then I will go ahead and do the complete opposite. I will buy the biscuit variant the Man I Keep In My Flat prefers, over the ones I prefer, because I know he thinks my sacrifice makes them taste even sweeter. I will never quite dare to cut the 'good' hair on my head short, even though I think it might look cooler, because I tried it once in the early nineties and some man whose name I can't even remember told me it was prettier longer. I won't drink full fat Coke.

I will do this because, with the best will in the world, I am not feminist in every act and deed. Not everything I do or think or say is done or thought or said because I think it'll help me, or any other woman for that matter, move closer toward the ultimate end goal of social equality. I am contradictory and messy and hypocritical, because I am alive, and that means, by definition, that I am not always as good as I should be. At almost everything, up to and including being a feminist.

Sometimes feminism and being a human clash, hideously.

Like when we just keep on sleeping with the ghastly man, over and over, because even though he's ghastly and probably really hasn't entirely finished with his ex-girlfriend, like he says he has – or just maybe *because* he's ghastly and he possibly hasn't finished with his ex – you have *really* good sex.

Or we get married and we take our husband's surname, which is tantamount to declaring he owns our ass, but we do it anyway because it's, I dunno, easier, or because we like his name better, or because we think it's cute.

Or you read COO of Facebook Sheryl Sandberg's *Lean In*, but it just makes you feel a bit knackered, because you can't do all those things Sheryl does, like taking your rightful place at the conference table at work or shouting down every man who tries to steal your thunder and your credit, or taking no more than a month's maternity leave, or keeping your eye perpetually on the next promotion. Even thinking about it makes you feel sleepy!

Or we end an argument with a man by crying, because (we tell ourselves) we just *hate* confrontation *so much* – only deep down we know it's because passive aggression and emotional manipulation have rarely failed us in the past.

Or we tell other women to stand up and be counted, to protest loudly on their own behalf, to love and value themselves professionally and personally and every other way . . . while knowing damn well *we* don't do this for ourselves.

Or we feel momentarily completely validated because some bloke at the bar sent us over a drink.

Or we let the sexist backchat slide because the sexist backchatter is driving our cab, and we just want to get home.

Or we'll de-hair every millimetre of our poor, raw, over-scraped skin because we're worried society will hate us if we don't.

You know,

That kind of thing.

So yeah, here it is, my gift to you:

Your big, fat feminist right to fail. To fuck it the fuck up, and *still* call yourself a fucking feminist.

Love, Hairy Scary Mary.

10

Thin

___

Admit It, You Hate Me Because I'm Thin

Polly Vernon, *Observer Food Monthly*,
Sunday 14 September, 2003

I didn't mean to get so thin. I liked food, especially supermarket top-end ranges and expensive freebie work lunches. And I didn't have an eating disorder. Just the usual understated body image issues; that low-level discontent most women experience on watching the stars on a glossy Channel 4 American import go about their whip-thin, fragrant business. Aka *Sex and the City* syndrome.

But thin wasn't something I actively pursued. Thin happened to me. Firstly, there was some heightened life turmoil. A new job, a very ill mother, general unease about where I was going now I had hit my thirties. None of which made me inclined to eat. Secondly, I became 'accidentally Atkins'. I fell spontaneously out of love with carbohydrates – with the pasta and bread that used to make up most of my meals – and in love with protein. I discovered fish, properly, for the first time ever. Sea bass, tuna steak, swordfish, yes! Went a bit yoghurt-based for breakfast, carpaccio of beef and rocket for lunch, fancy wilted spinach salad for dinner. In six months, I lost nearly two stone. On a clothes shopping expedition, I realised with vague interest that I'd gone from being a size 10 going on 12, to a size 6 going on 8. This tipped me and my five-five frame into the realm of what's technically referred to as 'probably a bit too thin, lady'.

What I didn't realise was how massively Thin would impact on my life. Beyond the predictable scenarios (mother fretting, lover wondering out loud if I was 'bulmenic' [sic]), other things changed. Rather excitingly, I was embraced by a fast and glam super-thin super-class. I was summoned for a drink by a group of women I used to work with on Vogue, a place where thinliness is not just next to godliness, it rates way, way above it. They practically applauded when I entered the bar. 'How did you do it?' asked the people who eat nothing (give or take the occasional pistachio nut – which, apparently, are the thin person's preferred bar snack because the time it takes to open them, multiplied by the possibility that you might break a nail on the shell, means you won't consume nearly as many as you might if they were, say, cashews). 'Stress, grief, a bit of abject misery, accidental Atkins,' I told them. 'Wow,' they said. 'Brilliant.'

We spent the night drinking cinnamon Bellinis, the Diet Coke of the cocktail world. We waved away the canapés on offer. We didn't eat: caramelised red onion and soured cream blinis, mini portions of sausage and mash on big china spoons, California rolls, mini lemon mousses in shot glasses. Everyone hung on my every word because I was newly, truly thin, and therefore authoritative.

Not everyone was so impressed. Old friends started watching me when we lunched together. I could see them thinking: why doesn't she have any bread? And why is she only having a starter? That's the oldest trick in the book, that is! They stealth-ordered extra portions of fat chips for me, in the vain hope I wouldn't notice. I did.

Men, in general, do not approve. Builders accost me on the street, telling me I could be a 'good-looking bird, if I ate a bit more'. They wave their sandwiches at me, in case I am a bit hazy on what food looks like. When I was loudly declaring my love of dark choc Baci in my local Italian deli, I heard the man in the queue behind me mutter, 'Yeah, right.' In short: you get thin, you become public property.

Our culture is obsessed by thin and by The Thin, by the obesity versus anorexia debate, by our (women's, obviously) constant taboo pursuit of thinness. A celebrity who isn't incredibly thin isn't generally considered 'A-list'. It's not right, but there it is. Everybody wants to be thinner. Whatever they say. And now I am, and I love it. I lost weight by accident, but I could have put it all back on again by now if I'd wanted to. But I don't.

Contrary to popular belief, being thin has made me happy. I've spent probably 16 years wondering if I would look better if I were skinnier, and now I know for sure. I do. But then almost everyone does. I like the way clothes fit me. And I like having cheekbones (although I admit I can look a touch gaunt in harsh lighting). As one of the most astute women I know said to me recently: 'You've lost too much weight. God, I love it when people say that to me.'

And weirdly, I like food more, now that I am untroubled by Sex and the City syndrome. I certainly think about it a lot less. I don't waste time calculating that day's fat intake, totting up calories consumed absent-mindedly on the corner of a Post-it. I don't need to. I know it's not that much: that's sushi for you.

My friends have re-christened me Thinny Girl, and I love it. Thin is part of who I am now and I thoroughly intend to make the best of it. With no apologies.

I wrote that article – *column*, technically – over a decade ago. It was printed in the opening section of *Observer Food Monthly*, the supplement which accompanies the *Observer* newspaper, where I was employed full time as a writer and editor; and oh my! It caused seven shades of bother. A burst of hate mail, which reduced after a week or so to a steady trickle, some of which continues even to this day. A wave of online evisceration; although this was the lost, dimly remembered era of TTBT,[1] so, in retrospect, could have been much, much worse than it was. Still. I got death threats; entire websites devoted to detailing my badness, my stupidity, my presumed decline into anorexia nervosa. A small envelope of suspicious looking white powder was sent to me anonymously through the post, as a result of which the entire newspaper was closed down for an afternoon while a forensic-suit-clad set of cops descended in the belief that the powder might be anthrax. (Chemical analysis showed that it was custard powder. 'Which was ironic,' a

---

1 The Time Before Twitter

trade journalist wrote of the incident, 'because everyone knows that Polly Vernon doesn't eat.')

Readers revolted. Letters of complaint rolled in, in their – I dunno – forties, fifties, maybe even hundreds? Enough to ensure that the readers' editor of the *Observer* wrote an apology for my column (which ran in the subsequent issue of the paper; over which, I still fume). Serious Questions were raised about the judiciousness of printing such a profoundly controversial piece in the first place, during the newspaper's morning conference sessions. ('Not everyone "wants to be thinner", actually!' one female editor raged. 'Do you?' asked another editor, a mate. 'Yes,' said the female editor. 'Like: half a stone?')

Colleagues who'd never paid me much attention in the past started looking at me funny. Interns furtively eyed up my lunch choices; I caught one of them snapping a pic of it, as I unpacked it on my desk one day, on her smartphone for posterity. Girls Aloud – then, newly formed — signed a copy of their first ever CD for me: 'To Miss Skinny, love Cheryl, Nicola, Nadine, Sarah and Kimberly XXX.'

Admittedly, I loved that.

But still. It all got a little tough for a while.

I called it Skinny-Geddon.

I did not see it coming. I probably should have done. But I didn't. It was the first time I'd ever caused any sort of a furore in journalism. I'd originally written the piece because an editor had some space to fill; her regular columnist was on maternity leave. She clobbered me en route to the tea trolley (I was seeking Minstrels; oh the irony!) and she said:

'You're thin! You should write about it for me!'

I should make it clear that this particular editor is a genius and a good friend, whose capacity to convince writers to write things they simply wouldn't dream of writing for anyone else in the land is unrivalled.

Anyway: 'About being thin?' I said. 'Me?' I said. 'OK!' I said, because I was a compliant little soul in those days – a little less so now – and also because I was, and remain, something of an egotist, and columns are the easiest, quickest and laziest way for a journalist to show off. ('Mind vomit,' my friend C – a reporter, or "proper journalist" – calls columns. 'All columnists are mind vomiters.') Two hours' work, little or no research, and you get your face blown up big on the glossy pages of somewhere or other. How gratifying that is for the thin-membraned, danger-ously over-inflated balloonish ego of your average features writer!

Except, of course, when everyone hates you for what you've written. Then it's awful.

When the column was published, and the backlash hap-pened, and *kept* happening . . . Well, it made me profoundly uncomfortable for causing any bother ('Oh God, oh God, I'm so sorry! Forget I said anything, yeah?'), then defiant ('Erm, OK guys, I just reread it, and seriously: it's not *that* bad. Is it? I mean, it was *meant* to be funny.') and ultimately: kind of tired. Internet search me to this day, and Google will prompt you to enter criteria relating to my Twitter account, my age (How Old Is Polly Vernon anyway?) and then: Polly Vernon Skinny, followed closely by Polly Vernon Diet.

Was I wrong to write that column? Insensitive, offensive, antagonising, irresponsible, even? Should I have known better?

Maybe.

I mean, as hard as it is for me (still) to believe anyone else would ACTUALLY BELIEVE there's a 'fast and glam super-thin super-class' out there (there isn't) or that I was embraced by it (I wasn't, on account of it not being real), I do now see that my gags were potentially obscured by the contentiousness of my subject matter.

In my defence: 2003 was a different time as far as weight was concerned; a time before weight became a cultural property, a time before thinness-celebrating and fat-shaming, size zero horror/envy. Before thinspiration sites, lollipop headed celebrities, red circles of shame on magazine covers and reality TV stars locked in an eternal circle of fattening and slenderising, a 'journey' they document rigorously for the delectation of whichever magazine or TV production company will pay them the most to be shot in a bikini. None of that had really kicked in. It was getting there. I realise that now. I probably realised it the day that column was published and Skinny-Geddon erupted. But it was definitely simmering away just beneath the surface at that point, waiting for its Moment.

It was also a different time in terms of newspapers and their online presence. Neither me, nor my editor, fully realised that this really quite silly piece of work was destined to hang around on the internet for an eternity, nor that it would turn me into an early example of the modern journalistic property known as 'click bait'. Click baiting is when a writer, generally female – ladies make the best click bait, for the idea that we might have opinions worth printing at all is still considered somewhat incendiary apparently – publishes something counterintuitive, contrary to popular perspective, and provocatively headlined,[2] with the aim of driving heavy, outraged, spuming and fuming online reader traffic towards the newspaper's website, where it'll result in much sweary comment, viral link-spreading and so on and so forth.

Still, if I'm to believe even *some* of the backlash: I caused pain with this piece. People have told me that it made them hate themselves – right before they got around to hating me. Twenty-something women tell me they read it as young teenagers and foreswore sweets on the spot.

Yikes.

Would I take it back if I could? Knowing what I know now, about the grief it caused others, never mind the grief it caused me?

I don't know. Censorship is not an elegant vibe, and I

---

2 A headline the click bait herself won't have written. Journalists rarely, if ever, write their own headlines.

maintained at the time – and I still maintain – that there is truth in that column, in as much as: what are we doing going around telling each other that we should love our bodies whatever and however they are, when we're also simultaneously going around venerating images of extremely buff Victoria's Secret models? That sickening schism is not helping us to work through our collective issues with weight.

And heaven knows: we have collective issues about weight!

Dudes! We are fucked up about this! Screwed. Bonko. Fifty shades of cray! Far more than we should be, if you think – really *think* – about what we're talking about here: the padding on our bones, the stuff which keeps the vital organs and the blood and the increasingly crazed thoughts on the inside. It isn't a religion or a political belief system, or illness or war. It's weight. It's just weight.

Except it isn't 'just' weight. It isn't 'just' anything. It is complicated and escalating, it is about class (the connections between obesity and the socially underprivileged are well-documented, politicians are not beyond using obesity as a stick with which to beat certain sectors of society) and it is about mental health (too thin? You're probably mad. Too fat? You're probably depressed).

Which is why we're *so* uncomfortable about it. Our own, and others'.

Stigmatised and stigmatising, judgemental and judged. All of us. Not just me. Not just the thinspo brigade, or the documentary-inspiring, crane-to-winch-me-out-of-my-apartment, morbidly obese. Not just the duckfaced, teenie selfie-inclined crew, or Claire from Steps or Kerry Katona or thingy from *TOWIE* or any of the other women whose entire career trajectory depends on their capacity to gain and lose and regain weight and make TV shows all about it . . . *All of us*. The slightly chubby and the naturally slim, the size 14s who dream of being a size 10 and the size 6s who dream of thigh gap; the women who know without having to think about it that they're a size 8 in Gap and M&S, but a 14 in Topshop; the ones who know, absolutely *know*, they'd be 100 per cent happy with their bodies if it weren't for their cankles, no! Back fat. No! Second and third chins, muffin top, knee chub, et cetera.

I mean, I say this isn't a war – but sometimes, it feels like it, no? Like we're at war with ourselves over the construction and rightness, or otherwise, of our own bodies. Like we're at war with cultural ideals on weight. Like we're at war with an incredibly powerful food industry, which can't help but actively try and make us fatter and fatter, with bigger portions, BOGOFs, sugar added to pretty much everything . . . Those insanely huge bags of M&Ms and mini Twixes and bitesize Wispas and Maltesers which supermarkets dangle temptingly from the display units that line the run-up to self-service tills, and which are marketed as being for sharing purposes, but which we all know we'll work our way through, all on our own. (Oh those bags of choc! Which are also labelled as 'Treats', only they're not really treats, are they, so much as habitual; those bags of choc which are frequently sold, on offer, at the bargain knock-down price of a teeny tiny singular quid a go, which, when you compare it with an average – what? – 80p for a normal-sized Twix? makes them begin to seem like actively sensible choices in terms of value for money at least, and which also fosters in you warmish glows of good feeling towards the people who so generously slashed the price on your choc, only of course, what they're actually doing is getting you accustomed to the idea that this serving is how much choc you now require in one sitting.)

And we feel like we're at war with the women who are thinner than us (neurotic, anorexic, controlling bitches!) and the ones who are fatter (lazy, weak, undisciplined, unhealthy, oh God, what if we're going to get as fat as them one day?). At war with the diet industry, the health and fitness industry, and the beauty industry, none of which are ever likely to encourage us to think our bodies are fine just as they are, because that is not how capitalism works.

We are bombarded by completely contrary messages about weight, every day; our own, that of teenage girls, that of the increasingly morbidly obese underprivileged underclass, that of models, celebrities, royalty and the occasional dieting politico. On the one hand, we're subjected to a world wallpapered by visual imagery that celebrates the super-thin, a relentless, one note, hip-jutty notion of physical perfection which monopolises our TV screens and our billboards and which, I'm pretty sure, has become skinnier, even, in the course of the ten-plus years since I wrote the very questionable column, to the extent that I'm probably not all that skinny any more by modern standards. *Then* we're told that we should learn to love ourselves as we are, whatever shape we are, because that is the greatest love of all; and anyway, guys don't dig skinny chicks, so just think about that!

Meanwhile, the government dispatches task forces to assess what kind of psychological damage is being wrought upon our body-conscious teenagers, many of whom are reported to be unhappier with themselves physically than they have been in years (although I've gotta say, no one ever asked me how happy I was with my body when I was a teenager. I'd definitely have said: 'not very', had they). And *then* it dispatches other task forces to try and establish what on earth we're going to do about the burgeoning obesity crisis, the one predicted to impact over 50 per cent of UK adults by 2050, entirely destroying whatever's left of the NHS by that time. It cooks up half-baked, unrealistic, unenforceable, unkind policies that threaten to take away benefits from those who are obese to the point that they can't work.

We're told, quite definitively, that faddy diets never, ever work (not really, not long term), and then we're told this new one that all the famous people in Hollywood are doing is medically proven and, like, *totally* effective, you've *got* to try it! We're told that carbs are the enemy . . . No, sugar!

No, fat! We're told to eat five portions of fruit and veg a day, nope, sorry, seven! Only: more veg than fruit, eh? Because fruit's full of sugar, and sugar's the enemy, so . . . Oh no, hang on, it's carbs again. Down with bread!

And yeah, we are taught to be highly suspicious of thin people. Thinnies. They must definitely be approached with extreme caution.

Because thin people must be weird. In this environment of drive-thru Maccy D's, and donuts sold in twelve-packs, and vast quantities of mayo added to any takeaway sandwich you care to mention, and sugar – so much sugar! – screwing with our capacity to metabolise so completely and utterly, repressing our brain receptors' ability to recognise when we're full; sugar, added wilfully and willingly to almost all packaged food because it's perpetuating a mass addiction, from which the food industry profits handsomely!

Thinnies must be weird! Controlled and controlling, neurotic, humourless (how can anyone have a sense of humour when they're hungry?), probably ill, certainly joyless, definitely smug. Thin people walk around, judging every person who is not as thin as them, because being thin is all thin people think about, right? Thin people have less integrity than the less thin, and they are less likable, no? Like, for example: remember that time Graydon Carter, revered editor of *Vanity Fair*, told the world that the famously thin, generally beleaguered actress Gwyneth Paltrow had once asked him how she could make herself more appealing to the general public, and Carter said:

'Gain twenty pounds?' And he was right. Though she didn't. If she had, she'd presumably have lost acting roles, because the public might like a little extra weight, but Hollywood does not.

And therefore wanting to be thinner is bad juju. Wanting to leave the ranks of the little-bit-chubby, in favour of the suspiciously skinny, is tantamount to desertion!

Right? RIGHT?

Well: no. Obviously, I'm going to say no. But: no! Wanting to be a little bit thinner is just wanting to be a little bit thinner. It doesn't have to be an unsisterly act of simpering compliance with a restrictive physical ideal. It certainly doesn't have to be about making women sick; either sick with sadness because we think we're not thin enough, or physically sick, because we've been driven to acts of disordered eating by this non-stop contradictory scream of perspective on weight. It can also simply be a choice, one you're entirely capable of making as a feminist, because: hey. It's your freakin' body. Being a little thinner, or wanting to be a little thinner, or taking measures to be a little thinner, doesn't make you more stupid, less sincere, less authentic, less You. It just makes you a bit thinner. Don't stress about the politics of it. Don't fuss about your potential to fail.

Just do it, as someone once said, quite a lot, in an advertising campaign. Do it not because you hate your body, but because you're starting to love it.

*

Of course my friend Bryony Gordon, the brilliant broadsheet writer and even more brilliant memoir author, and the face of a YouTube channel called One Fat Mother (with which she spearheads the anti-Yummy Mummy movement), would say I'm talking nonsense. In 2014, Bryony published a column in the *Daily Telegraph*, about how much she liked being fat. Having struggled to remain thin all through her twenties, Bryony got unexpectedly and deliciously pregnant in her early thirties, had her daughter – and then just didn't lose the weight she gained during pregnancy. Fourteen months on, she was still fat, a fact she celebrated with this column. 'Now,' she wrote, 'I'm fat and I'm happier and healthier than ever . . . I weigh something like 210 lbs and my dress size is an 18. I can no longer shop on the high street unless I fancy wearing a Zara handbag as a glove, or a Topshop belt as a hairband . . . and after all those years of fearing fat, I find it wonderful.'

Her column was published, and, inevitably, Bryony got eviscerated online and via her work email account; in exactly the same way that I had when I published the skinny column, only times about ten, because when Bryony published we were no longer enjoying the relative calm of TTBT.[3]

'Do you think our haters are the same haters?' I asked

---

3 The Time Before Twitter. We've been through this already. Do concentrate!

her, as hers reached peak bile, and she tried to remain philosophical in the face of people hurling abuse at her in 140 characters or less.

'Probably,' she said.

'Ugh,' I said.

'You know what, though?' Bryony continued. 'I don't think the actual problem is you talking about being thin, or me talking about being fat. I think the actual problem is that we both, as women, had the brazen audacity to tell the world we like our bodies. I think that's what makes people so mad.'

Bugger me, I thought. She's right! After a decade of being convinced I was the target of mindless skinny-phobia, it turns out I was quite wrong. I'm the target of How Dare You Say You Like Any Aspect Of Your Body, Madam? And In Public, Too!

I haven't risked saying that I like my body, not for a while. Not in print, not even out loud. Twelve years after I first lost weight, and first blew up the internet (well, a bit) by writing a column about my experiences as a thin woman in a chubby world – I'm kinda over the grief. Over the fake anthrax, over the online comments, over the hate mail, over being That Woman Who Wrote That Awful Article. In the current climate of generalised and widespread weight-angst, the only acceptable stance to hold on your own body, as a woman, is to consider yourself on some sort of Emotional Journey,[4]

---

4 Ugh.

away from out-and-out loathing it[5] towards a quiet, Zen acceptance of it. *That's* where we're supposed to be with our bodies. But we're not supposed to actively like them, are we? To consider them entirely good enough? That wouldn't be cool. That would be hubris, or vanity, or smugness. That would be dismissive of other women's experiences of, and struggles with, their bodies, somehow. That might seem unsympathetic, unlikable, unrelatable – unfeminist, even.

And yet – oh God, help me – I do like my body. I do.

It is still thin. Still a size 6, going on 8. It's older; inevitably, age has altered it. It's a little more dimpled around the thigh than it used to be; the skin tone isn't quite as peachy, it moves a little differently; gravity marks it, here and there. But it is still thin. My weight is a little harder to maintain, but I'm putting that extra work in. Not working out precisely, so much as *walking* out ... (I'll get to that shortly). I am putting the extra effort in, striving a little harder, focusing a little more, working for it not because I hate it, not because I seek to diminish it, to whittle it away to virtually nothing – but precisely because I *like* it. I value it. I think it's worth it.

I like my body because it is well and it carries me around just fine. I like it not because it is perfect (no such thing as

---

5 Which is considered to be a somewhat pathetic and unenlightened position to maintain.

a perfect body), but because it is definitely good enough. I like it not because it complies with some sort of societal ideal on thinness, but because that shape – my shape – is the result of that work I put into it, of care and attention and exercise, which always pays off, and there's a dependable, reassuring, cause-and-effecty sort of a logic to that. I show it some love and some respect, and like anything – dogs, plants, children, careers – it responds positively.

I like it because it works in clothes, and clothes, as we've established, are important to me. I like it because it is *not* a classically man-pleasing sort of a body, actually (too skinny, not curvy enough), and I feel there's, just maybe, some subversion in that.

I like it because it is me, and it is mine.

I like my body.

Which just shouldn't be a terrifying sort of a thing to put out there, but – is.

The twisted decree on any woman ever openly liking her own body is hooked into that contradictory, unwinnable modern attitude towards the female form, the one which simultaneously implores women and girls to stop hating themselves, to think of themselves as beautiful whatever they look like, to strive for higher physical esteem . . . And then slaps them down the very moment they demonstrate any, by telling them they should in fact be humble and modest and that there's nothing uglier than a girl who knows she's fit and 'oh my God, how much does *she* fancy herself?'

The screaming hypocrisy and damned-if-you-do-damned-if-you-don't-iness of which, now I come to contemplate it, makes me more determined to say this again:

I. Like. My. Body.

And while we're on the subject: I like yours, too.

11

The Feminist's Diet
and Exercise Plan

Y ou don't want to lose weight? Don't. Absolutely,
categorically, don't you dare! If you neither need
nor want to, then brilliant. Truly, like, *brilliant*.
There's a thing I didn't put in the Skinny-Geddon column,
which I probably should ... and it goes like this: while
being thin has made me happy, it's only made me happy in
terms of how fat my thighs aren't. It hasn't made me happy
Full Stop. I'm not anxious or sad about my arse or my upper
arms or my belly, but I am anxious and sad about a trillion
other things. Of course I am. I'm alive and human and that
is by no means an easy business; nothing as daft as a single-
digit dress size is going to change that.

So don't lose weight on my account. No no no no. You
keep your body. Wear it well. Reject all those infernal,
absurd, revolving thoughts, the ones which direct you to
diet and deny and despair at the soft padding which escapes
over the top of your jeans. When you catch yourself
squeezing critically and furtively at some flesh, just stop.

When you encounter yet another advertising image of an impossibly buff model, see it for what it is: a picture. Not a basis for comparison, not an end goal. Know that not even Victoria's Secret models look like *that* most of the time, that the bodies you associate with them are the end product of a brief period of intense training, a regime which is unsustainable long-term; that they get match fit directly before a catwalk show or campaign photo shoot, like any athlete does, but they can't and don't maintain it afterwards. Stop thinking of your body as a long series of trials and possible-blights and maybe-issues, of Do I have cankles? and Yikes! Is that knee fat? Of cellulite and muffin top, paunch and bingo wings, so on and so forth. Think of it instead as complete, as a whole.

Know that the world just *is* going to keep trying to press your body-anxiety buttons with anxious exhortations about joining bikini boot camps and applying creams and how your upper arms aren't toned enough and so on and so forth, but remember that these are *your* buttons ultimately, and it is within your power to stop them being pushed. Break that difficult taboo which I keep breaking: actively *like* your body. Admire it. Respect it.

But if you *do* want to lose weight, first: stop beating yourself up about wanting to lose weight. Stop thinking even thinking about your weight is a morally dodgy, feministically-speaking, suspect waste of your brain. It's not. It's fine. It's an inevitable consequence of being surrounded by so many mixed messages about fat, and you know. Whatevs.

Second: I can help. Come closer. Listen up. Let me tell you how losing weight is done.

Not with diets. Diets are fairy tales and lies dressed up as New Year's Resolutions; not a single one among them really works, not long term, and also: dear God, they're drab.

So don't diet.

Don't count anything and don't weigh anything and don't sign up for lighter meal deliveries. Don't revolutionise your eating habits overnight because you read this one book or you saw this one show or you went to this one group meeting.

Just eat less.

Like, 20 per cent less. Twenty-five, max. Never eat McDonald's or KFC or Burger King. It's not like they even pretend to be worth it, and that's just contemptuous. Don't eat the free food that washes into most offices during the course of the working day like flotsam disguised as substandard cupcakes. It never tastes as good as it should. If you do find yourself struck by a convincing urge to choc (yes, it's a verb) or crisp (also a verb), then hunt and forage for the choc or crisp. Leave wherever it is that you are, head out into the world beyond and ensure your quest for choc or crisp involves no less than fifteen min-utes' walking about.

If you're out for brunch or dinner, order exactly what you want – just don't eat it all. Stop eating when you're fullish. Don't wait till you're stuffed; straining and uncomfortable, exhaling and regretful. Don't be afraid to leave food. Don't worry about how it'll look or what people will think. Just step away from it, once you're done. No one cares; no one's watching that hard.

I'm aware that, at this point, it's customary to offer health warnings here, to advise anyone thinking about altering their eating habits with a view to getting thinner to take care and be cautious and see doctors and so on and so forth.

But I'm not going to. I'm not going to patronise you with talk of making sure you have a healthy BMI, not going to spout empty rhetoric about the dangers of anorexia, the horror of disordered eating. You know all this. The established tradition of invoking it while talking to women about their weight is infantilising, and women are infantilised enough already.

I *am* going to say: Don't obsess about food. Don't talk about it. Don't talk about calorie content (dull, not sexy), don't tell people you're on a 'fasting day' (dull, not sexy), don't comment on the food choices of friends, colleagues, female relatives, et cetera (inherently judgemental, dull, not sexy), don't brag about how little you ate the day before or bemoan the fact that you ate loads and, therefore, today you must be Good (dull, not sexy). There are so many other things to talk about. Telly! Have you seen telly? It's amazing! Talk about telly! Or books, or news, or the weather, or anything at all other than what you are and are not eating.

And you might want to live according to my single major food decree, which is this:

Life's too short for mediocre carbohydrates.

There. That's what I think about food.

Ah, but now! Here comes the good bit. It concerns exercise. Bear with me. Many of our collective weight issues are associated with our increasingly sedentary lifestyles; the fact that our jobs tether us to our Macs and to daily commutes, and our TVs and our Twitter accounts tether us to our sofas. The inevitable consequence of hours and hours spent sitting on our arses is arse enlargement.

So, clearly, we need to be less sedentary. A lot less sedentary.

How?

Not with yoga.

I mean, some people like it, sure. Me? I've always found yoga classes to be something of a twat-magnet.

And not with spinning. Because spinning's ever so hard, and in my experience, 95 per cent of the population of the world is destined to give up on doing something, sooner or later, if it's ever so hard.

Not with Zumba, either. Not that I've ever done Zumba, but I have a fundamental mistrust of it on account of its name, which sounds a little too much like something trying to seem like it's considerably really really a lot more fun than it actually is.

Not with cross-training (also hard, see spinning, above).

Or weights (bulky, retro, but not in a charming way). Or personal training (the catalyst of many profoundly dysfunctional relationships) and bikini boot camps, and definitely not with gyms.

Oh, fuck gyms! Cathedrals constructed in the name of impotent, ineffectual narcissism and seven kinds of foot fungus!

And fuck Pilates.

Actually – don't fuck Pilates. Don't fuck Pilates at all. It's doing wonders for my back. And I'm beginning to suspect I might be quite good at it.

But you get the idea. Don't do any of that crap, not until you've tried this one easy-peasy thing, which you already know how to do, a Thing that is both free and simple and not especially tiring, but preposterously, miraculously effective (I know, because it's the real reason I'm thin, the real reason I keep being thin); a Thing that will mean you lose weight in the healthiest way imaginable, and keep weight off in the healthiest way imaginable, and then, on top of that, you'll find you're cheerier and more sane and more sunny and more engaged, and oh! if there were a way of packaging this Thing, marketing it, and selling it on at a profit, I would, I really would, and I would be richer than God.

But there really isn't any way of doing that.

Because, you see, the Thing is walking.

I'm not talking about doing anything fancy. My walking is bog standard, run of the mill, low impact, uncomplicated, one foot in front of the other, lift leg, slap foot down squarely on the road in front of you, lift other leg, delight as trainer sole bounces satisfyingly off the tarmac, repeat several thousand times until you've completed – well, in my case, between ten and twelve miles a day, because that's how much of a raging walking addict I am, although I reckon you could do about three miles a day and notice a spectacular difference in your body and head within three weeks, and incidentally, I found out recently that Charles Dickens used to walk twenty miles a day, which makes me feel . . . competitive, mostly, which is absurd, given that Dickens is dead. Has been for a while.

Walking is my great weight secret. It's given me thigh gap (not something I ever aspired towards, mostly because I didn't know what it was until someone on *Made in Chelsea* got it, but, meh. I can live with it) and a flat stomach and decent posture and serious endurance capacity.

But it is better than that.

Walking is my religion.

It's my grace.

It's time to compose myself and compound my sense of self. Time to create or resolve or get so thoroughly immersed in an audiobook I very nearly collide with a cyclist who really shouldn't be on the pavement in the first place, but that's cyclists for you: lawless. Utterly lawless.

Walking calms me down and chills me out and literally and spiritually grounds me; and all of these things help with the ongoing quest for fanciability. At the very least, they help with the not-going-mad-on-account-of-the-myriad-angsts-and-stresses-and-sorrows-modern-life-throws-at-us-all levels.

I started walking twelve years ago, at the very beginning of the 2000s, when claustrophobia drove me off London's tube and towards its buses, but then fury over the buses recurring and unbridled lateness drove me towards the remarkable power of my own legs and feet. I started tentatively, walking from bus stop to bus stop along my usual route, and on the assumption that sooner or later my on-foot arrival at a stop would coincide with the arrival of an actual and relevant bus, which I'd then board. But that didn't happen – busless bus stops came and went, I kept on walking – and I discovered that it didn't take me so very much longer to walk than it would have done had I managed to get a bus. An extra half hour on top of the standard bus journey time, max. I was a tad late for work, but I've always suspected that a subtle and judicious amount of lateness in a professional situation, handled the right way, can inspire a degree of respect. Though don't quote me on that.

So I persevered. I began getting up earlier (I'm a morning person, AND?) and walking with purpose and with full observation of the weather forecast, which I fully digest before choosing an outfit (my ability to dress well and in accordance with the frantic vacillations of the British weather is, I'm confident, unrivalled). After a few weeks of averaging three or four miles a day on the walk in, depending on the route, I realised that my new regime was doing some fine work in the field of sculpting my thighs, lifting my arse and rearranging my stomach muscles. At which point, I started walking home, too.

The seasons changed, I adapted my dress accordingly – and realised I could never not walk. Ever. Partly because when you've seen your town or city – your Place – flicker, breathlessly and insanely subtly, from the bleak, scrag end of winter into the earliest hint of spring, when you've noticed the light change in fractions of degrees from early dawn to early dawn, when you've watched things sprout and be born and get made new and clean and hopeful and bright again, in front of your very eyes . . . you'll never not want to see it happen the next time. I swear it.

Mostly because walking wrought miracles in my head. It dampened every hangover into submission. It de-pranged any anxiety. It soothed heartbreak and quietened the washing machine churn of arguments and injustices, re-visited fruitlessly, over and over, in my head. It lightens every mad, bad mood you care to name. It lifts sadness. It engages you with the strangers you encounter, every day at roughly the same time and roughly the same geographical point, to the extent that they start seeming a lot less strange – and you! You start feeling a lot less strange, too. A daily walk will give you reason to laugh at least once, maybe because someone trips over a paving stone and then does the self-conscious follow-up dance of recovery, a manoeuvre which, when you think about it, is one of the most singularly endearing human things any of us is capable of doing. (Every person on this planet feels exactly the same in that trip moment: vulnerable, childlike, mortal, humbled, silly.)

Maybe because a wild-eyed four-year-old cuts you up on his scooter.

Maybe because of a dog.

(It's often because of a dog. You can rely on dogs.)

Whatever.

Walking gives you a major, blessed, delicious break.

Walking does, without a shadow of a doubt, keep me skinny. Ignore almost everything in the Skinny-Geddon column about accidental Atkins and chip avoidance. It's the walking that did it, that continues to do it. But compared with the other stuff – the calm, the laughs, the mood management, the witnessing of season shifts – the skinny thing is merely a bonus. Not a bad bonus. But definitely, just a bonus.

12

Old

___

The very moment I stopped worrying about being a little bit too chubby, was the very moment I started worrying about being too old. Seriously. One anxiety died and, whoa!, another anxiety reared up to replace it, a huge, fanged, psychological snake-bitch of a notion, which didn't even pause before striking.

Take that, skinny bitch! You might be thin, now; but are you not also . . . *Old*?

Oh, come on! It's not like I've ever claimed to be well-adjusted.

Mad as the box of snakes that are simultaneously striking me down with constantly emerging body issues, me.

Of course, the fact that I had just hit thirty-one, might have been a contributing factor in my warp-speed move into a brand new physical anxiety format.

I'd breezed through thirty. I'm young for my school year – late August, I've got disastrous handwriting, which I pass off as a consequence of my motor skills being only partially-developed at the time I was first taught to hold a pen;

and I'm habitually abandoned on my birthday by mates answering the call of a Bank Holiday weekend, final fling mini-break. But a late birthday also meant that all my peer group had already dealt with thirty, with that transition into earliest middle age – or at least, away from anything that could truly be considered pure youth – before me. I'd watched them do it, one by one; been to their parties, witnessed their defiance, their widely varying crises, and grown accustomed to the whole scene. When it was my turn, it just wasn't a big deal any more. My already-thirty friends had got used to the whole trembling on the brink of a new life stage thing; most of them weren't even trembling any more . . . And me? I would always be younger than them.

But thirty-one – thirty-one is a bit tougher. It's a bit less celebration, a bit less novelty and gags and a last hurrah, a bit more: ah. This is actually happening, then? It's no thirty-four, admittedly. thirty-four is when the shit really hits the fan in my humble exp; because thirty-four is the age at which women start having babies in earnest, rather than by mistake, much to the surprise of their friends who aren't yet having babies, who aren't even necessarily in relationships, who feel utterly abandoned and weirdly betrayed that the people to whom they are perhaps closest have, without any consultation whatsoever, abandoned them wholesale in favour of a minuscule, squealing, shitting excuse for a human they've only just met, so how can they possibly like them better?

Yeah. Thirty-four's the killer.

But thirty-one is not without challenge. The mad scrabble of your twenties to prove yourself, to tick off the boxes marked Relationship! Career! Home! has calmed a little. Life is suddenly a little less about frantically pursuing goals, a little more about, Is this it? Am I an adult? How much of what's already happened is undoable, and how much of it means anything at all?

And yeah: you just *are* a bit older. In my case, for whatever reasons: older than I'd ever really imagined I'd be.

On top of which, I was now thin. And as fun as that was in some ways, it did also come with the downer of my looking younger, from a distance, than I actually was.

This surprised some people. This unnerved and alarmed and terrified others. Like that one guy – nineteen if he was a day, pallid and poxy, in tired grey marl trackies, not what I'd call a looker – who catcalled me all the way up a hill one dreary day in my very earliest thirties, only to draw level with me, gaze fully upon my face for the first time, witness the full horror of the ancientness which marked it with . . . I dunno. A crow's foot, a forehead line? At which juncture, he blanched (as much as his habitual pallor would allow him to blanch) and rescinded the harassment on the spot, with some vigour, clearly under the impression that I would have leapt at the chance to go to Nando's with him, had he not – which I certainly would *not* have done, had I been nineteen, or indeed, ninety.

Then – shortly afterwards – came the IT support man,

who asked me if I was worried my boyfriend would leave me for a younger girl. I was holding forth, mid-office, about how preposterous it was that Hollywood consistently paired older men with younger women in its films; with particular reference to Michael Douglas, probably, when: 'I'm no psychologist,' said the IT man, who was fifty, and had one hand up my (Apple) Mac, which always makes me feel vulnerable, 'but I think you're projecting some personal anxiety onto the wider cultural moment. I think you think your boyfriend is going to leave you, for a younger woman!'

'I'm thirty-one!' I objected.

'Yeah, well,' he said, 'thirty-one's a difficult age.'

And if precious little moments like these weren't enough to plant the seed of 'Oh God! Am I old now?' in my mind; well, I could always rely on online comment to do the rest.

When I started my career as a journalist, the internet barely existed. I mean, technically (ha!) it did, somewhere, for some people (Tim Berners-Lee and a couple of his mates, one presumes), but in terms of impacting my – or any of my colleagues' – professional life, it didn't. We may have heard of it vaguely, rumours and the such-like of a vast electronic matrix destined to revolutionise our existences, but if we were hooked up, no one told us, and we wouldn't have known what to do with it had they done so. I remember getting email in the office for the first time, circa '97, and using it exclusively as a device via which to pass comment on the colleagues I didn't like to those that I did; as if I were passing mean notes at school. Shortly after my editor excitedly announced she'd received her very first bit of work-related email (a big moment, the office applauded). I remember another journalist saying: 'Oh, there's this really cool thing called "Google" you should try.' I remember buying my first book on Amazon and marvelling when it actually turned up.

The internet crept up on me over the course of the very late nineties, infiltrating my life, coiling its digital tentacles round my every thought, deed and working practice, softly, softly, as it did with all of us, until we were so hopelessly in its thrall by – I dunno, 2001, or so – that nothing and no one could save us. We couldn't move without it.

However, it wasn't till 2006 that the internet's one true purpose became clear, that being: to stick it to journalists!

In 2006, the *Guardian* newspaper – sister to the *Observer*, my employer at that time – launched 'Comment is free', an online venue for the *Guardian* and the *Observer*'s comment and political editorial pieces, which also boasted room for additional contributions from other writers; and, crucially, the opportunity for 'below the line' contributions, for readers' responses to any given article, and for readers' responses to other readers' responses to other readers' responses, and so on and so forth.

Bloody hell. That was a can of worms.

Other newspapers followed suit, opening up their online editions to reader feedback. Soon enough, everyone was at it. Then Twitter fired into life, and the jig was well and truly up (the jig, in this instance, being journalists not ever knowing what their readership really thinks about them).

Like pretty much every journalist I know, I wish it hadn't happened. I wish we'd retained our lordly privilege of being able to talk and talk and write and write without ever knowing quite how ridiculous people thought we were. How stupid, how wrong, how bad, how unpleasant, how ugly – how old. Honestly? I could have carried on without that.

None of us took kindly to the comment revolution. None of us. Some of us may lie about it now, claim we welcome the democratisation of opinion, and that we delight in the cut and thrust of online feuds. But you mustn't believe them, they're lying because they think it sounds good. Fact is, it's shit, all that.

It's not much fun now we've had time to get used to it; when it first started, it was *awful*.

I mean, there we all were, accustomed to getting the occasional legal writ from some interviewee, convinced they didn't say that thing we said they definitely *did* say (and directly into our Dictaphones, at that); or the odd, offensive and offended letter, handwritten, according to the ancient cliché (one of those clichés which becomes a cliché for the reason that it is also truth) in green ink, self-evidently the product of a slightly deranged mind . . . I once got one that was not only in green ink – it was in rhyming couplets. This was a particular fave. But that was all. The lawyers dealt with the legals and the green inkers went in the bin, and no one said anything more about it.

It came as something of a shock to discover that, once the writers of the angry letters to journalists were afforded the ease, the immediacy and the opportunity of an online comment box or a Twitter account, once they no longer had to find the paper and the green pen, compose the rhyming couplets, work out the address of whichever publication was harbouring the lying crap shit old journalist they'd taken against, find an envelope AND a stamp AND a postbox, maintaining a heightened level of fury all the while . . . Once those obstacles were out the way, well! Those occasional letters would translate into hundreds of comments, written by the hundreds of people, all super-keen to hurl abuse at us every time we published anything at all.

Suddenly, journalists were subject to a whole new hideous lexicon of loathing: BTL (Below the Line), Haters, Flamers . . . Trolls. And now? Now it's virtually a way of life. Every time I publish anything, I brace myself for the onslaught. Every time, it surprises me a bit in its vehemence.

At this juncture, I feel I should make an admission: I have never been trolled. A lot of the modern feminist debate is caught up in the issue of 'online trolling', the peculiar variety of anonymous invective directed at women. The historian Mary Beard has been a high profile target of misogynistic trolling; so has the feminist campaigner

Caroline Criado-Perez. Loads of women journalists have suffered too: rape threats, death threats, barely-literate tweets expressing the tweeter's hope that the woman journalist in question gets cancer very very soon. It's led to much despair, to the occasional mass abandoning of Twitter by women keen to protest those nasty, lone, horrifically persistent troll voices. Some have tracked down their trolls, and tackled them, face to face, over their sorry, spleeny internet proclivities. Others have had their trolls prosecuted and sent down.

Me? I haven't had a single troll experience, in all my long years of writing stuff. Not a one. To the point that I'm almost ashamed of my troll-free life. Why don't I provoke the trolls? Why don't they mind me? Why don't I wind them up, inspire them? Am I caught in some ghastly allegiance with them that I don't know about? Do I, somehow, *please* them?

God, I hope not!

What I *do* get, in large dollopy dollops of quasi-bile, is a newer, less readily-identifiable form of online bother. I get Snarked, and I get Trashed. Snarking and Trashing is another school of online aggression altogether. It's distinct from trolling, in that it's generally not anonymous, it's not nearly as unhinged, and it's not typically male – indeed, if anything, Snarking and Trashing is most often unleashed by women, *at* women. In tone, it is sneering and it is supercilious, it is superior and it is pompous. It seeks to discredit whoever (me! Not just me. But definitely quite often me!)

by attacking them as a person, rather than challenging the article they just wrote, or the point, or the perspective, or the argument they just made (which would be entirely legitimate. I never write anything without knowing I'm probably at least a bit wrong, never publish without accepting that readers have an absolute right to disagree with me. It blows my mind that anyone would ever think they're completely right. About anything, frankly).

Snarkers and Trashers achieve this with huge, sweeping statements about their target:

@womanjournalist1 is SO STOOOOPID; how bad, how wrong, how thick, how crap is @womanjournalist1? @womanjournalist1 is literally everything that's wrong with journalism! SHUT UP @womanjournalist1, JUST SHUT UP.

Or by gratuitously misunderstanding a point:

Everyone knows @womanjournalist1 hates all fat people.

Or by rustling up some cod objection to the target's entire being

@womanjournalist1 is JUST SO SMUG don't you think?

@womanjournalist1 is too white/middle class/
common/hungry/did I mention stupid? TOO
STOOOOOOOOOPID for anyone to care what she
thinks.

You can just tell @womanjournalist1 totally loves
herself, can't you? @womanjournalist1 is probably
drunk again.

@womenjournalist1 has, like, zero self-awareness.
God, @womanjournalist1 is AWFUL.

Or with the 'v' word, specially reserved for Snarking at
women when you don't have any specific criticism to raise,
but don't see why that should stop ya:

@womanjournalist1 is SO vacuous!

They may also adopt some wanton and irrelevant sanctimonious high ground:

Why is @womanjournalist1 boring us with celebrity
crap when the Ukrainian crisis is dramatically desta-
bilising Europe?

Or instead, opt for some casual undermining via a tactic
that someone clever named 'Whataboutery?':

@womanjournalist1 writes that she worries about the rape statistics in the UK, but what about rape as a weapon of war in Sudan?

So no, no online trolling for me. Not yet, anyway. But really: more than enough in the way of Snarking and Trashing.

Do I sound terribly sorry for myself? I do, don't I? 'Dear anyone who's interested: you are cordially invited to Polly Vernon's non-stop pity party, there will be mushroom vol au vents and woe, and dancing wistfully in circles alone; coaches at midnight, unless you want to stick around and watch her cry herself to sleep, as she does every night.' OK, stick with me while I rustle up a bigger argument. Because there is one:

Snarking and Trashing might be subtler and far less vicious than Trolling, but they have the same end goal in mind: to shut down whoever they target, to reel them in and slap them down. In this sense, they're as corrosive and uncool as Trolling. And it is by no means just, erm, @woman-journalist1 getting it in the neck, from the Snarkers and the Trashers. Snarking and Trashing has become standard practice in online comment, a go-to fallback register for interacting with almost anyone, which means that we're actually all getting Snarked and Trashed, and worse yet: *we're all doing it*. Precisely because Snarking and Trashing isn't as blatant and unhinged as Trolling, they're easy modes for most of us to slip into periodically without pausing to question ourselves – cos at least we're not trolling, right?

We'd never troll! – or even, really, noticing. A lot of feminists Snark and Trash. A lot of feminists get Snarked and Trashed. Feminists are not beyond Snarking and Trashing other feminists, in the very name of feminism. Like this:

> OMG can't believe @womanjournalist1 calls herself a feminist! She's such a fat shamer!/et ceteraaaah, et ceteraaaah.

Why are feminists also Snarkers and Trashers? For a load of reasons. Because of FOGIW, the Fear Of Getting It Wrong – specifically, in this instance FFOGIW, the *Feminist* Fear Of Getting It Wrong – which drives us to judge others before they judge us. Because we feel territorial about feminism, and can't always accept that others may think and feel about it, and practise it, differently. We Snark and Trash, in those instances, in an attempt to establish ownership over feminism. Because Snarking and Trashing is easier than articulating the real reason we're mad when we post that tweet, the true heart of the beef we have with @womanjournalist1 or whoever (in my case: BECAUSE SHE WROTE THAT THING ABOUT BEING THIN AGES AGO AND I VOWED TO HATE HER FOR EVER BECAUSE OF IT ONLY NOW I CAN'T REALLY REMEMBER WHY I HATE HER I JUST DO OK?). Because we have a shitload of feminist wrath built up within us, and sometimes we misdirect it.

Something like that, anyway.

Point is, we should probs give it a rest. Not sure it's helping.

But I digress.

The other thing I have taken away from online comment is that I am old. So old! As I've said, I started being officially old at thirty-ish, which may or may not have something to do with my also starting to be officially thin. Maybe 'fat' and 'old' are the two fave insults anyone wanting to take a woman down a peg or two will chuck about, switching between the two at will; or maybe they're just the two I am most attuned to hearing.

But yeah, there I am, a smidge past thirty, and older than the hills, according to the internet. 'Fifty-two years old with a face full of Botox!' wrote one – a woman, as I recall; how the comments stay with you, eh? – in response to my byline shot, which showed me aged about thirty-two and quite Botox free. 'Who does Vernon think she is? God, she looks rough!' wrote another. 'Shouldn't she have been put down by now?'

I potentially didn't help matters one little bit by launching the *Observer Food Monthly*'s Cocktail Girl column at around the same time.

Cocktail Girl was ostensibly a recurring bar review article, in which I visited fancy bars dotted jauntily around the world, got drunk in each of them in turn, then wrote about the experience in the guise of a high-living, amoral, past-her-best party girl with a dwindling trust fund and a taste for premium vodka. (Ideally Grey Goose, which I discovered in Toronto while interviewing the Olsen twins. If ever you want to impress a bartender, request Grey Goose by name.)

It was a wheeze, co-created with my editor, for two ends:

End one, to get some levity and silliness into the mag, to break up the long runs of recipes which made the title incredibly successful, but which could look a little textually dense to the casual flicker.

End two, to get me free accommodation in various cities when I was wandering round the world, interviewing or researching articles for other parts of the paper, which should explain why so many of the bars Cocktail Girl visited were attached to hotels.

(I also had a secret third end: I felt, on the quiet, that Cocktail Girl was making a point about women and boozing. The early 2000s proved quite a puritanical time if you were a women who liked a drink; much thought and print and public tut-tutting was given over to warning the ladies that we were drinking almost as much as men these days, and that only bad could come of it! God, that annoyed me! An example of how women are perennially expected to be the world's grown-ups, the serious, staid, sensible ones charged with keeping the men in line, because silly men can't really help themselves, they will just keep chasing fun, given half a chance!)

(Oh, and then, of course, there were echoes of my previous life working, not as a waitress, in a cocktail bar, on which I could draw.)

Each Cocktail Girl was accompanied by a photograph of me, dolled up to the nines in whatever frock I'd managed to buy for 20p (sadly, the dresses were not on expenses), draped wantonly over the bar – or barman – of the month. A cue many readers took to tell me, again, how absurdly old I was.

'Wrinkly old lush, who cares?'

'I'd tell her to get some beauty sleep, but it would take more than mere sleep . . .'

Et cetera.

On the 'plus' side, Cocktail Girl engendered some sort of a fetish following. Some bloke once phoned the *OFM* picture desk to find out if Cocktail Girl produced a calendar; even now, some years after the column was cancelled, a certain kind of middle-aged man will blush deepest red on being introduced to me for the first time, and go: 'But you're COCKTAIL GIRL!"

Yup, so that's what my early experience of online comment taught me; and that's what it's still teaching me.

That I was – am – old.

Question is: why did I care?

Why did it hurt?

Why can I *still* remember, in raging Technicolor, *those* hurtful comments, and not the squillion other hurtful comments directed at my lack of talent, lack of integrity, lack of truth?

Why is 'old' one of the snidiest things you can accuse me of? Me – and many other women? Why do the online trolls know to hurl it about like a swear word, shutting down their adversaries with one, fell, three-letter swoop? Why do they never use it on the men; why does it operate as a gender-specific slight? Is it because no one thinks a man – any man – is ever especially old? Men are 'mature', 'dignified', 'silver foxes', 'craggy', but rarely 'old'. And certainly not at thirty-one – I can't imagine a thirty-one-year-old man being accused of being old, can you? Or a forty-one-year-old man, for that matter. Or is it that men don't hear a reference to their aging as a slight?

Goodness knows, I do. Despite myself.

But why? Why was I more offended by the pallid and poxy youth's announcement that I was too ancient for him to sexually harass, than I was by the initial harassment? Why is the first thing I tell any make-up artist who's preparing my head for a shoot: 'I don't care what you do, just make me look less old?' (Incidentally, a female make-up artist once told me she marvels over the recurring gender divide she witnesses in those she works on. 'The women sit down, look in the mirror, immediately start telling me what's wrong with them, regardless of how beautiful they are. The men sit down, look in the mirror and give a gentle, self-satisfied head nod, regardless of how average they are.')

I mean, I am old. I've seen a birthday or forty. And, if I'm not exactly *old* – I am definitely *older*. Clearly older than I used to be. That's how life plays out, innit? So why do I care if it's pointed out to me? All anyone's effectively saying when they call me old is: 'You're older than some people, and definitely older than you used to be!'

Which I already know.

And ultimately, I know – every last one of us knows – that 'older' is a preferable alternative to 'not getting any older', because that is death.

Why then, does it sometimes seem like such a close call?

13

Old is the New Witch

I decide to hold a sort of conference for some of the women I know, so that they can tell me everything they think about getting older, about being older, about how people react to them being older, about why old is a bad thing. I lure them in with crisps and fine wine.

This is what they say:

'Mate! It's the modern equivalent of shouting "witch" at a woman because, as we get older, we know more, and we're less scared, and that makes us *scarier*. Men shout "Old!" because they think it will discredit us, diminish us; because with age comes professional advancement and knowledge and power and just getting so bored of their bullshit, and they know it, and they know *we* know it, and they don't like it, so they call us old!' says Cara, who is forty-one. She pauses to take a drag on her fag; Cara is the only person I know who has not given up smoking.

I take your point, Car, but women call other women old all the time, I say. I reckon more women call me 'old' in the meany mean way online than men do. A lot more.

'Because we're all subject to that man-oriented way of looking at life, so we pick up their prejudices; because men still run this show, but only *just*, so we're all still jumping through their hoops on what's OK.' Puff, puff. 'Trust me, PV. "Old" is the new "witch".'

'Yeah, but, not all men are freaked out by age,' says Leanne, who is thirty-eight, and going out with a twenty-seven-year-old, so she should know. 'Some men think it's actively hot. When Tommy hit on me, we were in a bar and it was pretty dark, I thought he just couldn't see how old I was. I remember being really glad we'd met in November because there were fewer daylight hours and so he only ever really saw me in low artificial lighting. I was like: give me enough candles, I can totally spin this out until spring! Then I found out he was short-sighted, which was even better . . . But then he *did* see me in daylight, with his contacts in; turned out that as far as he was concerned, me being older was like me having, I don't know, excellent tits. An actual bonus. Men dig it.'

'*Younger* men dig it,' says Antonia, who is thirty-nine, 'because they're maybe a bit more enlightened than men our age, and because of all the MILF porn they get mainlined to their laptops, for which I have to say, I'm the tiniest bit grateful. Older women are a sexy archetype to that lot.'

'Plus they haven't started to really witness the physical indicators of age in themselves yet,' says Cara, 'so they're less inclined to see them as threatening – to even recognise them – in women our age.'

' *Also*,' says Antonia, 'there's that thing where girls their age want to settle down and get commitment and domestication, and women our age have probably done all that already and are bored to tears by it, and just want to have loads of sex. Which means women our age and boys *their* age have something in common. We want loads of sex.'

('Do we?' says Cass, who is thirty-five and seven years into a relationship. 'Not sure I can be arsed.')

'Oh my God! Men my age have such massive issues with me going out with Tommy!' says Leanne, who never really stops talking about going out with Tommy. Which is half cute, half intensely annoying; we've given her another six weeks to get through this stage. 'They're always telling me how imminently he's going to leave me for a girl his own age. Pisses me off.'

'There's a word for women like you,' says Cara to Leanne.

'Yes, and I love it,' says Leanne. 'How can it be stigmatising to go: "See her? She's one of *those* who sleeps with beautiful young men!" I'll take "cougar". I don't care.'

'Right, but isn't "cougar" also just another way of pointing at you and going: "See her? She's old!"' says Cara.

'No, it's another way of saying: "See her? Beautiful young men fancy her,"' says Leanne.

Why do we think 'old' automatically has negative connotations, I ask? Is it because it's physical evidence of encroaching death? Us rotting away in front of each other, reminding each other it's all basically futile?

'Cheery,' says Cara.

'But if that was it, men would be as sensitive to it as women; but they're not, and they aren't expected to fight age, and fear age, in the same way,' says Cass, whose boy-friend is nine years older than her. 'Actually, men should hate aging *more*, because they die earlier, statistically.'

'I think they *do* hate it, they *are* as sensitive to it as we are though,' says Cara. 'I think, men are terrified of aging. Terrified of aging physically, terrified of what it means in terms of the drip drip dripping away of their virility, terri-fied because of what age does to their erections. But instead of facing up to this terror, they try and outsource aging onto women, make it exclusively a women's problem. If it weren't for men, women wouldn't have such an issue with aging. We just wouldn't.'

Is the female issue with aging maybe intertwined with ideas about dwindling fertility? Are women judged harshly in terms of aging, because we're *still* only really valued in terms of our ability to have children?

'Maybe. I do think about my age more, because I'm thirty-two,' says Hannah, 'and that means I should prob-ably be thinking about having a baby, but I can't even work out if I want kids or not, and that makes me feel older, in a panicky way. Should I freeze my eggs, by the way?'

'Fuck no,' says Karen, who got pregnant by accident for the first time at forty-one, on a one-night stand, because she'd read so many articles about how her fertility levels had been in freefall for the last seven years so she hadn't even bothered with a condom. 'I'd thought the only thing I was risking was chlamydia. Or AIDS . . . Anyway Polly, you've never wanted kids, so why would you be bothered about aging because of that? Surely, you should get happier and happier as you get older and therefore less fertile?'

(It is quite true, I've never wanted children; I've been perfectly clear on that point for as long as I can remember, and I've gone to some lengths to maintain my childfree status. I'll come back to this soon-ish, assuming you're interested.)

Dunno, I say. Maybe that fertility subtext is buried so deeply in our instinctive bleurgh of aging women, we no longer realise that's what it's founded on.

'Do you know what I hate?' says Karen. 'What I really fucking loathe? All the Invisible Woman chat; which says we stop being visible to men when we hit a certain age; they stop turning their heads to watch us as we walk down the road, they don't chat us up at parties, we just: pouf! Vanish from the face of the planet!'

Hannah looks alarmed. 'When does this kick in?' she says.

'It doesn't. Well, unless you think it does,' says Karen, 'so: don't think it does. It's a self-fulfilling prophecy and it's not one I'm buying.'

Me? I think the Invisible Woman myth is part of a cod-feminist-liberal-concern trolling movement, in which people (almost always of a male persuasion) want to seem politically correct while simultaneously making sure women feel a bit crappy about themselves, and so they wander about loftily decrying: 'Isn't it just *awful* the way women virtually disappear from sight, vanish from the male gaze, once they turn thirty-five? It's almost as if they become irrelevant once they can no longer bear our children, isn't it?' And then they'll try and mitigate it all by saying something like: 'Which is frankly ridiculous! I *adore* an older woman! I mean, Helen Mirren . . .! *I SO WOULD!*' just to make it clear that they're better than that, more evolved, only – sweetness! You're the one who brought it up! Also, you don't have a hope in hell with Mirren.

'Women remain as visible, or become as invisible as they choose to, somewhat regardless of age,' says Karen. 'I've chosen visibility. As you can tell.'

Which, you can.

Also: 'Visibility is contextual,' says Cara, who is a lawyer. 'If I'm less visible now to some random geeze on the street than I was at twenty-two, but far more visible in a law court because I'm the one in the wig and the gown: I can definitely handle that.'

'Who's invisible? What?' says Leanne, who has been texting Tommy.

When did we start worrying about aging, I ask?

'Now! I just feel like I can't get away with things so easily any more,' says Hattie, who is twenty-six. 'I don't think I can mess up, and then go: But I'm only young! Because I'm not only young, any more. Am I?'

'YOU'RE TWENTY-SIX!' says Cara.

'The first time I felt old, I was twenty-four,' says Cass. Why?

'Because some bloke said I looked older than twenty-four. I've been convinced I look old for my age, ever since.'

'The morning of my twenty-fifth birthday,' says Hattie, 'the 23-year-old in my office asked how it felt to know I would be in the ancient Overs category if I ever entered the *X Factor*. Which I had no intention of doing – can't sing – but the thought of being one of Louis Walsh's people!'

We all shout loudly about how preposterous that is, while simultaneously remembering that people – all manner of men, plus younger women (to whom we *do* seem old, because they couldn't even dream of a time when they'd hit twenty) and older women (slightly too eager for us to feel older than we already do; I clearly remember a colleague – about eight years older than me – telling me, on the day I hit thirty, that no one would distinguish between her and me in terms of age demographics any longer) – started calling us 'old' in our early twenties, too.

It's like a way of slapping us down, of making us watch ourselves and not get too full of ourselves, of ensuring we assume the habit of thinking – worrying, stressing – about aging, I say: calling us 'old' even while we are stupidly young.

'Yeah,' they all say, because I am *incredibly* wise.

Does it matter if we try and hide our age, then, I ask? Or does it make sense?

'By lying?' says Hannah.

'I never do that,' says Antonia. 'I think it's ridiculous. Also, you're risking looking old for the age you say you are, which is entirely counterproductive.'

I lied down by a couple of years when I was filling in a permission form before I got my upper ear pierced last week, I admit. I sometimes get amazed by the raw fact of my age, struck by how very ancient it seems when it is literally on paper; I felt ashamed.

'Twat,' says Antonia.

Fair comment, I say: though I was actually wondering what we feel about disguising our years with surgical interventions.

'Botox? I've had that,' says Antonia.

Wait: you won't lie about your age with your mouth, Ant; but you *will*, by having a toxin shot directly into your crinkled up forehead?

'Yes,' says Antonia. 'And what of it?'

I haven't tried Botox – not because of a moral stance, but because of fear. I think it'd make me feel claustrophobic if I couldn't move my face. I once tried one of those Frownie stickers, which I'd heard would smooth out the perma-grumpy line I've developed in between my eyebrows. Frownies are a specially-shaped piece of adhesive, which you wet, stick in place, and leave overnight, so that it releases that particular wrinkle. But it gave me a migraine and made me a bit panicked, so I took it off after twenty minutes. Surely Botox would be like that, like you're trapped in your own face, a flesh head of a vice?

'Pussy,' says Antonia.

'I don't think I'll do it,' says Hattie. 'It looks fake. You can tell. And I think it's mental when girls my age get it done.'

'While it is truly mental that girls your age get it done,' says Cass, 'you will find you get less hardline about such matters, as the crow's feet gather.'

'I won't,' says Hattie. 'I really won't.'

I understand celebrities doing it, I say. When so much of your job is being looked at, keeping the stuff people are looking at in a decent state of repair is par for the course. Same as me making sure my Mac is upgraded and my Dictaphone works. Plus, the industries in which they operate – TV and film, the 'looky-atty industries' – are especially youth-fixated, especially age-averse. I just don't think you can beat up anyone involved in those scenes, if they do take steps to cheat age. I think our tendency to mock them if they age, and mock them if they try not to age, is cruel.

'Yeah, except half the time they look worse with Botox and fillers, like they're wearing their own frigid death mask,' says Karen. 'On top of which, their appearance sets the pace for everyone else, even us. If I know such and such a movie star is my age, but has half my wrinkles, I'm going to feel bad about my wrinkles.'

Why? I ask. It isn't your job to have fewer wrinkles; but it *is* the movie star's job.

'It's a movie star's job to act!' says Karen.

Yes, I say, but being looked at is part of acting, and so inevitably, maintaining the stuff everyone's looking at becomes part of acting.

'But men actors don't have to try as hard as women actors,' says Karen, 'and all of them should be allowed to wrinkle and sag and bag – at least a bit – without it affecting their work!'

Which is true. Mind you:

I'm thinking I may have a facelift at some point, I say. Not yet. But one day.

'Are you *mad*?' say Cara and Cass.

Potentially. I have started a facelift fund, though, because I'll want something really good and expensive. I just think, there's nothing wrong with lifting it all up at some point in the future. Y'know. If I want to.

'But, but . . . you'd have to get KNIVES STUCK IN YOUR FACE!' says Cass. 'Just so: what? You stave off the jowls for a few extra years? They'll get you in the end, you know . . .'

'KNIVES! IN YOUR FACE!' says Cara.

I know, I say. But I would be asleep.

'Can a feminist have a facelift?' asks Karen.

Not sure, I say. It does destabilise the fundaments of my argument for Hot Feminism, I can see that – for sexiness extending well beyond the boundaries of one's drooping jowls. On top of which, I am really not finding the aging process as offensive as everyone always said I would. I can remember being nineteen and thinking it'd all be over for me, physically speaking, before I was twenty-nine. Then I remember feeling hotter at thirty-three than I did at fifteen – like, *much*. Who knows how much I'll fancy myself at fifty-five? It could be literally loads, far too much to allow me to undergo a facelift. It really *could*. I do seem to be on an upward trajectory of self-fancying, reverse age-related body dysmorphia or something. The only thing that's been a downer for me so far is all those people trying to tell me how absurdly old I am, all the time.

'INNIT!' says Cara, and Antonia, and Karen, and Hannah. 'Is it?' says Hattie.

'Tommy says he'll leave me if I have any work done,' says Leanne. 'Tommy says my wrinkles are sexy.'

14

How to Get Older, By Someone Who Keeps Getting Older

G et your first tattoo after thirty, no earlier. Good taste kicks in around about your third decade, therefore you're in with a much better chance of avoiding tatt-regret, if you wait to get inked.

Though you should definitely get your first tattoo *before* you're forty. You're welcome to have more, afterwards; but doing it for the first time post-forty is a bit crisis-y. Body piercing's fine post-forty, on the other hand, because jewels are more appropriate the older you get, regardless of where you're putting them.

Never wonder if you look 'a bit mutton dressed as lamb'. Just don't ask that question, of yourself or anyone else; don't subscribe to that fear. The idea that some clothes are age appropriate, and others are not, is spurious as hell, and based on the notion that blanket rules are ever a good thing. As long as we're individuals, who look and age differently from each other, this is flagrant nonsense. Never ask: is this too young for me? Only ask: does this suit me? View aging not as taking away your right to wear hotpants, but rather as *giving* you the right to wear different clothes. Some things just make more sense once you're over thirty. Or over forty. And so on. Pencil skirts. Tailoring: especially blazers. Gold, tortoiseshell, trench coats. Pedicures, blow dries and couture. You earn these pieces, with birthdays.

You have to be at least thirty-eight to qualify as a cougar. And that is a moment to relish; certainly worth the struggle of the intervening years to attain. Oh and by the way: technically, to achieve full cougar status, your lover must be half your age, plus five years; anything younger and it gets a bit weird, anything more and it's 'just a bit of an age gap', not an actual verifiable cougar situation. This is Cougar Maths.

Never ask anyone to guess your age (crass); never describe anyone else as 'looking good, for her age' (just 'looking good' will do nicely); never tell people that other people think you're younger than you are.

Don't think in terms of aging gracefully, or disgracefully. Think in terms of accumulating power.

Get yourself an age icon, someone between five years and two decades ahead of you, someone you think is handling it beautifully. Mine is some combo of Jenni Murray from *Woman's Hour*, Robin Wright in *House of Cards*, Charlotte Rampling in general, and Chrissie Hynde. Think: *that's* what getting older means: becoming more like *them*.

Also, get yourself a man age icon, a male pin up who's roughly the same age as you. Be aware of how 'old' – or not – they're considered; and recalibrate your thoughts and feeling about your own age, so they're in step with that guy.

So my man age icon is Don Draper from *Mad Men*, or rather the actor Jon Hamm (although I tend to think of him as Don, because it adds drama). I age in step with him. If no one's calling him old (which they aren't), then they sure as sin shouldn't be calling me old, either.

Choose happy over Botox. If happy's an option: embrace it. It does more for your complexion – eases your wrinkles, and the worry groove between your brows, lights up your skin – than injectables ever could. Happy isn't always possible, but when and if it's on the table – choose happy.

If you ever find yourself wondering whether you've lost your mojo to the relentless onslaught of age, take it from me: you haven't. You're having a bad day. You'll get it back. Trust me. Mojos never go, they just go into hiding periodically.

15

PS: PGP

So I'm halfway up a skyscraper in Shanghai, waiting to interview a world-renowned fashion designer; his PR – a sweet, corporate, non-camp gay man in his early forties – is telling me about Pretty Girl Privilege. PGP.

'The thing about pretty girls,' he says, 'is that they don't even know how lucky they are. If you're pretty, you have no clue how sweet your life is; how often you're given an easy ride; how much bigger your tips are if you're waitressing or how much more likely you are to get a few free side orders chucked in if you're being waited *on*; how much nicer people can't help but be towards you; how much easier it is for you to get served at a bar or hail a cab or cross a busy road; how much trouble you get yourself out of, just by flashing a smile . . .'

My first thought is: does he think I'm pretty; does he mean me? Does he? Does he does he does he does he? God, I hope he does! Does he, though? Does he? DOES HE? Et cetera.

My next thought is: I'm not sure he's right.

I think about Fran, my unremittingly beautiful Keira Knightley-esque friend who is riven by Fit Shame, who dresses dowdy for interviews with prospective male employers so she'll know that, if she gets the job, she did so on merit; who only really likes fancy dress parties because then she can legitimately 'ugly up', who feels her intrinsic sisterliness is diminished by the amount of men who check her out while ignoring her flatmates, every time they go to the pub together. I think about the amount of times I've seen other women react badly to Fran's beauty – bristle and recoil to be even in its proximity – and how much that's upset her.

'They're just jealous!' I've said.

'There's no "just" about it!' Fran replied, and she's right. Other women acting aggressively towards you is always other women acting aggressively towards you. Knowing it's because you're beautiful doesn't make that any better. It's still an unreasonable, uncontrolled, angry response towards something you – and Fran – have no control over, i.e. your head.

I think about Kamille, a girl I knew a little bit at university. Kamille was – presumably still is – a beauty, too; tall, blonde, slender, northern European. Kamille was in the habit of greeting everyone she met by kissing them on each cheek, as was the European way; a cultural fillip which proved furiously exciting to the Brit boys she encountered in her first term, all of whom fell in lust with her on the spot, and – ignorant of European kissing customs

227

– convinced themselves they were in with a chance with Kamille: why else was she kissing them? Ah, but when they discovered Kamille was kissing *everyone*, not just them, they flew into a communal rage; their admiration for Kamille quickly transformed itself into malicious derision.

They started calling Kamille 'The Campus Bike', which was how I first knew of her. She found out inevitably; she was devastated. Inevitably.

And I think about Eddie and the work experience girl. Eddie was a journalist on one of the papers on which I worked, and – despite the fact that he ruled over one of the Man desks (Sports or Foreign – I forget which) –, we got on. He'd swing by my desk for chats and choc regularly. One day, Eddie appeared and immediately started whinging about his new work experience girl. 'She's totally fit and she totally knows it and she spends her whole time flicking her hair about and it's really annoying,' he said. 'I hate her.'

I gently pointed out that the work experience girl was all of nineteen years old, on her own in a totally foreign, totally adult and extremely male environment, and quite probably saw Eddie and his band of merry hack man friends as hazy impressions of blokes a bit like her dad, rather than sexual beings who might be impressed by a hair whip. 'Maybe you should be nicer to her?' I suggested. 'Maybe she's intimi-dated and you being moody with her on the grounds you've convinced yourself she knows you fancy her and is rubbing your nose in the fact that you don't have a hope in hell with her (and BTW Eddie, you are literally two-and-a-fifth times her age), isn't helping things?'

'You're wrong, PV,' he said. 'She knows.'

I saw her later, trying to work out how to negotiate the office canteen system: a very pretty little thing, who startled and blushed when I smiled at her, then flicked her hair, to hide the blushing.

And I think about my friend D who is a stone cold fox, and a very talented comic broadcaster. D has listeners rolling in the aisles when she's on the radio, she's won awards, and plaudits from the mouths of the snottiest, most reticent male stand-up comedians. But the moment she gets in front of a TV audience, with her long lady hair and her big eyes and her wardrobe of tightly tailored, bum-embracing Roland Mouret dresses . . . no one laughs. They can't seem to accept D's funniness, in conjunction with her straightforward fitness. 'It's like it fuses their brains,' D sighs.

Then I wonder if there are any palpable, quantifiable benefits in being a pretty girl.

It might earn you some dosh if you're a model – but if you're a model, you're also destined to earn an average of about £20k[1] a year over a career which spans around seven years, and will be over by the time you're twenty-three, so, y'know . . . there are more lucrative, long term ways to earn

---

1 $27, 830 as of May 2011, according to the US Bureau of Labor Statistics.

a buck. And yes, there's some research to suggest that being above averagely attractive will mean you're more likely to get a job and more likely to be paid slightly more than a merely averagely attractive female colleague – but also, there's research which suggests this only applies to women who work in industries which aren't dominated by men; and that for above-averagely attractive women working in male-dominated industries, the reverse becomes true. They are paid less, and promoted less readily.

And good looks hardly guarantee anyone power and wealth, do they? If they *did*, all the politicians and all the multimillionaires would be exclusively fit. The Houses of Parliament were not noticeably a hotbed of wowsers, male or female, last time I checked. Ditto the boards of the FTSE 100, the British aristocracy, the movers and shakers of Monaco's yacht scene. Actually, if I might swing back to the issue of politicos for a moment . . . The prettier variety of MP often finds herself (and occasionally, *himself*) at a disadvantage when operating in such a male-dominated environment; the object of suspicion and derision, accused, like Eddie's work experience girl, of playing on their looks to get ahead.

I suppose one could argue that genetic beauty makes you more likely to be picked up by some rich man in search of a trophy wife, someone who might override his genetic defaults with your DNA and provide him with some hot offspring; and that therefore, materially, it can pay off. But, assuming we overlook the obvious flaws in this plan (in which you kid yourself that a bank balance makes sleeping with someone for whom you don't care all that much palatable), it also means you're dealing with the kind of man inclined to divorce you in a heartbeat the moment a shinier trophy comes along.

And good looks do not guarantee you love or happiness or peace or self-esteem or confidence. Beautiful people get dumped or ditched after a single date, or ignored on Tinder, or scorned after a one night stand, every day. They fail and they fall, they suffer self-doubt, anxiety and depression, same as the rest of us. That stuff gets doled out on a strikingly egalitarian basis.

And I think of all my female friends who made the tactical error of dating men who aren't nearly as attractive as them, under the misapprehension that they'd presumably be nicer than the good looking guys with whom my friends had kept breaking up, up until that point . . . Only to discover that:

'Ugly guys aren't nice! They aren't nice at all!' says Maggie, my most recent fool mate to attempt this gambit. 'They're just furious and bitter because they feel permanently spurned by the hot girls, and they think it's only a matter of time before you spurn them too – which you do, but not because they're ugly, because they're mean. *And* they're also weirdly entitled because they've grown up watching films and TV shows and reading books in which the geeky socially inadequate brainbox outsider eventually wins round the beautiful head cheerleader with his gentle, understated charm. Only: what gentle, understated charm, exactly? And also: what brainbox?'

And then I think of what my friend Jem and I have identified as I Didn't Fancy Her Anyway syndrome, in which men become suddenly, incredibly aggressive towards women they find attractive.

'So they'll see a girl they fancy,' Jem explains, 'and in their heads, they're all: "Wow! She's amazing! I think I love her! Do I love her? I'm not sure . . . But: Wow! I *definitely* fancy her! Maybe she fancies me? No. No, she'd *never* fancy me. I don't have a hope in hell. I'm not good enough for her. Oh my God! That girl thinks I'm not good enough for her! That *bitch* thinks I'm not good enough for her! How dare she? I love her and she's too shallow to care! Just because she's beautiful! Who the fuck is she anyway? She's not all *that* beautiful! She totally thinks she is, but she isn't . . ." Meanwhile, the girl in question is wondering if she's going to have chicken goujons for her tea again.'

And then I list all the pretty girl scripts, all the clichés, all the cultural and social archetypes doing the rounds, the same ones which have been doing the rounds for years, decades, generations, centuries.

Pretty girl = bitch

Or

Pretty girl = spoiled.

Or

Pretty girl = vulnerable princess in need of rescuing.

Or

Pretty girl = arch minx, seductress, boyfriend stealer.

Or

Pretty girl = stupid, vain, vacuous.

Or

Pretty girl = dead on the inside.

Or

Pretty girl = dead on the outside in the context of a horror film, when she's generally the first one to get it.

Or

Pretty girl = some bloke's idea of a trophy.

Or

Pretty girl = peaks early as the queen of the popular crowd at school, after which her life slides to a standstill – she never leaves her small town, she gains weight, she gets divorced, because that's justice.

And

Pretty girl = easy target, recipient of minimal sympathy;
                oooooh, don't hate me because I'm beau-
                tiful, et cetera.

And I think: Pretty Girl Privilege? It's a little bit more complicated than that.

But I don't tell the straight-acting gay fashion PR any of
this. Instead, I find myself thinking: does he mean me,
though? Does he? Does he? Does he?

PART FOUR

MEN, WIVES, BABIES

16

Men – An Overview

Y̲ou know those feminists who hate men?

No; me either. Not sure they exist, truly.

OK. So you know those feminists who *don't* hate men?

I'm not one of those.

I am one of those feminists who likes men. Like, really, *really* likes men. Like – *loads*. I am one of those feminists who likes spending time with men and teasing men and flirting with men and sleeping with men. I like working with them (though not *for* them, that dynamic doesn't seem to suit me) and drinking with them and chilling with them. I like it on a personal level, and I like it on a political level. I think if men spend time with feminists who really, really like them, things might progress.

You could think of Hot Feminism as the diplomatic corps of the feminist movement, if you like.

Men, though! *Men*! Aren't they just hilarious! Silly and funny, cute as buttons when they try; wearying as PMT rewrought in flesh when they don't. Forgive me if I veer down the road of vast, sweeping generalisation at this point, won't you? I'm doing it for laughs, because men are an easy target (which I am not beyond exploiting), and because damn it all! There is some truth in those sweeping generalisations.

Sometimes handsome (and, preferably to my mind, pretty; I have a terrible weakness for a pretty man), and sometimes useful (ref: sperm, superior muscle mass, increased propensity for creating body heat, which can take the edge off a frosty flat interior come wintertime). Somewhat limited in emotional range; not entirely eager to let it all hang out in terms of the feeling of stuff, though there are exceptions to that, I'll allow; and what they can't do in terms of crying when it's appropriate, they do make up for in terms of being the essential components of any given boy band (see? Terrible weakness for the pretty man! *Terrible*!).

Oh, men! Flawed to hell of course and ever so testoster-oney, which can make them irrational and hairy, but to be fair, so am I. Let he/she who is without inadvisable hormo-nally-perpetuated impulse (and overactive body hair follicles) throw the first stone. And then there's that thing where every last one (up to and including the gay ones, the urbane ones, the reconstructed ones, the metrosexual, the perennially and unashamedly southern . . .) carries with him some inclinations towards alpha behavioural patterns, which he'll unleash sporadically, quite as if he's unaware of what a raging cliché that makes him.

My fave of all possible alpha displays include (but are

not limited to): the swinging of an invisible sporting imple-
ment (golf club or similar, the subtext on which being I
PLAY SPORT I AM MAN); the wiiiiiiiide spreading of
thighs on public transport seating (a dual purpose display
of alphafication, it's colonising and territorial, but also has
a light subtext of: I have a big penis everybody!); deployment of loud booming man voice (because the louder you
talk, the cleverer you sound, right?); and out and out blagging (because when you're a man, you can probably do
anything at all! Even if you actually definitely can't, even if
you lack the necessary experience and qualifications, you'll
probably pick it up before anyone notices because YOU
ARE A MAN!).

I like the way they can't dress as well as women, especially when they try, really hard, to dress as well as women.
I like it when they express vulnerability and inadequacy as
rage, because: cute! And also: ineffectual! I like it when they
try and civilise themselves by acquiring one of the set of
recently approved-for-use-by-men life skills, the kind of
thing which might have seemed a tad effete a year or two
ago, but is now terribly fashionable, to wit: 1) knowing
something about cocktails, 2) attending a weekend residen-
tial course on learning how to bake your own sourdough
bread, 3) ostentatiously growing out very specific areas of
facial hair, 4) cycling while wearing head to toe Lycra, 5)
making more dapper sock choices, 6) using emojis in text
messages. I like how incredibly gratified they become when
they manage to do one of the things they all think a Real

Man should be able to do: fix something, carry something else, eat a hot chilli, avert total disaster by damping down the barbecue fire before it gets out of control.

I have fancied vast swathes of their number. I could write my autobiography in terms of men I fancied through the eras: I started circa '78 with Luke Skywalker, graduated on to George Michael, Morten Harket, the man who held the baby in the black and white Athena poster I had on my bedroom wall (because I'd have failed at being a teen of the 1980s if I hadn't), the two Nicks (Kershaw and Kamen, though admittedly, Kershaw was a 'Nik' not a 'Nick'), the one no one else wanted in Bros (the non-twin, my rationale being: if no one else wanted him, I was in with a better chance), Keanu Reeves in *Bill & Ted's Excellent Adventure*, Jason Priestley as Brandon in *Beverly Hills 90210*, Val Kilmer when he played Jim Morrison in the 1991 film *The Doors*, every last member of the early incarnation of Take That on rotation (pretty boys, pretty boys . . .), Alex James from Blur (whom I'd work with a decade after that crush first raged, and God *that* was complicated) and so on.

Currently, you find me in the rabid throes of fancying everyone from Ryan Gosling to the absurdly handsome cobbler who mends shoes and cuts keys in the tiny cubbyhole of a shoe repair and key cutter establishment situated directly across the road from the offices of *Grazia*, at the easternmost point of Shaftesbury Avenue. (He's famous for his fitness, is that bloke. For miles around they call him 'the fit cobbler of Shaftesbury Avenue'; all women in a two-and-a-half-mile radius of the shop only take their best shoes in to him to be reheeled, in the hope that their choice in designer branding will impress him. Not a single one among us knows his name: there's a general sense he'll maintain more mystique if we don't.)

Yes. I like men. I fancy them and I think they're funny. I've studied them for years in all manner of environments, kept them as friends, boyfriends, flatmates and pets;[1] fought with them, loved a few of them, battled for professional supremacy with others. Partied and eaten and slept with and messed about with. Adored and objected to and bullied and, yup, even feared.

Got that one in my flat, somewhere.

Hot Feminism believes that men are trying to be better. *I* believe that men are trying to be better! I do. Some of them, for sure. The one who apologised to me for using the word 'chick' (even though I didn't mind). The one who said *Game of Thrones* made him uncomfortable because of the sky-high tit count. The one called Calum Best – son of the footballer George Best; reality TV star and notorious womaniser – who once asked me what I meant when I said I was a feminist, and then listened to me, intently, as I coughed up what was, in retrospect, a very early stirring of a version of Hot Feminism.

---

1 Not really as pets. Well, a bit. No, I don't mean it. (Or do I? No. Maybe?)

They are trying. They are.

And it's tough on them. I get that too. It's not like they even know exactly what they're trying *for*. I mean, for heaven's sake, if we don't know what constitutes definitively feminist behaviour patterns, if we haven't reached consensus on this lark (and we haven't, nor will we ever, what with it being vast and complex and ever-shifting and entirely dependent on our own individual experiences and situations, sensitivities and requirements), then how on earth can we expect them to?

On top of which: I get why men aren't handing over their longstanding privilege all that wilfully. I understand why they aren't going: you want equal pay? Sure! Have some of mine, that'll even things out! Or: you want people to listen to you in this meeting, at the expense of them listening to me? No probs, I'll hush my mouth! Or: you'd rather you didn't do most of the tedious drudgery of the housework any more, on top of working a full day? You'd like to feel as wholly entitled as I do when I stride down this street, a bit like I'm a king and everyone else is a loyal subject? You'd like me to give up my deeply held conviction that my opinion of your arse is the only one that truly matters, and that you dream of securing my approval of it, and that's why you keep going to Pilates really, it's got nothing to do with sorting out your lower back issues like you keep telling people?

I know why they aren't all going: cool! Let's make that happen right now! Because: who in their right mind would?

It must be so nice to feel those things! It must be *brilliant*! Why would you want to stop?

And of course, even if you did get to the point where, as a man, you find yourself thinking: OK, fair's fair, time to share this world-/power-/money-/rights-/shit out equally with the ladies . . . How do you stop thinking the world is right-fully yours to own and run? If you've been raised to believe that's the case in a million different ways (starting with the fact that boys are encouraged to run and jump and girls are encouraged to smile and comply); if pretty much your every experience of being alive reinforces that idea that it is truly yours, if you're told, over and over, that your very male-ness relies somewhat on you winning, beating, conquering, owning, monopolising, shouting, and definitely not cheer-fully relinquishing your assets and your status to the next chap, particularly if the chap is a lady. How do you Just. Stop. Doing. That?

I can't swear that, if I were in their shoes, I'd do it any more freely, any more graciously, any more readily. I mean, I haven't yet handed over a single one of the privileges I was born with. I'm white and I'm Western and I was born in the late twentieth century, as opposed to a more pox-ridden and less liberal time, and even if I wanted to give up any of the advantages those factors bestow upon me, I wouldn't have the first idea how. I'm middle class-ish, I wasn't raised with money (no ponies, no private education, not much in the way of foreign travel unless a single French exchange expedition counts, which I can't think it does) but I was raised with the expectation that I'd read a load of books, probably go to university and have some manner of career. You cannot buy that kind of entitlement; nor can you give it up.

I am not about to apologise for these things. I am not about to flagellate myself on account of 'em. But I acknowledge them, because I know the renouncing of privilege is hard. I acknowledge them, because they mean I understand why men haven't yet allowed women in, or through, or up, or on-board, in so many bloody respects.

I acknowledge them, while also thinking: you really are going to have to work with us to even things out, men. I know it's hard and I know it's weird, and I know it involves really quite a lot of sacrifice on your part. I know it'll mean the renouncing of part of your very identity, the part that is big on conquering, overpowering, dominating and owning. But the thing is, we want our due. We want it and we need it, we kind of just *are* coming for it . . . And also, I think it will be good for you. No! I *know* it will be good for you. We intend to take your supremacy from you men, but we're offering you equality in exchange, and dudes! That's a really good deal.

Men are suffering now, too. I have no doubt about that. Their mental health issues are deeply troubling, their suicide rate is horrific – three-and-a-half times that of British women, according to latest figures from the Office of National Statistics. In 2009, I lost one wonderful male friend to the tragedy of those suicide stats, it absolutely broke my heart, and I am fucked if I ever lose another one.

I believe that a more female-skewed society would be a society that talks more and suppresses less, that de-stigmatises expressing vulnerability and asking for help, that devalues stiff upper lip and celebrates heightened emotional intelligence. More sweeping generalisations about the default settings on the genders, perhaps, but seriously ... If more women are allowed to rise higher and higher in professional situations, and more men are allowed to stay home and raise their children, if ancient and irrelevant expectations about the husbands and fathers being the prime breadwinners are eliminated, if the stresses and strains of our lives are redistributed evenly among the sexes: surely that's going to help everyone?

Whenever a serious social inequality is righted, it just *is* better for absolutely everybody.

17

Actual WAG

When I was twenty-two, I went out with a footballer. Well, I *say* 'went out with'; but truly? What transpired between me and him represented something marginally more involved than a one-night stand, but probably incorporated less in the way of commitment, emotional sincerity and total time elapsed in each other's company than a holiday romance.

I first saw him on the telly, playing in some match or other. I was – and remain – completely unarsed by the allegedly beautiful game, which, I've always contended, has significantly less to offer in terms of passion and narrative breadth than your average episode of *The Only Way is Essex*. Men run this way, then they run the other way, and the most you can hope for is that a ball gets projected into the back of a net, maybe three times in total, and that someone falls over? Seriously? 'Not just a game,' they say, but as far as I can see, it isn't *even* a game.

But my flatmates at that time were fans, there was some major tournament occurring, I was otherwise occupied doing something that made them feel bad because they should have been doing it too, but weren't (specifically: revising for my university finals, even Hipster University makes you take exams in the end), and so they summoned me to join them as they watched a match of particular significance (no idea which or what or why) by telling me there was a sexy man on the pitch.

It turned out that they were quite right.

I'm not going to name him. I'll allow you to think this is as a consequence of some finer moral impulse, that I'm choosing to protect his identity because it wouldn't be fair to tell my side of the story without allowing him the recourse to tell his. Actually, it's because if I don't specify, your imagination will run berserk and lead you to conclude he's considerably more dreamy than he actually is. In fact, I think I *know* who you're beginning to think it might be (bearing in mind the timescale we're talking about, having perhaps done some hasty maths). I know whose name and whose flawless profile you're conjuring up. And I am more than happy to let you carry on with that delusion.

This one wasn't *that* hot, though he was, undeniably, very hot. Tall and elegantly crafted in the way of anyone who trains for a living. His thighs were buffed and turned like works of art. His face was pleasing. Symmetrical, dark; his eyes were intense, his brows were thrillingly furious. He was, apparently, good at football – Premier League, my friends! – though that was neither here nor there as far as I was concerned. I found that I did, however, enjoy watching him run. A lot.

When he came into the cocktail bar in which I toiled after university, some months after I'd first seen him on the telly, I got rather flustered. He was quite as pretty in the flesh; and quite as alluring. One of the many gorgeous things I've learned through interviewing famouses is that you almost never fancy in real life the ones you thought you fancied when observing them from afar. I have a long and proven history of being totally wrong about the boyband member I was convinced I had the hots for, the one over whom I'd swooned on TV, the one whose face I'd fixated on on album cover art . . . up until the point I met him, at which point I discover it wasn't him at all – oh no! – it was that other one, the one to whom I'd never given a second thought, until I stood in his presence, breathed in his smell, looked directly into his eyes, saw how he moved and smiled and deployed the vernacular, and realised that he was by far the funniest and brightest and sexiest of the collective. It happened with Take That, it happened with McFly, it happened with One Direction, it even happened with Blue (although that time, it turned out I didn't fancy any of them at all), and it happens because, as I lovingly reflected in the course of my whole On Being Fancied treatise, a chapter (or nine) ago, merely being physically attractive never made anyone truly, deep down, sexy. Tip of the hotness iceberg is physical attractiveness. Assuming hotness can come in iceberg form.

But in the case of my footballer: unusually, his telly appeal translated into life. The superficial physical charm was accompanied by other compelling vibes: a smartness, a sweetness, and probably best of all – minor indications of an interest in me.

It is always easier to fancy someone who clearly fancies you, don't you find? One has to at least entertain the possibility that the attraction is mutual, however briefly.

So there I was, uncapping overpriced bottled beer and slipping it over the counter towards him, blushing furiously, while he looked at me for milliseconds longer than he technically should have done.

'Fuck me!' goes Jules the Goose, my friend, my then-colleague in cocktails – and one of the flatmates who'd lured me to the TV and away from my revision that time with promises of hot footballer flesh. 'That's **** ******, and he is *looking at you*!'

Clueless of how to proceed, too flustered to speak, totally discombobulated by how fantasy on-telly world appeared to be crashing headlong into my experience of reality, I did the logical thing and took myself off to hide in the loo for a bit. When I walked back into the bar to resume my duties, I heard Jules the Goose triumphantly announce my re-emergence to the footballer, thus:

'That's her! There! That's the one I was talking about! And YOU are the only reason she watches football!'

'Really?' said **** ******. 'Why's that, then?'

'Um,' I said. 'Um.'

For I am charm personified.

'Because she thinks you're fit,' goes Jules the Goose.

And so I killed her.

No, I didn't. Very hard to kill, Jules the Goose.

I can't entirely remember what *did* happen next, just that it culminated with an exchange of phone numbers, and a week or so later, the next time **** ******'s team played in London, he popped round to Jules the Goose and my Hammersmith pad to pay court.

Hooray!

Stuff unfurled from that point, as stuff is sometimes wont to do. There were Moments and rufflings of clothing and bedlinen, intertwining of limbs and quite a lot of tongue; a couple of outings which might have qualified as proper dates, though maybe not . . . And then I played it cool (or tried to) and then he did (or tried to), and then I *think* someone[1] may have written a letter which was supposed to be cheeky and seductive yet smart, but almost certainly was none of those things, though fortunately the author of the letter[2] can't remember much about the content. Except that I wrote it in bloody French.

It was by no means an intense affair, to no extent a meeting of minds. The whole thing was definitely one of those romantic adventures you pursue on account of the stories you and Jules the Goose can tell all your other

---

1 Me.

2 Me again.

mates, rather than because you're experiencing a connection with another human that is so pure, so truthful, you
have no choice but to see what happens next. Oh, it was
quite fun, I think; though I do also think that (in a complete reversal of the way such businesses are supposed to
play out) he was a bit scared of me. I think he saw me as
a bit fast and 'London'. He was quite straightforward and
terribly northern, and there I was, with my catsuits and
my Wonderbra and my faux cockney accent (I'd had such
wild success in ditching the Devonshire accent on arriving
at Hipster University, I'd fallen into the habit of adapting
whichever fake accent most suited my ever-changing environment), perhaps being a bit overwhelming. I know we
went to a KFC once and the boys behind the counter
nearly exploded with giddiness over him. Another time, he
brought Jaffa Cakes by way of a love token. Another, he
knocked over a cup of tea onto Julie Goose's rug, and she
and I referred to the resulting rug damage as '**** ******'s
stain' for the rest of the time we shared flats together.

It fizzled in weeks, due to me being a bit daft, but it left
me with a mild fondness for that one footballer in particular
(he's a pundit now, he flickers up on my radar/TV sporadically), and also: a most unlikely affiliation with WAGs in
general.

When I was doing whatever it was I was doing with my
footballer the terminology 'WAG' was at least a decade
away from being invented (by an editor at my mag alma

mater *Grazia*, I believe, as a fleeting point of interest). When I was doing whatever I was doing with my footballer (an exercise in mutually beneficial lechery? Erotic rug staining? Blatant star-fucking?), the phenomenon of being romantically involved with a footballer hadn't yet been enshrined in popular culture as a desirable, or risible, or generally fetishise-able, notion.

This was the early nineties remember, this was five years before Posh and Becks got engaged at Rookery Hall in Cheshire; twelve years before media coverage of the Baden-Baden World Cup became infinitely more fixated on the antics of the players' assorted missuses than it was on the tournament; fifteen years before Coleen Rooney gave birth to a son called Kai, learned that her husband Wayne Rooney had slept with a prostitute while she was pregnant, forgave him anyway. Football was in the first stages of being gentrified, of having its brand identity wrested from the grasp of a loud, violent, terrace-disrupting and pitch-invading underclass, so that it might be spruced up and sanitised for the delectation of the middle classes.

When I was doing whatever I was doing with my footballer (showing off to my mates, reluctantly eating KFC, trying and failing to care about the offside rule), football was still somewhat niche, and its players weren't in any sense mainstream celebrities, which meant their lifestyles weren't scrutinised and obsessed over – which meant their women were inconsequential irrelevances.

*

WAGs became a Thing in the mid- to late-nineties, when football started saturating the mainstream. This happened because footballers discovered they could cash in their competence on the pitch for advertising and endorsement deals with companies that had nothing to do with football – and a lot to do with cars, shampoo, watches, sunglasses and so on – but who rather fancied gussying up their brand identities via a paid-for association with some Contemporary Paragons of Masculinity (henceforth, CPMs) or other, and heaven knew, footballers were *that*. Footballers stopped merely being sportsmen and became fully fledged celebrities. As celebrities, their lives off the pitch became as intriguing to the media, and all interested parties, as their lives *on* the pitch, and a hefty element of that off-pitch involved their wives and their girlfriends.

All of which would have been brilliant – especially for me, because I'll be honest: I have *a lot* more time for the wives than I do the players and the game itself, they tick far more of my boxes than a bunch of men running around a bleak field ever could – if the WAGs (who officially became 'WAGs' through the course of the Baden-Baden World Cup tournament of 2006) had not also ended up as one of the world's most legitimised targets for unbridled women hating.

It is my firm conviction that, as the planet tries really hard to moderate its sexist impulses, so it also becomes inclined towards identifying a smattering of individuals of the female persuasion whom it feels entitled to hate. It's like we – all of us, men and women, feminists and otherwise – seek out a safety valve on our base misogyny, a get-out-of-jail-free card on it, as if we think:

'OK, we know we're not supposed to feel unjustified and instinctual loathing for *all* women, *all* the time, so we're going to get rid of any we've built up and suppressed by expending it on a very few of them. In order to pull it off convincingly, we'll rustle up some pseudo liberal argument in our own defence, and then no one will ever notice! We'll say how sad it is that these women seem capable only of existing through the prism of marriage and wifeliness, so that it'll seem as if we're somehow defending most women while slagging off these very particular women – which is the special genius of this act!'

Models often get it on these grounds, and so do It girls. At least three actresses/singers from any given generation of A listers suffer from it especially badly. (It seems to be Miley Cyrus, Gwyneth Paltrow and Anne Hathaway at the time of writing. It was Keira Knightley for *years*, but then she got married, at which point we decided she'd become suddenly more likable, because: oh, who knows why? We realised she truly wasn't interested in stealing our boyfriends after all? How rational!)

Plus I estimate that an average of three female randoms a year also get it. I'm thinking specifically of the curious case of Ruby Tandoh of 2013's *Great British Bake Off* reality TV competition, a woman who was, apparently, just too pretty for us to accept she was also good at cooking, so we did the sensible thing and vilified her. Mainly on the grounds we thought she 'looked a bit moody' and that competition judge Paul Hollywood fancied her, which we seemed to think was her fault, rather than his.

And of course, any woman attaching herself romantically to a prominent footballer is considered entirely fair game.

Why? Because WAGs are awful, right? Gold diggers, basically whores; the willing trophies of those overpaid, preening narcissists we can't help but admire because they're so damn good at kicking a ball about! WAGs are wantonly consumerist, and such terrible role models for young women, on account of them perpetuating the idea that success is achieved through attaching yourself to a young man of great talent and wealth, having his babies and turning a blind eye on his serial infidelities, while sidelining your own potential, your own talent, your own ambition, because who needs to do anything that tiring when you can marry your way through life? WAGs! With their handbags and their premature Botox, their hair extensions and their flint-eyed social ambition! WAGs, who only ever distract their noble menfolk from the truly important business of the day, which is winning football matches!

Yeah, well, except: bullshit. I've met some WAGs – the furious, brittle French one with a law degree and a terrifying desire for vengeance (long story, I was implicated, yes). The doll-like blonde creature with one of the most deliciously foul mouths I have ever encountered. An extremely irreverent one who referred to her Premier League husband as 'man-bait', because all other men were persistently bedazzled by him, drawn to him like moths, and it made her laugh . . .

I've met some WAGs. I've even almost kind of been one. Turns out WAGs – like all women, like all humanity – defy clichés and categorisation; and anyone hating them on principle might as well hate all women on principle, which means they might as well hate all people.

Because WAGs are people too.

I suspect much of our antipathy toward WAGs stems from the hilariously transparent homoerotic crush male football fans tend to harbour for footballers. Football fans hate WAGs, because WAGs do what they're trying really hard to stop themselves from wishing they could do, specifically: have sex with footballers.

OK, OK, I may be overstating the case.

Though possibly only a little bit.

I do definitely think anti-WAG sentiment is symptomatic of the extent to which we extend terrible reverence towards any aspect of popular culture that appeals predominantly to straight men (sport, guitar music, brrm brrms, sorry – *cars*), while dismissing those aspects which appeal predominantly to women and gay men (pop music, celebrity culture, fashion). This is the reason we think, for example, that football *matters* – football inspires and dignifies us, football unites us and brings us transcendence! – while fashion diminishes us, restricts us, renders us stupid and probably anorexic. You could translate it, thus: the things men care about are FAB because men are FAB, while the things that women care about are stoopid, because women care about them, and women are stoopid.

Seriously: who's to say that a soap opera-ish fascination with the wives of footballers is a less legitimate concern than the on-pitch antics of some bloke who dropped out of school early so he could get really, really good at chasing a ball around? Not me, buster! And, while I'm on the subject(ish), why is it that we commend a middle-aged man for becoming passionately engaged with a football match, while sneering at a teenage girl for becoming passionately engaged at a boy band concert? As far as I can see, there's absolutely no discernible difference between some bloke sobbing over defeat at 'the' Arsenal and some young girl sobbing over Harry Styles mid-ballad . . . These two are as silly and wonderful as each other, both transported by the spectacle of their own chosen demigods, cavorting around in front of vast, adoring crowds.

But I digress.

My bigger point is this: WAGs should not be routinely belittled, or vilified, or dismissed – because we are all WAGs. Live long enough, love a bit, and sooner or later, lady: you too will end up a WAG.

*

I am a WAG. And so are you. And you, and you and you . . . Not in the literal female accoutrement of a footballer sense, of course. Not unless you do go out with a footballer. Which – you might. I did, for heaven's sake. But no, I'm thinking more in the sense that we almost all of us experience a spell – or several spells, or something which is less like a 'spell' and more like 'a substantial portion of your life' – as a Wife or a Girlfriend to someone or other. Technically, I'm a 'G', for I will not marry the Man I Keep In My Flat, on account of deep-rooted fear of flouncy frocks and also commitment, and how much I hate organising Events. I am, and will remain, a girlfriend, a 'G'. Even if it means I have to pay inheritance tax on the flat we bought together because he dies first (which I really think he will).

We all end up being, to some degree, and at some point, defined by the fact that we're in a relationship. That we share a bed or a home, a surname and some children, a tax return and body fluids, a Facebook page and hopes and dreams for a combined future, with some man – and this becomes part of our identity.

Even if we're not active WAGs right this moment, we've most of us got a latent WAG buried in us somewhere. If we're just out of a relationship, if we've been out of one for some time; if we're single but well aware we're raving serial monogamists and therefore our situation might be best described not as 'single', but as 'between relationships', if we've made peace with the idea that we just really would rather like a boyfriend, OK? – and we're going to some lengths to find one ... We are WAGs. Ex WAGs. Future WAGs. WAGs in waiting. Wannabe WAGs. WAG without portfolio.

And that's all a teeny bit tricksy. Feministically speaking.

Being with a bloke is a compromised state.[3] Being in love is a compromised state. They want things and we want things, and sometimes those things clash, and if we let them have the things they want at the cost of our having the things *we* want, then we're not just caving in on a personal level, we're losing out in a bigger battle: as a woman, to a man.

In addition to which – and forgive me for this trite, predictable observation, I swear I wouldn't make it if I had any other choice, but I don't, because it seems to be so terribly, tediously true – most men will revert to a state of near-childishness, when placed in the context of a long-term relationship, particularly if that relationship occurs in a domestic setting. Men see the trappings of home: they see fridge, they see mugs, they see cushions, they see the remote control, they feel cosy and protected and warm; they look at the adult woman who shares this space with them, and they think: MUMMY! Even though they know damn well

---

3 Being in *any* relationship is a compromised state. If you're in one with another woman, don't think I underestimate the issues and complexities implicit in that. I don't. It's just that the battles those issues and complexities produce aren't generally fought along gender lines.

that chick in question is actually their partner, their lover, their missus, their significant other, their co-signer on the mortgage docs.

I don't know when the transition occurs, precisely. Maybe it's six months into a relationship. Maybe it's on the first anniversary of your relationship. Maybe it's the day after you move in together. Maybe it's when you have his child.

I don't know.

But I do know that it happens. One day they're your boyfriend, independent adults entirely capable of muddling through on their own; the next: they've had toothache for two weeks and won't book an appointment at the dentist because they're too scared (although they say 'busy'), and so you do it for them, self-consciously making the phone call, apologising to the receptionist because you know how absurd this seems – then you end up accompanying them into the surgery, to ensure they go at all.

Or they seem to have become completely blind to the fact that the recycling bin is overflowing (actually, truly blind, it's not that they're wilfully ignoring it, it's just that they can't see it) and so you deal with it *again*, huffing and puffing with passive aggressive rage so not-entirely contained it verges on being actual aggressive-aggressive rage.

Oh *and*: they refuse to get *anything* dry cleaned, because they're convinced dry cleaning is a scam, that all those guys ever do is hang stuff up for a bit in a breeze, spritz its hot spots with Febreze, pop it in a plastic garment bag and charge you £7.50 for the pleasure – so you end up doing it, instead. Dropping it off, collecting it, paying for it, and pretending you haven't, because if you do, you'll get dissed for falling for the Great Dry Cleaning Scam. Why do you do this? Why do *I*? Because we tell ourselves 'someone's got to', without even really knowing what that means? Because we don't want them turning up to so-and-so's wedding smelling like a tramp, on account of how that will reflect on us (though will it? Really? They're independent beings ultimately)?

Somehow – and you're *really* not sure how or when this happened – but *somehow*, the buying of birthday cards and gifts for anyone the two of you know as a couple, falls into your jurisdiction as The Woman. (At a push, they'll sign the card you bought – but only if you put it in front of them, with a pen, and often only after telling them exactly what to write.) And despite yourself, you're the one who ends up managing his relationship with his own family – talking to his mother more frequently than he does, having coffee with his sister-in-law while remembering her children's names – because you're pretty sure all connection between him and them would fizzle out and die if you didn't.

Which is not to say that, the moment any given man enters an adult and domesticised environment, he'll become entirely useless. He won't. It's my experience that while many of them start failing, instantaneously and miserably, in terms of physical and emotional upkeep once cosily

embedded in a long-term relationship, they'll simultaneously start excelling at what I think of as the Dad Arts.
They'll produce power tools as if from nowhere, and start
putting up pictures you're not entirely sure you want on the
hall walls in the time it takes you to have a quick shower.
They'll deal with the Wi-Fi when it drops out. They will do
the things which need to be done to the taps.

And you let them get on with it.

And then, and then . . . You'll find yourself sometimes
using a tone of voice you don't recognise while asking them
repeatedly to do one of the things you keep doing on their
behalf, and then you think to yourself: bloody hell, am I
nagging? Is this actual bloody nagging?

And you'll marvel as they grow increasingly deaf to your
demands, increasingly likely to find twenty-seven tasks
more pressing than the one you think they should do first
(number seventeen of which = put up more dodgy art in
the hall).

And *then* you'll let them get on with it even more.
Because it's easier. Or rather, because it seems completely
inescapable.

Which is fine, except: is it? Is it OK to be a feminist and
accept that this is how we roll in our romantic lives? That
traditional roles just will kick in, regardless; that the ladies
will cover the caring and the gents will do the DIY, and we
may nag, and they may ignore – quite as if it's the 1950s in
our hearts? Because there's something about loving someone
which circumnavigates the feminist in us, fuses it, views it

as an affront to that one bloody man; the one who can sometimes seem so vulnerable, so lost, so ill-equipped to deal with pretty much everything – never mind how gender roles really are shifting in the world at large? Does some part of us seek to protect them from the feminist revolution we're simultaneously perpetuating elsewhere? Because we're not entirely sure they can handle it?

I am a completely inadequate WAG. Traditionally, WAGs cook, clean and child raise, yet I perform none of these functions.

I am, by no stretch of the imagination, a domestic goddess. I'm what can only really be described as a 'truly shit cook'. I had no interest in the culinary arts as a younger woman; the foodie revolution struck the UK circa 2002, bringing with it all manner of olive oil and high end cheese, and leaving me, if anything, more determined than ever to remain a shit cook. I'm a stubborn, contrary article by nature; and so it was that as I witnessed the rest of the world losing its mind over something I'd never given a fig for (food), I redoubled my efforts to know less even than I did before. I retired what had passed, up until that point, as my signature dish (Thoroughly Mediocre Chilli con Carne). I resolved to never know anything more about wine than: it gets you good and drunk. I wore the fact that I had never cooked a roast like a badge of honour (still do); a year ago, when I interviewed the UK's resident Queen of Cake, the amazing broadcaster Mary Berry, I paused to reflect on the fact that I was probably the only hack on living record to have not told her I'd had enormous success in recreating her famous lemon drizzle cake. (Because I hadn't even tried.)

I'm not sure if any of this is an expression of feminism, so much as pure inadequacy undercut by a pronounced lazy streak. Although I do often think of the thin friend who once said to me: 'the problem with food is, it makes you fat. The better you are at cooking, the more you'll eat your own food. Remain bad at it, and that avenue of temptation will be firmly shut down.'

Also, you do know you can ring people up, and demand that they bring you piping hot food which they've cooked on your behalf, in these excellent little aluminium cartons, sealed with cardboard lids, from which you can eat using plastic cutlery, which means you don't even have to wash up afterwards?

It's super cool.

Admittedly, my culinary incompetence makes reciprocating dinner party invitations tricky – though not really, because I just never do. Curiously, I still get invited to other peoples' dinners (many of which, to be fair, are catered by the man-aspect of that particular couple), though I think this is because I earn my keep in other ways: risqué parlour games and moments of outrageous indiscretion, mainly. I believe that in life, people are either natural hosts or natural guests, and I have made it my business to be an exceptional guest. I arrive on time with two bottles of prosecco minimum, I make delicious conversation, I am a charming drunk. I'm pretty damn good at guesting, though I say it myself.

Anyway. It may not surprise you to learn that I don't clean, either. I pay someone else to do that (a woman, inevitably; do male cleaners even exist?) once a week. I feel guilty enough about that to vacate the premises while the cleaning process happens. This amuses the Man I Keep In My Flat no end.

'You're so transparent,' he says.

And I'll get to the non-child raising shortly, though that's a whole other chapter.

This, then, is how you can avoid compromising some of your feminist politics within the confines of a relationship: by remaining a childless, dreadful cook and an uninterested cleaner, who is big on outsourcing.

But I acknowledge that this is a very particular way of proceeding, and also: it isn't just about that, is it?

18

The Selfish Wash

'**D**o you ever feel as if you'd have no communal social life if you left it up to them?'[1] says Annika. 'Like: I don't think we'd leave the house if he was in charge of our friends. Or go on holiday. Or go to a party, ever ever. He can barely answer a text message summons to the pub from his brother.'

'We'd have no social life, no emotional life, and I also think our child would be dead,' goes Sadie.

'Same,' Annika says. 'Well, we have no child, so there would be no child death, which is good. But we probably wouldn't talk to anyone else ever, if I didn't have our joint social interaction interests covered. I'm like our social secretary. And I'm not even that sociable.'

'I have to pretend Matt earns more in front of certain of his friends, when really, I earn, like, *much* more,' says Zara. 'And he's never asked me to do it, I just do; because I'm scared I'll emasculate him if I don't, but seriously: what the

---

1 Them = men.

fuck? I emasculate ten men before lunchtime at work! I *like* emasculating men at work. It's what I do for fun! Why, then, do I go to such lengths to avoid emasculating this one specific man in a gastropub on Sundays?'

I have to pretend I care that he's at the pub again while I'm home alone watching *Made in Chelsea*, I say, when in fact, all I want is to be able to watch *Made in Chelsea* in peace. But if he can't tell his pub mates that he's in the pub, as some act of defiance perpetuated against the grumpy, controlling Other Half, then he'll look and feel I dunno. Unloved? Unwanted? And also, and for the same reasons – we've somehow silently come to the joint decision to allow everyone to believe that although in fact neither one of us want to get married, I secretly, deep down, really really do, I'm just sucking his non-proposing up in the name of keeping him, whatever the cost.[2]

'Men just *are* manipulative fuckers,' Sadie says, 'but they'll come over all: "men are so straightforward, women are so complicated and never say what they mean!" Which means they're being manipulative about being manipulative, manipulation squared.'

'Matt wilfully manipulates me into making tea for him every morning,' says Zara.

'How?' goes Sadie.

'He asks me what my plans are for the day, which is his way of making me think about my schedule – where I'm

---

2 I may have just blown that myth, eh?

going to go, what I'm going to do – which in turn is his way of reminding me he likes it when the first thing I do, each and every day, is make him tea, even though I don't drink tea myself, ergo it is an act of sacrifice on my behalf, which is what makes the tea taste so sweet.'

'The bastard!' says Sadie. 'You should leave him!'

'Well I would,' Zara goes on, 'but I quite like doing it. It means I don't have to be as nice to him with my words and other actions, because he thinks the tea alone is proof of my affections. Also, I get him back by doing a selfish wash.'

'A selfish wash?' asks Annika.

'I wait till he's out, go through the dirty laundry basket, separate out our clothes into two piles, then only wash mine. Selfish wash.'

'Oh yeah, I do that,' says Sadie, 'but then I feel guilty and end up ironing his shirts after he washes them. Is that bad?'

'Depends,' says Zara. 'Do you hate ironing?'

'No, I quite like it. I find it de-stressing in its methodical way. Plus it gives me a sense of achievement.'

'I think that's fine,' Zara says.

'Even if Gray *really* likes it when I iron his shirts? Even if it makes him *really* happy?'

'Hmmmmmm,' says Zara. 'Maybe not.'

Annika says she thinks it's all relatively uncomplicated when it comes to household chores, in that it's fairly obvious if one of you is doing more than the other one, and if you're doing more than the other one *while also being a woman*:

'then that's clearly not cool. The facts of it are straightforward, and the unfairness of it is quite straightforward. It might not be straightforward to stop it happening – but you both kind of know where you're at with it.'

Might that also just stop happening as an inevitable impact of general increased equality, I ask. Like, when I get super-busy at work, I just *do* stop doing even the small amount of housework I usually do, because all I can do is work, stress, sleep. I stop being able to see that the recycling bin's overflowing, too. Which of course might just mean I'm trembling on the brink of all-out domestic disarray . . .

'Entirely possible,' Annika goes on. 'But what's *really* difficult is loving them. How do you love a man without totally screwing up your principles?'

Go on, I say.

'OK, so . . . Say they've fairly obviously drifted off into some quasi-depressive slump and won't talk to anyone about it because they're men and they do not talk, so you end up having to practically do an intervention with a therapist to stop them falling even deeper into despair. Or that thing we were talking about before where they just will not maintain their own social life, or your joint social life, and you know they'd just give it all up and go total hermit in a heartbeat, so it falls to you to do it. Or you book their doctor's appointment because they won't. Or you tell them they really do need a haircut, they're showing you up, and then you book that. How do you avoid those clichés of wifely behaviour when you do also just care about them, when you do also just love them, and if you didn't do all that cliché wifely behaviour shit, they'd be a total mess? Except then you think, am I just enabling their messiness with my clichéd wifely behaviour, would they be better off without me? And then you start to cry softly to yourself.'

I don't know what the answer to this is. I know I struggle with getting the bit of me that loves the Man I Keep In My Flat to coexist with the bit of me that's feminist – so I thought I'd ask Lena Dunham.

Dunham is twenty-eight years old; the creator, writer and star of the HBO series *Girls*, a precocious prodigious talent who is famous for getting her pretty, chubby, non-Hollywood compliant naked body out on TV in the multiple interest of protest, realism and laughs. She's award winning and successful in a way that makes almost everyone else in the world look a bit like a failure relatively; and she is irrefutably feminist. Feminism saturates her perspective and her TV shows and her vibe in one of the most complete, convincing, instinctive and practically applied fashions I've ever seen. I met her when she was in London publicising her book, *Not That Kind Of Girl*; and even though she's considerably younger than I am, and even though I have presumably had more experience of relationships by sheer dint of my knocking around the planet for longer . . . Dunham still seems like something of an oracle on life, she's got a big brain and a sharp wit and heightened emotional intelligence quotients.

I am keen to know what she thinks about how we play romantic domesticity.

We talk about her relationship with the musician Jack Antonoff, who she lives with. I asked her:

Is it possible to be a feminist and be in love?

'Yes, I think it's really possible to be a feminist and be in love!' she says.

We're sitting in the café of the Soho Hotel, bang smack in the middle of London. I am drinking coffee and she is drinking green tea and contemplating eating the tiny muffin which arrived, propped up against the side of her cup. Dunham's hair is a washed out green colour and she's got a massive stress-related mouth ulcer; her speaking voice squeaks off into Marge Simpson-like octaves when she's hamming a line up to make a point. She isn't even slightly cool and she doesn't even vaguely care, which makes her cool in a way I haven't really seen before

Go on, I say.

'I think it's a really cool thing to be a feminist in a relationship and figure out how to make that work and how to put your politics into action . . . Or sometimes, retire them for a moment.'

Is retiring them for a moment OK then, I ask; thinking of all the times I do. Like when my computer screws up and I go running to The Man I Keep In My Flat to fix it. Like when he picked our mortgage provider, even though half the money in question is mine. Like when I pay the cleaner, even though I do not clean – because, apparently, the responsibility for things being clean is still ultimately mine.

'Yes!' says Dunham. 'Sometimes, there are certain gender dynamics . . . I do not ascribe to fixed ideas of gender, but there a certain things that dudes do in relationships, and there are certain things that women do in relationships, and they're stereotypes for a reason. You can try to override them, but . . .'

You'll end up doing them anyway?

'You will.'

Like?

'Like . . . I feel like in my relationship, I can fulfil a more traditionally dude-like role. I'm the person who's in bed, distracted, thinking about my work. Slightly unavailable. My boyfriend's really great at leaving [work-related anxieties] at the door. But there's certain things we can't get over, which is me being like . . .' Dunham puts on a whiny, high-pitched nagging voice: '"I called the person who is fitting our blinds three times, and I have not gotten any support from you, and I need you to pick a sample!" And I'm this person who I never thought I'd be screaming at my boyfriend about blinds! And how there's "a difference between off-white and white! And you have to pick one, or the blinds will be off-white and you'll say you wanted white!" And I hear myself and think: Oh, I should just jump off a cliff right now, with all the other lemmings.'

The nagging! The nagging we never thought we'd do, then we all do anyway, even if we're Lena bloody Dunham!

(Which is not to say we aren't subject to nagging in return, of course. When people share a confined space, they will all end up in the nag zone, irrespective of gender. It's just that when men do the nagging, it tends not to be recognised as nagging, more as 'a request, repeated a tedious quantity of times'.)

So what *do* we do?

'You've just got to run with it. You've just got to own it. Being a dog owner [which Dunham is], being a homeowner, being a girlfriend, there's certain things, patterns you fall into, that you never dreamed, feminist or not.'

This, then, is perhaps the blurriest of the battles feminism is fighting. The laws on progressing professionally and socially seem straightforward, relatively: we want more money and more power, we want to occupy more space in public life. But at home, where it isn't about power or dominance, where it just can't be about power or dominance because that isn't how personal relationships work ... Where money isn't a marker of worth, but rather a desperately prickly issue, a top predicator of divorce ... What then? What *there*?

Embracing the WAG you just are, as opposed to the WAG you think you should be, is a solid Hot Feminist jumping off point. I feel no shame about my domestic failings – I revel in them, rather – but nor should you feel any shame about your domestic accomplishments. Go with the aspects of trad-WAGery which suit you, the things you're good at, the things you enjoy and find fulfilling; gleefully, wilfully, ditch the others. You cook but you don't clean? Bravo! You interior design but you don't cook? How nice! You wash but you don't handwash, you hoover but you don't dust, you childcare but you don't do anything else . . .? Carry on! Never feel obligated to acquire any of the domestic arts which don't come naturally to you. Never allow anyone else to tell you you really *should* be able to cook a roast/clean a stain/hem a duvet/bake a cake, you know . . . Why should you? Why?

In time, the idea of gendered domestic duties should dissipate. I've seen cooking become a Man Thing over the course of the last decade alone, which might have been mainly due to the arbitrary whims of fashion – but which has also had some significant, real consequences in the positions all men and women occupy in their own homes, in the division of duties within them. Blokes now just do feel it's their place to cook. Next up: childcare? It could happen; if more women start occupying higher, better paid positions professionally, if paternity leave becomes more than just a token two-week break for the chaps – then it *will* happen.

Otherwise: practise what a girl friend of mine calls 'periodic tactical ball-dropping' on the truly drudgey stuff. Play chicken on the overflowing recycling bin (will he break first? Will you?); wantonly disregard the accumulating post mountain. You know, just out of curiosity. Just to see.

Reel in the mummy duty moments: definitely leave him to deal with his own dry cleaning.

Ditch the 'good family man' narrative. Nothing winds me up like this: our capacity to congratulate men for having the astonishing decency not to ditch his Mrs and the kids for some spangly piece half his age, for turning up for bathtime periodically, for being fun at the four-year-old's birthday bash. Nothing else demonstrates how much higher the domestic bar sits for women than it does men. You never hear a woman congratulated for being a 'good family woman', because, well! We expect nothing less from a woman than that she sticks by her man and her kids! So either we stop bandying about the expression 'good family man', stop telling men they're pretty much heroes for fulfilling their side of the domestic bargain – or we start calling women 'good family women', too.

Take on the more dude-like roles, if and when the more dude-like roles suit you. Be quietly proud and happy to be the one who earns more, even if you *do* then lie about it in public; for now, anyway. It seems likely that, as women progress professionally, so the possibility that we earn more than our husbands and boyfriends do will be assimilated into our personal lives, and stop being a source of stigma or awkwardness. Cherish your own tendencies towards emotional unavailability when work stresses override you.

Ensure you pick a good one. One who will not take advantage of your retiring the politics sporadically, who will allow you the dude-like moments when they suit you, who will accept the Selfish Washes.

Hot Feminist Wag practice. Definitely a work in progress.

What Do We Call Them

What do we call them, that isn't cheesy? Or smug? Or cliché? Or simpering? What do we call them that isn't over-formal, or self-conscious, or dramatic, or daft? What do we call them that isn't old-fashioned or childish, ambivalent or super-technical? That will somehow communicate our affection and our long-term intentions, without making us sound clingy or reverent or proprietary, or triumphant or daft.

It's an issue, which is annoying. Men don't struggle with what to call their women, because men don't struggle with being defined by their relationships with women – because they *aren't*. We are still, somewhat. Drab, but true. Which means that our names for them are weighted down with subtext and greater significance.

Let's consider some possibilities:

Boyfriend
Just does sound daft when applied to those older than thirty, particularly if you're cohabiting.

BF
No.

Boyf
Marginally more acceptable than BF, on account of it being retro; still, it's hardly ideal if it's being applied to an adult relationship scenario.

HAB

Lacks the conviction of 'WAG', probably on account of that final, relatively soft 'B'.

Fiancé

Awful! Unforgivably French, unnecessary deployment of an acute accent, more twee than candyfloss, as smug as smug gets with its hefty top note of: some man wants me! *Me*! For ever and ever and ever and therefore I have won The Race! Bow down before me and my newly-burdened ring finger! If you're v'ey v'ey lucky, you too may end up occupying this enviable position one day!

See? Awful! If you find yourself in an engaged state, I recommend that you refer to your engagement as 'the in between' and your engagé as 'MY in between'. Or just stick with boyfriend.

Unless he's older than thirty.

Husband

OK, I guess, if it's an actual fact, though ensure you're not flinging it about wantonly as further evidence that some man wants you for ever and ever and ever and ever and ever and got it? Good.

DH (Online abbreviation for Dear Husband)

Comment deleted by online moderators due to obscene nature of content.

Lover
Yeah, yeah, but when you go with *that* one, you're basically hinting to the world you have loads more sex than it does, which is annoying, plus unlikely, because why draw attention to it if you really are?

Piece
Ooh, I like this one (though it is perhaps a little camp).

The Ball n Chain
Amusing reversal of traditional imaginings on gender roles within a relationship, redolent of a 1970s sitcom (rarely a bad thing). A little self-conscious for regular usage, though. See also: Him Indoors.

The Male Accoutrement
I've tried this one for size in articles. Heavy handed, potensh; also something of a mouthful. Nicely gay, on the plus side.

EPO
Entertainment Prevention Officer. I got this one off a cop I know. They do love a mnemonic, the police.

Business
How a friend of mine refers to her bits on the side. E.g.: 'Business is playing up, again.' Or: 'Business is going strong this financial quarter!' Or: 'I may have to close that

business down imminently.' Funny but very coded, and I suspect not that translatable into what passes for real life anywhere that isn't inside my friend's head.

Bo

Fine, if you're doing the vocals on a Nelly track from the early 2000s.

Bae

Fine, if you're Beyoncé. But you're not, are you? No. (Unless – you *are*? In which case OH MY GOD THAT'S AMAZING! I'M A HUGE FAN OF YOUR WORK, B! Can I call you B?)

Special Friend

I always feel like you're overhyping your situation with this one. Like: I'll be the judge of how special they *really* are, ducky. So, unless he does, I dunno, *tricks* or something as obvious and instantly impressive as that, you should probs avoid. Also, it can sound a bit like 'Invisible Friend', which is (hopefully) something different.

Partner

No one likes this. No one. It's cold, formal, sexless, loveless, ugh. I once attempted to use it, but ended up replacing it with 'thing'. 'Allow me to introduce my . . . Thing,' I said. It sounded better than 'partner' would have done.

Boy Toy

Fun, but risky. Know your audience before making free.

The One

Categorically no, on grounds of ickiness, factual inaccuracy and also off-the-hook delusional smugness levels. There is, in no universe, a One person destined to fulfil your every romantic and sexual and practical need, a day to your night, a yin to your yang, a tick for all your boxes, a nice neutral camel counterpoint to your fluorescent yellow, et cetera. Do not look for that, do not hope for that, do not intertwine yourself with another in the belief that they are that. They are not. Indeed, it's my opinion that in the course of any one adult existence, the average chick meets six people she could make some version of a life with, the only problem being she can't have them all, choices have to be made, options have to be narrowed down. But no one's The One. I'll accept 'One Of The Possible Six' (as in: 'I've met someone! And I think he might be One Of The Possible Six!') or 'A One', (as in: 'I've met someone! I think he might just be A One!'), but never 'The One'. Romantic claptrap destined to end in tears/infidelity, the very moment you meet your next 'The One'. And you will.

Man I Keep In My Flat

Does sound a bit like he's there against his will, admittedly. (NB He's free to come and go as he chooses. No. Really. He is.)

19

How Not To Have A Baby

I do not want children. I have never wanted children. Not having children was right up there with 'grow up hot' in terms of my early defining ambitions; and unlike the hot (which remains an evolving work; a quest that never ends, hotness being pretty unquantifiable, ultimately. It's not the sort of thing you can ever go: 'nailed it!' about), I *can* say with absolute confidence that I have definitely pulled off my ultimate end goal of not having children. So far.

Look at me! Thirty-five years old (depending on when you're reading this, though I'm lying anyway, so no matter) and I don't have a single kid to my name! Not *one*! Not even a really, really small one.

I do think I'm allowed to congratulate myself on this count. Indulge a little moment of celebration. High five my own soul, jump up and click my heels together; deliver a knowing, twinkly side-glance at the camera I secretly think is following me around and filming my entire life.[1]

---

1 Don't you think that too, sometimes? Oh, you do!

My childlessness[2] is an accomplishment of kinds. It has not been easy.

I don't mean physically. It's the *easiest* time not to have children *physically*, is this. Hoorah for freely available contraception and reproductive rights in general, and for women not having our entire destinies tethered to our biological function, because risking pregnancy each and every time you have sex can seriously mess up a lady's capacity to run the world/have good sex!

But emotionally and culturally, not having kids is difficult. A challenge, even.

I was very young the first time I thought: 'Yeah, about *that* . . . Not sure I'm mother material.' I was still a child; seven at the oldest. A neighbour had brought her newborn round to be admired, and I didn't see anything particularly admirable in it. It was small and obviously, anxious-makingly, breakable. It didn't seem to be on the verge of contributing much in the way of diverting chat. I watched it puke on a muslin cloth, which the neighbour had draped semi-permanently over one shoulder for the purposes of baby puke-capturing. I'd quite wanted to puke myself.

'If you're very, very careful, you can hold her,' said the neighbour, quite as if she were offering me some sort of

---

2 Or if you'd rather 'childfreeness', though I think that's a bit of a mouthful, plus for me, not having children is so self-evidently a good thing, I don't attach stigma to the word 'childless' – although I know some people do.

treat, as opposed to a go on a highly breakable puke-machine. 'Would you like that?'

'No,' I said, and then I made myself scarce, which no one noticed, because they were too busy gazing upon the wrinkled visage of the tightly swaddled highly breakable puke-machine, whom the neighbour was now threatening to breastfeed.

And so I had my first of many Babies? No thanks! moments.

The next one struck when I was eleven, and my mother gave birth to my youngest sister, Chloe. Though I understood that this child was fundamentally excellent as a person from really quite early on – highly amusing, jolly and quite subversive – I was also appalled by the stubby, bloody remnants of her still-attached umbilical cord. There seemed to be something horrifically *biological* about this whole procreation business, and on those grounds alone – I wanted nothing to do with it.

A sort of visceral bleurgh at the prospect of motherhood morphed in time. As I grew, so did my conviction that I was no kind of breeder, and so did my justifications for not wanting babies. I went from a sort of stubborn: but why *should* I? to a more enlightened: there's something fundamentally suspect about the way everyone talks babies to girls, but never to boys; to a militant: why would I do *that* to my body/career prospects/independence/finances? Why would *anyone*? Latterly, I've been able to season my baby-evading principles with a light dusting of environmental concerns, like so: the planet is horribly overpopulated already, why should I add to its problems with future generations? I'm not sure how sincere that is, however.

On expressing these perspectives – which I did, regularly – I was informed with certainty, and by almost everyone, that I was quite wrong and would change my mind.

I'd change my mind when I was older.

I'd change my mind when I fell in love.

I'd change my mind when my friends started having babies.

I'd change my mind because I, like all girls, was fitted with a biological clock, with a ticking hormonal time bomb of a prompt on procreation, which would erupt at some point, sure as eggs is (ovaries) eggs, overriding my intellect, reducing me to the baby-craving equivalent of a zombie, urging me to get myself the hell knocked up.

I'd change my mind, because to remain childless was selfish.

I'd change my mind because I just *would*.

Ha.

Guess again, mofos?

Now, aged forty-seven,[3] I can confirm that they were wrong and I was not. Hoorah for Me, being right about Me! I've grown older and more happy with my childless life, with

---

3 I could be forty-seven! I mean, I'm not. But I could be.

every passing birthday. I've fallen in love and thought: this is nice, but I do not seek to affirm this emotional conjoining of two people with the literal combining of our genes into one or more mini Us-es. I hung about as many of my friends had babies – and admittedly did feel left out (abandoned, betrayed even – unreasonably so, for sure, but still . . .); yet very sure this was not something I wanted a part of.

And I have never experienced so much as a fleeting millisecond of broodiness.

I just do not dig babies. They alarm me with their absolute vulnerability, and they bore me with their lack of wit. When I see babies, my first thought is: please don't cry, it's such an unpleasant noise. My second thought is, and please don't get hungry, because although I'm aware I should be super cool about women who breastfeed in public, I'm just . . . not. I wish I was. But I'm not. (This is another way in which I may appear to fail as a feminist, and also a human, I am quite aware.)

When people rave about the mystical, intoxicating, addictive properties of baby smell, I think: sick and wipes? *That's* what does it for you?

And I would refuse to believe women itch and shudder and physically yearn to hold random babies – babies they've seen *en passant* but they do not know, babies who've issued from the wombs of women they do not know – if I hadn't witnessed them itch and shudder and yearn to do precisely that with my own eyes. I have! And from where I'm standing, it's bizarre, because, mate! I have no *idea* what that's like.

When colleagues bring newborns into the office, and everyone crowds round for a peek and a snuggle and a practice hold, I keep well away, duck my head down, plead deadline, hope the visit will be over soonest. When people tell me they're pregnant, my first instinct is still to say: 'Bummer! But don't worry: I have phone numbers!' (I have learned, latterly, to not actually say these words.)

Babies. Just not my thing.

I do like (some) children. I find their characters, and thus their capacity to amuse me, kicks in at around eighteen months/two years, at which point I can certainly spend some time with them. But by 'some time', I mean 'an hour or two', as opposed to 'eighteen solid years, extending onwards into a lifetime of generalised worrying, caring and unconditional loving'. I just think I'd get bored.

Oh, I don't mean that. Of course I wouldn't get bored. Well – I assume I wouldn't. It's more that I am alarmed by the prospect of being eaten whole with my preoccupation for something that will never love me as much as I love it, because that's kind of the deal with kids, and *c'mon*, you've just got to really *want* something if you're prepared to sacrifice (in no particular order) your career, finances, body, relationship and life to it. All those things that men never have to consider when becoming parents. All those things which have made me think, often, that I'd *love* to be a dad. I think I'd make an excellent dad, I really do. I genuinely envy men their ability to be dads.

*

So this would be fine – I mean, objectionable of me, I can certainly see that; I do understand that a child means literally everything to its co-creators, and that my indifference to the small, squirming, noxiously fuming centre of their universe can come off a little harsh . . . But yeah, other than that, it *would* be fine, if the world didn't consider me a raving nut job on this point. A selfish, broken, unfeminine, responsibility-eschewing, life-progression-averse arsehole destined to die cold and alone because I am wilfully choosing to not do the one thing I am engineered to do, namely: make more of me.

That's where the challenge came in.

I am sitting in a café, writing; on the run from my cleaner who's going about her guilt-inducing duties in my flat, right now as I type. This café is one of my faves, a newly established cool li'l independent institution, parked in the midst of my generally run-down, non-gentrifiable London endz. It's got higgledy-piggledy wooden seating and charming baristas of an international persuasion, and the muffins are top notch. Because of all this, it's become extremely popular; busy on a permanent basis. I'm delighted for its owners. I've got to know them a bit, because I'm a raging Flat White addict and they are my most reliable dealers. They are good people.

But lately, things have got nasty. My café is subject to a bitter turf war; a territorial dispute rages here, as it does in chichi coffee shops all over the land. It is bloody and intense and fought with physical heft, moral entitlement, snide looks and barely suppressed rage. It is the battle between Mummies With Buggies and Freelancers With Laptops, both of whom seek to occupy maximum space, and make the other subset feel damned uncomfortable and like they shouldn't really be here, with a view, ultimately, to driving them out for good and ever.

I am team Freelancer With Laptop: silent, dead-line-dreading, eternally on the lookout for a perch near a plug, so I can power up my various technical effects, fearful that the Wi-Fi might drop out. Team Mummy With Buggy is encumbered with child plus kit and minimal sleep; she too seeks the seats with the most adjoining space, so that she can stash the kit and divert her child for the period of time necessary for her to consume an entire latte before it goes cold.

We do not coexist easily.

Freelancers With Laptops hate Mummies With Buggies because their children are loud, and because they pose a spill risk. Mummies With Buggies hate Freelancers With Laptops because they monopolise the good tables, taking up more than their fair share of space with their electrical goods and their air of entitled self-importance because I'M WORKING HERE ACTUALLY, OK? Their charger wires pose a trip risk to the toddlers, at whom they keep shooting filthy looks because it's easier to blame your lack of concentration on an errant child than it is accept that you're just totally lacking inspiration that particular day.

Mummies With Buggies perhaps think the Freelancers With Laptops are judging them for being Mummies With Buggies and who haven't gone back to work yet (and who might never go back). Freelancers With Laptops think Mummies With Buggies are judging *them* for doing nothing more significant with their lives than arse about on a laptop in the middle of the day, pretending to do some screen-writing or something. On top of which, everyone's off their tits on caffeine, which never helps a stressful situation.

No one ever says anything other than: 'Do you think maybe you could squeeze up and let me and my baby sit here too?' (through clenched teeth).

No one ever does anything, other than shoot dirty looks and roll their eyes, and perhaps deploy their toddler as a juice-wielding dirty bomb.

But still. It's very fraught.

You could cut the atmos with a cake slice.

Who's right and who's wrong? No one, obviously. We're all middle-class idiots who seek ownership of this warm, jazzy space which offers us some sweet relief from the claustro-phobia of our own homes, none of which are done up as beautifully as this here caff. We want the baristas to like us best, to remember our orders quickest. We're overgrown children seeking to dominate the playground.

But, in our petty, small-victory-seeking way, we are also playing our part in a much bigger game, expressing a larger, more generalised, more legitimate tension.

The chasm between women with kids and women without has never been deeper and wider and less bridge-able than it is right now. It's never been as dark and divisive, it's never been as problematic.

My café turf wars are the distilled essence of a larger cultural turf war, one being fought everywhere, all the time. In the offices of the land – where women with kids piss off women without by demanding first dibs on the holiday allocation, because if they don't do that, they won't get away at all what with the restrictions that school holidays impose on their schedules; and women without kids piss off women with kids, who think the childless among us are promoted more readily and valued more highly. On the pavements – where women with buggies graze the ankles of women without, and the women without resent holding doors open for the women with, because the women with are too distracted and tired to acknowledge and offer thanks. And in general chat, when women with kids say things like: 'I just only really feel like I can *talk* to other mothers now, do you know what I mean? Oh sorry – of course you don't . . .' And the women without kids wonder at what point those with forgot what life was like before. And neither one of them wants to share a plane with the other lot.

'PV, you're woefully ignorant, and naïve and rude and wrong,' says my friend Vicky, mother of two. 'When you have a baby, you simply no longer have the capacity to worry about whether your semantics are negatively impacting the delicate sensitivities of your childfree friends. You don't have the time or the energy, and if you did: you would not care. And if your buggy gets in the way of a passer-by, you are unlikely to even notice. It's like you're inhabiting this small zone of interest, and you can't really see beyond it, because all you are doing, literally, *all you are doing*, is keeping a new thing alive.'

Tensions shouldn't be running this high, but they are. It did not used to be like this, the chasm between women with kids and women without did not used to run this deep. As things stand, it's ripping a generation of women apart, and that is bad news from a social perspective, and from a feminist one.

In the course of the last fifteen years or so, over the precise period that I would have been having children had I been so inclined, ideas of motherhood have changed beyond all recognition. Mothers – and mothering and babies – have become fetishised to within an inch of their (capacity to create new) life. Where motherhood was once this thing that most women did, though some did not, a life stage that was likely and desirable, but in no sense the Only Game In Town – it's now become a cult. A heavily coded, incredibly intense, highly merchandised, strictly regulated series of tests. A bizarre hybrid cross between competitive sport, money-spinning cash-in opportunity and the root cause of a gazillion neuroses. All consuming and never ending, judged and judgemental, where no one's really sure what the end goal is, actually. Getting your child to Oxbridge? To Number 10? On track for a Nobel Peace Prize, the Young Musician of the Year Award, the upper echelons of the BBC; or just happy, fulfilled, well and kind?

Women are no longer merely 'mothers', they're adherents to some specific mothering discipline. Are they Tiger Mums (strict and ferociously competitive on behalf of their children) or Helicopter Mums (excessively anxious and over-involved with their child's academic progression)? Will they be leading lights of the school-gate fashion scene, or mumpreneurs (who evolve their advanced mothering skills into some manner of business, often cupcake or knitting related)?

Where will they stand on Push Presents and baby showers, on the controversial issue of whether it's OK to announce your latest pregnancy to the world by posting a snap of their positive pee stick on Facebook, or to use their three-month scan image as their Twitter avatar?

Will they be Yummy Mummies or MILFs? How extravagant will the party favours distributed at their children's birthday parties be, and how likely are they to set up their own free school in the fullness of time?

This is modern mothering. And it's mental.

By my reckonings, motherhood as crazy-making cult first stirred circa '99, the year Victoria Beckham gave birth to her eldest son Brooklyn; and I wouldn't like to say these things are interconnected, except that I think they might be, with special reference to the vast myriad of consumer opportunities new wave motherhood presents.

Where it's ended up is with women believing they can't merely be mothers: they have to be unimaginably perfect mothers. And btw: the accepted standard on what makes any woman even half decent at it is raised higher and higher and higher, and contorted into more and more contradictory and complex iterations all the time, so that anyone attempting to have a child ends up feeling like they're constantly failing in a billion different ways. Do you swaddle, do you hothouse, how much folic acid were you taking the week you fell pregnant? Why did you name your child *that*, why didn't you time its birth so that it'd be relatively old for its school year, and therefore likely to do better academically? How dare you drop less than a grand on your buggy, why wouldn't you dress your three-year-old in Stella McCartney, are you seriously telling me you haven't started it on baby French yet; bought it a special helmet to correct its allegedly funny-shaped head?

These pressures and shifting goalposts and growing demands and expectations transform women with kids into second-guessing, super precious, eternally anxious, overburdened and oversubscribed individuals. Frazzled and weary and so very judged. And they make those of us without kids – either by choice or by circumstance – feel ignored and irrelevant and like we're being excluded from the only game in town worth playing. Sidelined, lesser, constantly required to quietly step aside and allow the women with kids to monopolise the limelight, the priority seating, the broader cultural debate, the drama. We are reimagined as barren failures, or cold, hard, career-fixated mega bitches living a joyless, loveless half-life.

Nobody can work with this. Nobody. Nobody can triumph over it. Our twenties, thirties and early forties (and even later, now that IVF is making motherhood at fifty a Thing) have been transformed into decades-long, unwinnable wars; wars which we wage against each other – the childless/-free/-lite versus the women with children, yes; but also, all that Mum-on-Mum aggro! The Stay At Homes versus the Workings, the only-way-is-breastfeeders versus the breast-just-didn't-happen-for-me-don't-shame-me-for-that-I-feel-bad-enough-already-ers, Tiger Mums versus yogic organic mums, MILFS versus Yummies. We fight each other – and we fight the idea that whatever we do as women of childbearing age will, without question, be the wrong thing.

It's a shitty way to proceed: needling, aggressive, stress-inducing, isolating.

Like I say. It's a set up.

Who's set us up? No one in particular; or rather: everyone. The Mummy Wars are not the result of a conspiracy – unless we're talking about the forces of commerce, which some years ago cottoned on to the fact that the more neurotic you can make people about their parenting skills, the more easily you can take money off them. Say hello to cashmere eau de Nil everything, buggies worth as much as the family car, matchy matchy mummy-and-toddler lounge wear, brain training games for three year olds, the culture of gifts for teachers and epic birthday parties . . .

That *is* bordering on the conspiratorial. But you know capitalism. Creating new customer demographics and then tormenting them into buying shit is just its gig. You can't blame it for that.

More sinister, maybe, is the possibility that this version of motherhood reared up right at the beginning of this millennium, as a self-generating, self-sabotaging tax on how liberated women had become through the latter stages of the last one. Having peaked in terms of free-wheeling lady-libertarian lairiness in the Ladette-happy 1990s, we got slapped back into place – and, let's be honest, we slapped ourselves back into place – in the early noughties with this shifting and intense paradigm on sensible, grown-up woman behaviour.

The subtext on baby mania, mummy madness and the Mummy Wars can only ever be this: Women! Your main purpose – your only true purpose – is the bearing of children, and don't you forget it! Don't you go getting carried away with dreams of power and employment, money or creative gratification – or you will regret it!

All these rules and regulations, all these ideas and theories and notions, all this incredibly expensive STUFF, where there was none before . . . All of it is designed to make women feel less liberated, less empowered; to poleaxe them with doubt, fear and anxiety, while draining them of cash, because it's presented as the only thing that stands between them and an ill child, or a stupid child, or an underachieving, damaged, depressive, unpopular child, or no child at all; which would mean their lives would come to nothing,

Men are not impacted by any of this. Men are not told, repeatedly, that they are failing as fathers in twenty-seven different ways and counting. Men are not told that they should look a certain way when wielding a baby, subscribe to a certain kind of daddy tribe, aspire toward yumminess and/or fuckability, while simultaneously being fathers. Men are not described as 'daddies on the lash', when they leave their children at home with their baby mummies to hit a bar in the company of other daddies. They're just men, out for a drink. Men with children do not have awkward and stilted conversations with men without children about how they can no longer even remember their lives before the kids. Men win at fatherhood just by providing the sperm and being seen to provide; that alone will win them the screwy 'good family man' accolade I've already discussed.

Motherhood seems to be the battle feminism's losing – and losing out to – most rapidly, most completely and most willingly. Even those of us who don't have kids are being screwed over by it.

20

A Funny Story About Rape

I am eighteen years old and back in Exeter, on Easter hols (only, we call them 'vacation' or 'vac' now, which I really must try to remember) from my first year at Hipster Uni. I am heartbroken because my very first uni boyfriend dumped me days before the end of term, for reasons I hadn't been entirely able to fathom. He'd been the first boy I'd fancied on campus and the first one to ask me out, and: oh, I'd liked him very much! He was sweet and bright with this really cool baseball jacket, which was, like, his signature vibe, yeah? – more to the point, he was extremely good looking. Olive skinned and dark eyed with an Estuary accent I'd prized particularly highly, on account of how borderline allergic I'd become to Devonshire accents while growing up there with such limited success.

Anyway, yes; he'd dumped me with little to no explanation (nothing I'd properly listened to or assimilated, anyway; it's often better to ignore the people who are explaining to you precisely why you're fundamentally unlovable, I've found), and I'd stumbled home in a blur of sad, three snaps of him stowed safe in a Boots photographic envelope, so that I had an option on making myself feel sadder yet, in the unlikely event that I started to feel a teeny bit better. Because teenage girls HEART heartbreak. Also because teenage girls HEART the opportunity to boast about their handsome boyfriend, even retrospectively after he's dumped them, to all their old friends from back home, and photographic evidence of his fitness helps boost one's argument.

I'd taken my sad-sack dumped self, and those pics, to a very popular Exeter pub one late afternoon to meet up with a bunch of people I'd attended sixth form college with. We showed off at first about how different we were now – how sophisticated, how grown-up! – and how much better our experiences of university were, and then we re-bonded, ate cheesy chips and enjoyed the easy familiarity of each other's company, after so many weeks and months playing up to the new and relatively unknown social scenes we'd encountered at our respective colleges. I passed round the pictures of my ex, delivered a heightened and highly romanticised version of our brief but intense affair, and allowed everyone to tell me how handsome he was and how he was clearly scared of the intensity of his own feelings for me, which is why he'd had no option but to dump me. 'He's probably regretting it!' goes Helen. 'He's definitely regretting it!' says Susan. 'He's probably picking up the phone to call you right now to ask you back out, but then getting scared about how you'll react and losing his nerve, but then thinking:

"No! I have to win her back! I have to let her know I've made a terrible mistake!"' goes Helen. 'That is clearly what's happening,' says Susan.

'Is it?' says Cas, a harsh realist dressed as a 19-year-old goth; every girl gang needs one. 'Is it really?'

Convinced that Helen and Susan had a point, that Cas did not, and that I should get my hopeful, heartbroken ass back to my parents' home ASAP, so that I could be around with a view to receiving any stammering, nervous phone calls from my lovelorn and regret-addled ex, I left my mates-from-before in their pub, and began to make my way back to base camp (taking a bittersweet life check of a moment to wonder if that house did even qualify as base camp, given that a) my parents were in the throes of getting a divorce, and b) I didn't really live there any more, did I?). It wasn't late, half seven or thereabouts; though it was March, and so pretty dark. The pub was located halfway up a canal path, which was part of the reason it was so popular; it was picturesque as all hell in the summer. In the early spring, though, on a low key mid-week night like this one – it came off as isolated.

Do you have a feeling where this is going yet?

So there I am, walking along a quiet towpath in the almost-night-time; enjoyably mournful, my ex-boyfriend's photographs clutched to my chest, playing fanciful reconciliation scenarios over and over in my head. Maybe he'll weep! Maybe he'll beg! I am stone cold sober, my student funds had stretched to two Cokes and a part share on some cheesy chips that evening, and nothing more intoxicating; I am a bit chilly because it is a bit chilly, and I am very much in a jeans jacket sort of phase, it being a jeans jacket sort of a fashion era. What if he's met someone else and he's phoning to tell me that? Oh God, how awful that would be! And so on.

Ah, but then there's this guy coming along the same towpath, in the other direction. I am too busy calculating how the hell I'll respond when my terrible, wonderful, beautiful ex tells me he's seeing another chick now and how he thought it best that he warn me in advance of my finding out some other way, to pay the stranger much mind, though I do get a whiff of him (my age-ish, physically unremarkable, I wanna say his hair is . . . dark?) paying *me* some mind as we brush past each other on the narrow path. Seconds later, I hear him whistle after me. If only my ex wanted to whistle after me, I think. Why does this person think I'm whistle-able at, while my ex does not? Why? Unless . . . does he? He did once, not so long ago so . . . Could he? Might—

I am grabbed from behind, wrapped tightly in someone else's arms, so tightly that breathing's not much of an option; I turn, or am turned, to confront the person who is doing the grabbing, assuming it must be Helen, come to catch the same bus with me, because who else but a friend would touch me with such intimacy, unannounced. Only it doesn't feel like a Helen-ish sort of a thing to do, on top of which, I can sort of already tell it's a man. I am fully turned. It *is* a man. A man I don't know. The man who whistled.

He pushes his foot between my ankles, trips me and falls on top of me.

It all gets a bit vague and nasty-dream-sequence on me after that. Adrenaline and panic and fight instinct mingled with flight instinct, and a sheer inability to make sense of what's happening to me so incredibly quickly, muddle things up. Then there's the intervening years, of course.

Here's what I do remember:

Being crushed beneath his heft on the path thinking, he's not even that hefty! How ridiculous that I can't move! How preposterous! I'm so fucking weak! How am I so fucking weak that if some fucking random wants to trap me like this, beneath his not-all-that-hefty-even heft, he can? *How*?

Feeling the shape of the precious pics of my precious ex in their precious envelope pressing into my lower back; I'd dropped them when I'd been caught, and fallen onto them when I'd been tripped.

Thinking: it's good I know where they are.

Looking at the moon behind the outline of this guy's head (pushed so bizarrely close to mine); realising it was full, thinking: that's good. You can rely on the moon.

Him looking a *bit* like this guy Rab who was in my halls at Hipster, who I didn't know very well, but liked well enough. Rab was good friends with my good friend Giles, which was something of a recommendation.

This person was not behaving like Rab. Not at all.

*

I screamed a bit, so he put his hand over my mouth, and that was awful – additionally claustrophobic-inducing, on top of the already claustrophobia-inducing fact of his body trapping mine – so when he said (precisely as people often do on the telly, who knew?), 'If I take my hand away, you have to stop screaming . . .' I complied.

Then he said: 'Are you a virgin?'

(He had a Devonshire accent; my relationship with Devonshire accents – already fractured at this point – broke down irreparably.)

Was I a virgin? Well, no. In no way. The recently departed boyfriend and the formative, moustache-objecting one who turned out to be gay anyway could testify to that among, let's face it, a few others. But I figured maybe I was being offered a get-out-of-jail-free card here; that perhaps the whistling stranger currently pinning me to the dirt against my will was operating according to some manner of slut-punishing policy, and would leave off if he thought I was pure and untouched by man.

So I took a punt.

'Yes,' I lied.

'Good,' he said. 'I like it better that way.'

It was at this point that I started to get *really* pissed off.

It was at this point that I thought, Nah. I'm not having this.

It was at this point that the emotional equivalent of the Incredible Hulk stirred within me. Me! Little, anxious, self-esteem-lite, late-teenage me, who had until that very moment never rated herself particularly highly, never thought she was worth a great deal, who'd never really made a fuss on her own behalf about anything much, give or take that one time she got accidentally filed away into the thicko maths group during her induction into secondary school (when I'd pulled the teacher to one side at the end of the lesson and showed off my weirdly evolved mental arithmetic skills like I was speaking in tongues for ten minutes, after which he ejected me forcefully into the top set, a look of fear in his eyes); who was admittedly enjoying the cool-girl status Hipster Uni had started inexplicably bestowing upon her – without really, truly assimilating it into her deeper sense of self.

Me.

I went *mental*.

'Do you have *any idea* who you're dealing with?' I said. My voice was loud and grand and commanding and entitled. I channelled regal grandmother demanding better service at Claridge's tea room. I channelled unrecognised celebrity throwing a shit fit because the PR won't allow her access to the VIP gifting suite.

'Eh?' goes my wannabe rapist.

'Do you have *any idea* WHO I AM?'

Italics and caps, oh yes!

He tried to stick his hand up my top.

'What the hell do you think you're doing? You can't actually think you're going to rape me? ME?' I continued.

'Rape you or throw you in the canal where you'll drown,' he said. 'Rape or murder. Your choice.'

Well, I thought, at least we've established the parameters of our situation. Oh, but hang on:

'You can't do that,' goes my emotional Incredible Hulk. 'You really can't.'

'Why not?'

'BECAUSE OF WHO I AM!'

'OK,' he says finally. 'Who are you?'

He stops doing anything at all, other than lying heavily on top of me. He is listening.

Ah.

So half of me's thinking, well that's torn it because who really are you? Some girl they used to call Ugly Polly who's blagged her way into the It crowd at Hipster but will be found out any day now, who doesn't have enough dosh to get herself anything more than two glasses of tapped Diet Coke and a half portion of cheesy chips in a provincial pub, whose hair is only just now recovering from her maternal grandmother's attempts to cut it into curls a decade earlier, who likes writing stories and poems on the quiet but who's ever going to give a monkey's about *that*, whose main skill is an ability to learn the lyrics to any given pop song after one listening, which isn't anything anyone would ever describe as 'marketable'.

I'm not sure any one of these facts will deter a rapist.

On the other hand:

'My name is Polly Vernon,' roars the Incredible Hulk, 'and I am bigger than you will ever be! I am eighteen years old and I am at Hipster University and I am already big, a big deal! But I am going to be *so* big one day! So big! You have no idea! And you do not do this to me, because I am Polly Vernon and I am a big deal AND YOU JUST DON'T!'

I remember this with daft clarity, because they were not things I had ever thought about myself before. I remember this with daft clarity, because it was the first time I realised that some hidden secret part of me I'd never properly considered before *really* rated the rest of me; and recognised when someone had overstepped an un-oversteppable mark, and needed to be *told*.

Cool.

Ah, but hang on, because apparently, it hadn't finished yet:

'Also, my dad is the chief of police, and he will send his helicopter to get you.'

I know, I know.

'Right,' goes my wannabe rapist, and he pauses; which is when I found myself thinking: bloody hell, this one's gullible for a wannabe rapist. My dad is a furniture restorer. He does not have, and has never had, a helicopter.[1]

Yet the whistler seems to buy it. He becomes uncertain, loses focus for a milli-moment; his weight shifts, I am freeish!

I slip from his grasp, and scrabble away, skedaddling inches, then feet, along the canal towpath, off and away on my Doc Marten-shod feet, towards the main road, some ten minutes off.

---

1 To the best of my knowledge.

He catches up with me. He grabs me. He trips me.

It starts again. Me, pinned beneath him, him trying to get at the parts of me hidden behind second-hand Levis 501s and an M&S men's jumper (in fashion terms, I am mid-transition from Exeter indie kid to Hipster Uni fly girl incarnation) and the denim jacket; me, scared and squirming and fuming, the Invisible Hulk lashing out, using my fingernails to score his cheeks.

I have no idea how long this phase went on for. I know there was a brief moment when I thought: 'If I let this happen, it will at least be over at some point.'

But for whatever reason, I didn't.

And then . . . then he gave up. Suddenly. Completely. He gave up, got up, ran away along the towpath in the direction of the pub, away from the main road.

I ran towards it.

Then I turned, and went back to pick up the squashed pics of my ex-boyfriend, half buried in the dirt which marked the spot where I'd struggled so hard with some bloke I didn't know, my own rapidly developing sense of self and an Invisible Hulk I never knew I possessed.

The cops caught him.

I'd bumped into a couple of joggers, running down onto the towpath from the road, just as I was haring up towards it; told them what had happened. The police were called from a nearby house. They sent a helicopter up to look for my attacker (that'll show you!, I thought); meanwhile, a woman who lived in a house at the far end of that cursed section of cursed canal noticed a young man acting shady round her bushes, called the Fuzz. They zipped round, approached him, asked him about the lurid scratches he had all over his face, and he confessed on the spot.

Days later, I caught a train to London, and went to stay with a friend for the remaining weeks before it was time to go back to Hipster Uni. The friend picked me up from Paddington Station in her shit car.

'I think Devon wants to kill me,' I told her.

So there it is. My drab, funny, prosaic, everyday little almost-rape, which isn't an 'almost' rape according to the UK judicial system – it's not even an 'attempted'. It's a sexual assault so minor, my attacker – who carried right on confessing, all the way to court, which meant I didn't have to give evidence or anything ghastly – was let off with a suspended sentence and a compensatory fine of £500, which he saw fit to pay me in £5 instalments. Cheques arrived on my doorstep on a fortnightly basis for years afterwards, pink-slip reminders of what had happened to me. (A decade later, I would read a news story about a woman who worked in Boots who was found guilty of falsely accusing a male colleague of rape and ordered to pay him £400,000 in damages. 'I see,' I thought, 'so apparently, rape is so awful a crime, that if you make up a story about it happening to you when it didn't, you're in for four hundred thou; yet it's simultaneously so not actually that awful a crime that if you have a proper stab at committing it – find some chick, chuck her on to the ground, squidge her beneath your body and so on – then you'll only be down five hundred.')

It wasn't the worst thing that ever happened to me.

I might feel differently if I had been raped of course, I have no doubt that I *would*; but as it stands, it really wasn't the worst thing that ever happened to me. The physical scars were negligible, the emotional scars were minimal: I had a shaky, nervy few months, didn't sleep so well, went to Glastonbury far too soon and spent the entire festival convinced every skanky ill-hatted hippy in attendance had designs upon me. I became 20 per cent more sensible than I already had been. To this day, I have never left my home for an evening out without knowing exactly how and when and by what safe means I'll return; I have never gotten so drunk that somebody else had to deal with me. I still don't like it when people I don't know walk too close to me down a darkened road.

But those sad, harsh, weirdly comic scuffles had no impact on the way I felt about sex. I'll be honest, the moment I got back to Hipster, I exploited the whole tale to make people – with particular reference to men – admire me. 'You're so brave,' they'd say, before taking me by the hand and making sweet, sensitive liberal love to me (the ex a fading memory). I exploited my own attempted rape, to get me more hot man flesh. Oh yes, I did!

And why not? Shallow people get raped too! Plus, as far as I was concerned, rape had as much to do with sex as being punched in the mouth had to do with being kissed; the towpath scuffles were as related to the things I chose to do with my body as puke is to rainbows, so how could they have any bearings on my love life? They couldn't. (I still find the idea of 'consensual sex' a misnomer, because sex *has* to be consensual. If it's not, it's not sex. It's rape, and rape simply isn't sex.)

I bounced back; I didn't merely survive that attack, I capitalised on it. The good fortune of its randomness certainly helped. Some years later, I'd find myself in an emotionally abusive relationship, being lied to and manipulated so completely over such a period of time, I no longer knew if it was Tuesday or yellow. It took me far longer to recover from that determined, targeted, relentless attack on the heart of me, launched by someone who was supposed to care, than it did one haphazard slapdash moment of violence on a canal path, perpetuated by someone I just happened to be walking past at a bad time. This is how I know it's absurd to comment on the relative severity/impact of rape and sexual violence cases according to whether or not the perpetrator was known to the survivor. I can quite imagine how a non-stranger rape might screw with the survivor's mind, might make you feel more culpable, might make the act feel more horrifically personal, might absolutely railroad your ability to know when you're safe and when you're not, from that moment on. Which is why

Professor Richard Dawkins, who in July 2014 referred to the phenomenon of 'mild date rape' on Twitter, should STFU, ATYPS.[2] It just doesn't work like that, my friend. Rape is never mild, and knowing the person who's raping you does not necessarily make it easier to survive.

So: not-actually-being-raped wasn't the worst thing that ever happened to me. It awoke my internal Incredible Hulk and that was by no means a bad thing, and I did bounce back. But still: it happened. This horrible, weird, nasty, silly, bleak, lonely thing, that was ultimately a bit inconsequential (he didn't go to prison, I didn't go back to Devon much) . . . *That* did happen. And it, and variations on it – some of which are so much worse, so sickening and horrific they actually merit reporting in newspapers, though bloody hell! It pisses me off that I have to acknowledge that my non-rape is almost inconsequential in the grander scale of rape – happen all the time. Will keep happening. To you, to people you know, to the people you love, follow on social media, have a crush on, get annoyed by, think are a bit smug, envy, admire, hate (though you're not quite sure why . . .); consider funny, sweet, tough, intimidating, impervious, evil, warm, right, wrong, cool, clever, et cetera.

To them.

To me.

To us.

---

2 ATYPS = As The Young People Say

To one in five of us.

For fuck's sake.

The more I think about rape – the more I write and shout and rage about it – the more I realise that much of the problem with the rape debate is just this: that men's visceral fear of being accused of rape (either falsely and maliciously, or because they worry that something they did in the past might be re-cast in the light of new thinking, as a bit rapey, actually) clashes hard with women's visceral fear of being raped.[3] This means that men get defensive, and women get shouty – and no one gets anywhere.

We need to park that if we can. Reel it in, at least a little.

Next, we need to think properly about the issue of consent. The vast majority of rapes are non-stranger rapes. They don't have the good fortune to be as straightforward and unequivocal as my almost-rape; they're blurred by pre-existing relationships, by the fact that what ended up as a rape started out as a legitimate date; and by booze. This means that legally they rest entirely on the issue of consent, on who thought it was OK to have sex with whom under what circumstances – and who thought it definitely wasn't. And this makes rape incredibly hard to convict. Consent cases depend on the word of one person against another; on top of which, understandings of what even constitutes consent vary dramatically.

In January 2015, Alison Saunders, the UK's Director of

---

3 Not, I should add, that it's only women who suffer rape. It isn't.

Public Prosecutions, issued new guidelines on the investigation of sex offences designed to make it easier to prosecute rape cases – particularly rape cases in which the woman was too drunk to consent to sex. Saunders said that in the future police and prosecutors should put greater onus on rape suspects to show that the complainant really had consented to sex. This is cool and good and definitely a step in the right direction.

Thing is, I don't think the question of consent will ultimately stem the rape stats.

I think the question of enthusiasm might.

Enthusiasm's the thing, isn't it? Enthusiasm's what you're after! Not mere consent, not a gentle, meek, blushing: 'Oh, OK then, go on . . .' But a screaming, raging, ripping at the other person's clothes degree of unbridled lust! An unarguable demonstration that both parties are equally up for this, equally into it. Enthusiasm is what we need to propagate as a gold standard on consent.

We need to teach boys and men that the only sex they should ever pursue is sex with women who want it quite as much as they do, and who are loud, proud and obvious about this.

In turn, we need to teach women and girls to feel ultimately sexually entitled, to be, and to act, in a predatory way when they want sex with someone. To think of themselves not as sex objects – but as *sexual beings*. To make *that* the definition of 'being sexy'. Because it is, isn't it? It's certainly the definition of Hot Feminism. Empowerment through raging, shameless, sexiness; empowerment not in spite of your sexiness – but because of it. We need to teach women and girls that sex is not just about fear and risk, it's not about avoiding being slut-shamed online, or not feeling adequately respected after a one-night stand. It's about fancying the pants off someone – even if you don't know them that well, even if you've just hooked up in a pub, even if you are only looking at having a one-night stand with them anyway.

We need to undo some of the damage hot-and-cold running free porn has wrought on young people, how it's impacted us culturally, how it's corrupted our perception of sex, how that's changed us, with specific reference to rape. Morally, ethically, theoretically, et cetera and so on, I have absolutely no issue with the idea of people deriving pleasure from looking at images of other people deriving pleasure from each other. However, as it stands, pornography is made by men, for men, with aesthetics and narrative arcs and by depicting acts designed exclusively to titillate men.

The best that can be said of any women involved in the making of porn is that they are not entirely in control of the process. The worst that can be said is that they're being coerced or pressured or darker things still. This is very ugly for them – and very unhealthy for us. Porn is now so absurdly, freely available to anyone with a smartphone and a spare five minutes that it's permeating all contemporary ideas of sex, which means all contemporary ideas of sex are super male-oriented. Porn makes sex seem like the unique property of men; it perpetuates the idea that men are sex's prime consumers – while women are little more than its enablers. This is a terrible, toxic lie. Sex is ours. Really. Not theirs. *Ours*.

We need to stigmatise the rape of adults as we do the rape and sexual exploitation of children. We need to view rapists not as jack-the-lads who chanced their arm in a situation which was a wee bit shady, what with the girl being off her tits on Chardonnay (only what was she doing getting herself into that state in the first place, what did she *expect*? And she blatantly wasn't raped anyway, not *really* . . . she just woke up the next day with a guilt-infused hangover, and then freaked that her boyfriend would find out she got pissed up and cheated on him with that guy . . .) Instead, we need to start viewing them as proper nasty sex criminals.

We need to do something about the embarrassingly brief and light sentences passed out to those people who do get charged with sexual assault and rape; the five hundred quid and a non-custodial here, the year or two inside there. We need to recognise, in sentencing, that rape is a much more serious crime than credit card fraud or that thing where that guy faked his own death in a rigged up canoeing accident so that his wife could collect on his life insurance – the kinds of crimes which are routinely punished with several years' imprisonment, while, for heaven knows what reason, rape is not.

We need to understand that the fact that rape happens so often doesn't make it less completely bloody awful for everyone who endures it. Quite the reverse.

We need to do this. We really, really need to do this.

21

The Lady Lech

Q: What's the difference between being soul-shrinkingly objectified by the imperious, oafish, unsolicited, unwelcome gaze of the perennially entitled male and being deliciously, flatteringly, day-makingly appreciated by some guy you haven't met yet?

A: How hot is the man who's looking?

Of all the shaded, nuanced, intricate complications which govern the ways men and women relate, the ones which direct and inform their tendency to check us out are probably the trickiest. When is it OK, and when is it not? How did it start and how much do we want it to stop?

I was eleven, max, the first time some geezer had a good old look; not yet out of middle school, certainly not physically advanced for my age. He was a scaffolder (of course he was, they often are; I've since been told that scaffolders are inclined to live life on the edge emotionally speaking, on account of them living life on the literal edge of buildings,

315

which all conspires to make them edgy, generally), eighteen if he was a day. I was walking past him on the street, on the way home from school; he paused in his work (he was sitting on the edge of a pavement, I remember quite clearly, locking segments of metal tubing together), and he looked at me and he nudged a scaffolder friend who looked too, and then looked away less impressed.

I felt self-conscious and confused, unsure (was this *really* what was going on here? Could it be? Possibly?) and – oh dear – just a little bit flattered, because an actual man had seen me! And looked again! And then, oh dear, oh no! Because his friend had not considered me worth looking at, which meant I could enfold rejection into this heady package of feelings.

The moment was over in a moment, as moments generally are, but I recognised it for what it was: something new, something set to become a complicated part of my life from thereon in. Me and every other chick on this earth.

Because:

Oh bloody hell, *that*! The tedious, unknowable, inescapable non-stop-until-it-does-stop, freaky, demeaning, delighting, offensive, flattering, distressing, empowering Thing that is being looked at by men!

The weird, twisted power of it, of feeling visible, of feeling admired, of standing out; which then doesn't feel like any kind of power at all on those days when you want to be on your own, in your head, without being constantly reminded that you also have an exterior; or on those days when it feels less like being desired, more like being subject to a threat; or on those days when it doesn't happen at all and you're left going: *Wha*? Why not? What's going on? Am I too old/fat/spotty/frumpy all of a sudden? Have I cut my hair too short? And furthermore: WHY DO I CARE? I HATE MYSELF FOR CARING! WHAT HAVE THESE BASTARD MEN WITH THEIR BASTARD EYES TURNED ME INTO?

Or those days when it happens all the time and you have no clue why, and you find yourself thinking: am I wandering about with my tits out and on display or something? (And then you actually take a moment to check that you're fully clothed.)

Those days when it happens in one postcode but not the next, and you're all: I seem to be playing oddly well in the high street but getting nothing in the business district.

Those days when you think: does everyone want to fuck me, or am I completely deluded and misreading signals that simply aren't there, imagining eyes upon me when there really aren't any; is this the beginning of my inevitable descent into fully fledged madness?

Those days when it makes you lippy, and you find yourself screaming: 'What is your *point*?' at a looky-loo motorcycle courier, and quite enjoying the release, especially when he wobbles.

Those days when you steal yourself for assault-by-eyes (plus probable verbals) as you approach a building site manned exclusively by lairy-seeming blokes in cut off denim and high vis jackets, when you contemplate crossing the road to avoid the confrontation, the aggro, but then think:

dammit all, why *should* I? And you get closer and closer, take a deep breath to strengthen your resolve . . . And they completely ignore you, just calmly get on with their work and you feel abandoned.

The time I turned round to make sure there wasn't any traffic coming before I crossed the road, and the man behind me goes: 'I see you looking at me!'

The time I shot an absolutely filthy look at the man I thought was staring me full in the left nipple, then realised he was partially sighted (which was OK because of course he didn't see me make that assumption and shoot *that* look; but also, less OK, because the woman standing next to him *did* see).

The time I'm out with a mate and she's on the receiving end of all the looking and I'm not, and it makes me feel bad despite myself. The time it happens the other way round and I feel bad, the other way round.

Waiting for it to drop off as I get older, wondering if that's a good thing – given that I never asked for it in the first place – or the worst thing on the planet.

Dressing to thwart it because you're feeling vulnerable enough anyway that day.

The time my mate Charlie thought the US immigration official was fully eying her up, and then he pulled her to one side and threatened her with legal action because she was attempting to enter the country without a journalist's visa.

All those times I thought I was getting attention, and it was the hot chick behind me.

All those times I've liked it.

All those times I've hated it.

'If it's a white van man, I'm totally: fuck off,' says Other E. 'But if it's a fireman, I'm like: score!'

'That's because fireman are objectified themselves,' explains Original E. 'Society makes this big deal quasi porno hero myth out of them, and they are as battered about by that, as belittled and owned and monopolised and informed by it, as women are.'

'Nah,' says Other E, 'it's because of their uniform. And their inherent nobility.'

I tentatively raise my theory that being looked at is only truly an issue for us when the looker-atter is a minger, because: how dare the unattractive lie their eyes upon us? How dare they imagine they're in with a chance?

'Totally,' says Other E, who is still reeling from a recent assault-by-eyes perpetrated by an ugly man exiting Greggs: 'in a full-on filthy raincoat, eating a sausage roll so badly he kept missing his mouth, while simultaneously giving me the once-over. Up and down go his eyes, smack goes the sausage roll into the area slightly to the left of his manky mouth, puff pastry and sausage filling dribble down his literal filthy raincoat . . .'

'He quite possibly decided you weren't up to snuff, furthermore,' says Original E.

'Innit tho,' says Other E.

'While it is basically true that I'm OK with being checked out if the checker outer is a fittie,' says Original E, 'I would add two qualifiers: 1) sometimes I'm just not in the mood, even if they are fit, and 2) many of them seem to harbour insanely inflated notions of their own fitness so work on the assumption that their gaze is perpetually welcome, when in fact 90 per cent of the time they simply do not make the cut.'

'You're assuming they even care what you make of the way they look,' goes Other E, 'but I don't think they do. They're in it for the looking and appraising alone, for the proclaiming of their inalienable right to perve.'

I ask Rich, who is a man, about his motives in checking women out, and he says: 'I have been told I am horrifically unsubtle in looking at girls. My mate says it's like I transform from this mild-mannered bloke into a predatory lech with an incredibly penetrating stare, which is distressing, I had no idea! But as for my motives: I want them to see me looking. I think all men do.'

Really? Why?

'Because we are MEN and we are LOOKING!'

Because you think you're the superior species, observing the inferior species like we're beguiling wildlife?

'God, no! The opposite. We think we're inferior, and we're blagging it.'

Do you think you'll ever stop?

'Me in particular, or men in general?'

Men in general.

'No.'

*

I don't think they'll stop, either. I don't think any manner of feminism – trad, hot, Twitter-perpetuated or otherwise – will ever put an end to the checking out. I don't think men will ever be civilised or legislated out of it. When compared with being shouted at, or groped, looking is too subtle an activity to define or condemn. It's instinctive and deniable, and so bloody pervasive.

And so it feels like this awful thing they have the monopoly on; like we'll be eternally vulnerable to their judgement of our outsides, and nothing will ever stop it. How will we ever make peace with it? How will we ever overcome our conditioned responses to it, to feeling pleased when this hideous slight against our very souls is dished out to us or ignored when it isn't? How?

Well.

We can do it back.

Oh, sorry, did I say '*can*' do it back?

I meant: do.

We do do it back.

Don't we?

I don't think men realise quite to what extent we are objectifying the holy fuck out of their scrawny little arses, yet. How casually and meticulously we pick apart their clothes, facial hair choices, bone structure, eye colour; how routinely we assess their physical activity levels as evidenced in the lay of their pecs.

And it's my plan that they find out.

This is no longer their game to play exclusively. They may consider us the passive, powerless recipients of their visual attentions, but the fact is: we aren't. Fact is, we are also admiring, rejecting, lingering, approving of some bits of a particular male, while feeling disappointed by others. Puzzled to all hell by their shoes, feeling an electric thrill over the way that one's neck meets his chest so very pleasingly, getting lost in that one over there's lips. We have names for their different bum types, don't we? We fetishise their armpits. We think it's a shame when an especially pretty one lets himself go to seed. We prefer a flat stomach over a paunchy one; we notice who's self-conscious about the fact that he's losing his hair and we hope, for his sake and for ours, that he has the jawline and cheekbone configuration necessary to pull off a crew cut. We are the lechers. We are the watchers. We are the fanciers.

We look and we look and we look. And we must look more. More, harder and more obviously. They need to know we are doing this. They need to feel the might of our gaze. Because the more we look, the more we correct the assumption that a woman's place is to be passively admired while a man's is to do the active admiring.

Cos sweetcheeks, that just isn't what's happening here. Suck on it.

And while I'm on the subject:

Give women forty years of feminism, and what do we do with it? Go out with men fifteen years younger than us, that's what. We turn cougar.

OK, OK, this is not the only thing we've done with it, clearly. Some other good stuff has popped up as a consequence of our tireless fight for equal opportunities and rights and stuff.

But cougaring is perhaps the most *fun* thing we're choosing to do with it.

It's a relatively new development in the Hot Feminists' repertoire.

Sure, there were occasional incidences of older women dating younger men in the past – Mrs Robinson in the 1967 Dustin Hoffman film *The Graduate*, and so on. But they were rare, and unconvincing on a number of levels: for example, in the case of *The Graduate*, the Mrs Robinson cougar character was played by Anne Bancroft, who was only six years older than Hoffman, her 'cub'.[1]

Cougar as archetype of the way a woman may choose to conduct herself sexually was only really officially recognised in 2009, when it began happening really quite a lot. This was a time when artist and director Sam Taylor-Wood (then forty-two) began a relationship with actor Aaron Johnson (then nineteen); it was also four years into Demi Moore (then forty-seven)'s marriage to Ashton Kutcher (then twenty-nine); and two years before TV presenter Caroline Flack (then thirty-two) would start going out with One Direction's Harry Styles (then seventeen).

---

1 'Cub' is Cougar speak for younger lover. Don't ask me how I know this.

But since then, well! Hasn't it panned out deliciously for the over-38s[2] among us?

Sure, Demi's relationship with Ashton may have ended in divorce, but they got an entirely viable (commendable, even, in Hollywood terms) eight years together in there beforehand; and sure, Harry and Caroline were destined to split too, but when I met her she told me she has nothing but jolly memories of the interlude, give or take how badly she got hounded by rabid 1D fans and the paparazzi. Meanwhile, Sam Taylor-Wood has become Sam Taylor-Johnson, while Aaron Johnson has become Aaron Taylor-Johnson, the couple have had two daughters together and the few times I've stalked them round glamorous bits of London, attempting to gain insight into their romantic dynamic, they've looked entirely credible, not to mention really rather hot.

In other news, many of my friends are having a fine old time dating men who might still be reasonably described as boys. When Jem (thirty-nine) fell briefly for a twenty-seven-year-old, she said this: 'Officially I'm telling people I'd love to find a man my own age, but men my own age seem only interested in younger women, so what else am I meant to

---

2 Officially the earliest age at which one can consider oneself a Cougar. It's at this point that one becomes suddenly, mysteriously, highly visible to 26-year-old men. I remember thinking at the relevant moment: bloody hell! I was never this popular with 26-year-old men when I was twenty-six.

do? Unofficially, I'm delighted: HAVE YOU SEEN HIS PRETTY YOUNG FLESH, POLLY? HAVE YOU *SEEN*?'

Jules the Goose's fling with a youngster, only ever referred to as Jules the Goose's Youth Outreach Project, is the stuff of cougar legend (but you'll have to ask her for further details).

Leanne (thirty-eight), of Chapter Old, is still quite merrily engaged in her year-long relationship with Tommy (twenty-seven), although Tommy has lately started expressing concern that Leanne will ditch him the moment he hits thirty. Leanne is not being entirely generous in disabusing him of this possibility.

Me, meanwhile . . . hampered as I am in the pursuit of younger lovers by the Man I Keep In My Flat, I tend to focus my cougaring activities on a quasi-platonic social level; enjoying the flirtatious attentions of younger men as a mild-mannered ego boost. Oh, I *do* like hanging out with them – partly because they're so damned pretty, but also because they're so damned *not* the same age as my male contemporaries. The unmitigated pleasure of spending time with a bloke who is just never going to tell you he's started wondering What It's All About lately or with a bloke who isn't mired chest-deep in miserable midlife crisis, on account of not even being thirty yet; a bloke who sees possibility and light and fun and options round every corner, as opposed to prostate cancer!

Unsurprisingly, middle-aged men are taking this development horrifically badly. For aeons they've revelled in the notion that while they were hardwired towards seeking out younger, more fertile flesh than their own as they got older; the ladies were not. The ladies were not so superficial, not so lecherous. The ladies appreciated an older gent, with his sophisticated urbanity and his status. The ladies didn't notice sagging flesh and wrinkly faces, because the ladies do not operate according to such fickle, flighty rules. The ladies are more interested in a fine sense of humour and a general worldliness than we are physical beauty.

Yeah, about that.

Guess again, loves.

The creeping revelation that, as a gender, women are every bit as desirous of hot, young, unblemished and unjaded flesh/minds as men are and that, furthermore, hot, young, unblemished and unjaded flesh isn't entirely averse to a bit of *us*, does not sit easily with middle-aged men. Partly because it means the pretty younger female creatures they're currently considering hooking up with may well ditch them for pretty, younger male creatures of their very own in the fullness of time. Mostly because it suggests that women are not – as men had always supposed – the grown-ups of the species; the sensible, right-minded, grounded ones with a long-term plan and an eye firmly settled on a domesticated end goal, the ones who can be relied upon to keep wayward them on the straight and narrow, thus neatly freeing them up from having to do the right thing most of the time. Oh no. We're as daft as them, it'd seem, at least in terms of our libidos.

Good luck with that, everyone.

22

The Feminist Flirt

This is how we do it:

We never do a baby voice.

When men (who are not obviously odious) offer to buy us drinks, we accept graciously (assuming we want a drink). We don't consider the accepting of said drink to:

a) Compromise us as feminists.
b) Obligate us to do anything other than graciously accept the drink. Not even engage in follow-up conversation.
c) Cheapen us. It's just a drink.

We do politics, religion, war in our general flirtatious discourse. We do not subdue our opinions for anyone. We find that if we smile while maintaining our principles/perspectives ferociously, only utter twats will be turned off. Indeed, non-twats will be turned on.

We never hide how funny we are.

We listen, we ask questions, we prompt. But we do not indulge a man who doesn't listen/ask/prompt back, on account of how self-involved windbags are invariably awful in bed.

We can identify a Pick-Up Artist (those misinformed, mis-directed saddos encouraged to practise the dark art of seducing women far too good for them by the self-styled gurus of seduction they've encounter on online forums) at fifty paces. We know that any man who considers women to be 'targets' or 'prey' as opposed to 'other people' – who suffers under the delusion that it's OK to persuade women who don't really fancy you to have sex with you anyway – is to be pitied and/or shouted at, but *never* indulged. We are particularly attuned to the tedious act of 'negging', which is to say: all tactical attempts to lower our self-esteem to such a point that we will respond willingly and gratefully when they lunge in our direction (neggy little tongues extended). Oh, we are Teflon-coated against negs! And so, when they say: 'I bet hardly anyone tells you how pretty you are,' we say: 'People tell me constantly.' When they say: 'I used to fancy you, weirdly,' we say: 'I had barely any idea who you were, unweirdly.' When they say: 'Do you pluck your eye-brows? One of them's a funny shape . . .' we say: 'And yet still bigger than your cock, I'd imagine'.

We know they think we're sending subliminal signals with our hand-to-hair engagement, so we fuck about with that a bit. It keeps 'em on their toes. And anyway, if they knew that we were merely trying to uncomb the almighty bird's nest which has established itself, Winehouse-like, at the base of our skull, where our hairline and our neck merge, they'd be *so* disappointed.

We never try and boy-up our taste in music in the interest of seeming cool. Don't lay claim to a fondness for EDM if you are in fact all about Taylor Swift. It's dishonest, it's too easily exposed as a lie and (worst of all) it lends weight to the misapprehension that boy music has more merit than the music of the girls and the gays.

We do not mitigate our foul language for the delectation of man ears.

We understand that a tendency to boast is derived from a fundamental desire to impress and be liked, a twisted extension of the fear that we're not good enough. We forgive it in others, and we forgive it in ourselves.

We do not accept grammatical errors in sexts.

We don't deny our feminist politics should they arise in the course of casual flirty chat. Rather, we integrate them into the seductive process, thus: 'Yeah, I'm a feminist . . .' Pause;

lick lips, smile wickedly. '. . . Does that make you *very* nervous?'

If we lie about the quantity of our ex-lovers: we lie up.

If a man attempts to charm us by speaking ill of some other woman – criticising the hair of the nearest, prettiest waitress, say; or by referring to his ex as 'mad, mate; quite mad' – in the mistaken belief that this will in some way flatter us, or indicate that he considers us superior, or communicate to us that we need not feel threatened by said other woman . . . Then we show him short shrift. Oh, we show him *mini* shrift! Micro shrift!

We reject with calm serenity, and after having quietly acknowledged the substantial balls it must have taken to approach someone as magnificent as us in the first place – unless we have reason to suspect we are dealing with Pick-Up Artist, in which case, all bets are off.

We take rejection with calm serenity, having congratulated ourselves on striking a blow for Hot Feminism by risking it in the first place.

PART FIVE

SOME OTHER THINGS

23

The N Word

A nd so, my lovers, I begin the process of winding down. I've told you some – much, actually – of what I know about the part clothes play in my bid for empowerment and equality. I've told you about fancying and being fancied, about depilation and selfish washes. Cougaring and waxing. Aging and snarking. I've done WAGs and babies, men and facelifts, Wonderbras and body consciousness, FOGIW and PGP. I've described my kind of feminism – Hot Feminisim – in the hope you'll either adopt it, or parts of it, or bugger off and create your very own kind of feminism from scratch, as you are entirely entitled to do.

Oh, I could go on! I really could. There is so much more to say and a few more tales of the Funny Shit I Did In The 1990s variety to tell ... But you'd get bored and I'd get tired. And in the course of writing this book, I've had to start wearing glasses for the first time, having sacrificed my very eyesight to this greater cause; and oh dear, didn't *that* involve a whole fortnight of soul searching re the nature of aging, never mind the exhaustive opticians-searching re the nature of finding an absolutely perfect starter pair of specs. ('Beware the Scandi architect at the Venice Biennale vibe,' Other E instructed, 'also, Gallerina at the Frieze art fair. You can't pull either off'). I sorted it out in the end; of course I did. I went retro NHS with light subtexts of off-duty Charlie's Angel, since you ask.

So yes, I need to start stopping, before I lose some other faculty, or chip a nail, or develop a semi-permanent puffy under-eye area as a result of imbibing one can of dead-line-enabling Diet Coke too many.

I can already tell that it won't go well. I am awful at goodbyes. Separation anxiety mingles with a lifelong struggle to be sincere when sincerity is absolutely appropriate, and I falter in the act, do a runner even, if I think that no one's paying attention.

I am one awfully bad goodbye-er, let me tell you.

Yet there is a word I struggle with more, even, than goodbye. A word that is infinitely more important, I believe. A little word, an ostensibly banal, everyday sort of a word, which nonetheless stands for so much and resonates so hard. A word which is my first line of defence in so many situations.

The word is No.

And before you raise an incredulous eyebrow at my N word issue, before you even pause to think: well, that's a bit odd, innit? . . . Don't tell me you're any better at No than I am. I simply will not believe you.

I'm not big on telling you what to do. You may have noticed.

And yet, if I did offer you one piece of advice, it'd be this: say No more. Say it often. Say it loud, and with conviction, and like it's easy. And then say it again. Every time you're asked to do a thing, or go to a thing, or say a thing, or act in a way, or endure a situation, or indulge a social nicety, or perform a task that makes you feel uncomfortable, or awkward, or exploited, or which simply does not suit you at that particular moment . . .

Pause.

Breathe deep.

Say, 'No.'

Oh, I know for a fact that I am not the only woman who struggles with the N word! I am not remotely rare in finding it a bugger to pronounce those two letters once they're placed in conjunction with each other. I was trained this way. So many of us are. It's one of the shittiest things we do to little girls en masse, teaching them not to say no. Never mind whether or not we overload them with gendered toys, with pink plastic shit and dress up princess dolls and Girl's Worlds. Never mind the debatable wisdom of telling them over and over that they're pretty while forgetting to tell them they're clever or funny.

Urging them towards smiling compliance, to nodding and agreeing and submitting and perpetual people pleasing and cod-eagerness to do all the things someone else wants them to do the moment they tell them to do it . . . That's the biggie. That's the fucker. Intermingling all ideas of being kind, helpful and good with that compulsion to say: 'Yes!' 'OK!' 'Of course I will!' 'I'd love to!' (when in fact they mean: 'No!' 'Bugger off!' 'Isn't there someone else you can ask?') To respond to the opening gambit: 'Could I ask a favour . . .?' with: 'Sure! Anything! Name it!', as opposed to: 'Depends what it is, dunnit?'

That's what hurts.

I mean, I guess it might be fine(-ish), if we were a) teaching little boys to do it, too, and b) hard-wiring ideas of boundaries into everyone involved. But we're not. Instead, we're training up our little girls to have a massive disadvantage in all future life wranglings. To endlessly indulge other people's whims. To put absolutely everyone else before themselves, in all imaginable situations. To go waaaaaay out of their way to service the demands of other people, none of whom necessarily have the best interests of our little girls at heart. We're training them up to eventually go out on dates with men they don't especially fancy, just because they were so persistent in the asking, and it seemed cruel to say, 'Nah mate. I just think I'm too good for you.' To sleep with people they don't really want to sleep with, because they've somehow ended up kissing them and going back to theirs, and now changing their minds and summoning an Uber seems unthinkable; not least because whoever-he-is is so convinced that having sex with him is a fab idea, and who is that former little girl to contest his will, to 'no' him? To stay in relationships which no longer suit them, because they're completely inexperienced in the art of dishing out the ultimate 'no' – which is rejection.

We're training them to take on far more than their fair share of work, over and over again, because saying no to an authority figure – to an actual boss! – is among the most forbidden of nos.

To go for coffee with dullards who are good at making them feel guilty if they reach around for yet another excuse to postpone. To lend money they can't afford to lend, or don't want to lend, to people they kind of know will never pay it back. To take on chores which aren't really theirs to perform, to put their name to causes they don't honestly support, to indulge cold callers for far longer than they should.

And through all this, *because* of all this – we're doing something which is ultimately much worse than setting up our little girls for a billion individual intrusions on their time and energy. We're telling them that every last one of their own desires isn't all that significant, or reliable, or legit. Not when pitted against the desires of someone who isn't them, it isn't. We're dooming them to an eternity of hefty time taxation; of minutes, hours, days and weeks devoted to the service of others, all of which could have been devoted to the realisation of their own hopes and dreams, to the reading – or writing! – of excellent novels, to the studious learning by rote of pop lyrics, to blissful nap-ping interludes. We're also, in all probability, predisposing 'em to passive aggression on account of all the suppressed fury they'll harbour while feeling instinctively obligated to JUST SAY YES. And to seething, long-term holding of grudges. And to cancer.[1]

I bear the emotional scars (and the passive aggression, oh – 100 per cent with the PA!) of a woman who's spent a lot of her life saying Yes, when she meant No. Of saying 'Sure!', when I meant 'Go away'. Or 'Don't be cheeky!' Or 'I'm too bloody busy sorting out my own life, to pick up the slack on yours.' Or 'No I won't do you that favour, because I've already done you four on the trot, and I cannot think up a single time that you helped me out in any way at all.' Or 'Actually, I don't want to have a drink with you because you're depressing and spiky and you always leave me with a day-after-downer of epic proportions.'

My name is Polly, and I am criminally bad at No.

Oh, I'm trying to get better. I am! You find me about a year into a Yes Recovery Programme of my own devising. I am making something which approaches progress. I do this thing a friend of a friend suggested: every time I manage to successfully turn someone down in some situation or other, I make a note of it on my iPhone. At the end of a calendar month, I contemplate all the Nos, work out whether or not I regret any of them, calculate how much time I've land-grabbed back for myself, give myself the same time back again to fritter away however I choose.

---

1 No, I have no proof of this bit.

My No Memoirs run something like this:

6 Jan

Depressing S asks if we can have lunch. I say I've got a deadline. Depressing S goes: 'Maybe next week?', I go: 'Maybe!' while thinking: 'Never!' She goes: 'I'll mail you!' I think: 'I'll pretend never to get that!'

Regret Factor: zilch.

Emotional repercussions: healthy! I do not have to decompress from undiluted exposure to Depressing S's assorted neuroses, her conviction that K secretly hates her (which, btw, K *does*), her tendency to try and unload some of her self-loathing onto me via the medium of bitchy asides re my life.

Time re-appropriated: two hours, fifteen minutes, although lunch with Depressing S always feels so much longer than that, so in terms of emotional tedium avoided, we're probably talking, like, a full week!

14 Jan

K asks me to write a thing I do not want to write for his section of the newspaper. I go: 'I'm too busy.' (He goes: 'It'll take you an hour, max!' I go: 'No, it won't. The research alone will require longer than that AND YOU KNOW IT.' He goes: 'Oh, go on! It'll be fun!' I go: 'I don't think it will . . .' He goes: 'You promised me you'd do this when we had a drink.' I go: 'Did I? I don't think I did . . .' He goes: 'Totally!' I go: 'Even so, I've really got a lot on, it just isn't practical . . .' He goes: 'OK, but I'll get INSERT NAME OF PROFESSIONAL NEMESIS HERE to do it instead, and THEN you'll be sorry . . .' I go: 'I can live with that,' while wondering if I can. He goes: 'You *never* do the things I want you to do!' and finally gives up.)

Regret factor: minimal. I mean: I've given up cash money payment for the piece, plus I've willingly given it over to INSERT NAME OF PROFESSIONAL NEMESIS HERE, but I haven't had to go out of my mind attempting to meet two deadlines simultaneously, which is never good for the mental health, or the skin.

Emotional repercussions: I suppress mounting panic over having to repeat the No so many times, and some paranoia re the certainty I'll soon find myself workless and broke and wondering if K will ever ask me to write for him again given that I proved so unreliable that time . . . But I recover from both quickly.

Time re-appropriated: a day and a half.

Et cetera.

It's a process.

Here's what I've learned:

1) I find it easier to No people in a professional capacity than in a personal one, what with the emotional stakes being lower.

2) Excusing myself from something I don't wish to do by feigning illness, or by invoking the feigned illness in others, is not a great way to proceed. It's dishonest and it doesn't contribute to the ultimate endgame, which is the assertion of my own will. I have to own my No.

3) You can tell a lot about the person you're dealing with by how easily they tolerate your No. The very best among them accept a No with ease and good grace, without subtly punishing you on account of it (either in the moment, or later), without reading it as a bigger rejection of who they are and what they stand for and without attempting to get you to agree to some lesser variant of their initial request. This lot are the good eggs. Spend more time with the people you find it easy to No.

In addition to which, I am enormously enjoying playing around with the different forms of No. Different phrasings, different gambits, different tactics. I've discovered that, by allowing a few hours – days, even – to elapse before replying to a text or email demanding that I do something I don't much want to do, the initial energy in the request will dissipate, my reluctance will have made itself apparent and any No I issue won't come as much of a surprise to whoever. I've discovered that it's best to accompany a No with minimal explanation: more credible, more dignified, more succinct. I've decided that any request issued via the medium of a Round Robin email can be ignored immediately, not least because I loathe the expression 'Round Robin'.[2]

And I've discovered some extremely fun turns of phrase, all of which I'd like to share with you, with a view to you trying a few of them out for size.

No for Beginners

'I would, but someone got in first with a better offer.'
Which might be a joke. But then again . . .

'I'm a bit stretched.'
The Swiss Army knife of Nos, this phrase can be deployed in almost all situations, on account of its superb opaqueness. It could denote financial issues, or scheduling issues, or emotional difficulties; it hints at obligations more noble and dramatic than the one whoever is trying to inflict upon you. And it's always going to be at least a little bit true: who isn't somewhat stretched, by something or other, at any given moment in time? Precisely! (Stolen from M, who recommends using it sparingly for ultimate impact.)

'I don't do deals on the doorstep.'
A form of No originally developed by my friend Mag,

---

2 I also loathe the expression 'Secret Squirrel'. Something to do with the misappropriation of woodland creature references.

with the specific purpose of getting shot of anyone who cold-called her house and tried to sign her up to charity donation schemes, but which (I've since found) can banjax almost anyone attempting to get an unwilling Yes out of you, on account of it being simultaneously obscure and absolute. Plus, such glorious alliteration!

'I think, on reflection . . . I won't do this. You understand.'

This is a magnificently grand way of No-ing, which simultaneously flatters the person you're refusing with implied intimacy ('You know me well enough to know why I can't do this, we needn't be specific, need we?'), while also quietly suggesting that you're just slightly too important to waste your precious time on the whatever. Simon Cowell would use this No if he was trying to be nice. So would Dame Judi Dench.

'Problem is, I don't really see what's in this for me.'

Advanced No-ing, the subtext of which is: 'I can totally see what's in it for you, however.' Should be deployed if the person you are attempting to No has come back with three or more reiterations of the initial request.

Related:

'Well, I would, *but* . . . it isn't really very Me, is it?'

Subtext: I'm going to leave you guessing re the true

nature of Me, which should put you off asking me to do things I don't want to do for a while.

Also related:

'That doesn't work for me.'
Subtext: And things working for me *is* an issue, in case that wasn't clear.

'Bleurgh.'
Plus accompanying 'I'm being sick' gesticulation. Jolly, yet definitive.

'I don't really do that kind of thing. Blanket policy.'
Subtext: Nothing personal . . . I just have rules, is all.

'Oh, you are funny!'
A little beauty of a No, which suggests you can't believe the asker is serious, so cheeky/inappropriate/demanding is their request. With any luck, they'll roll with your assessment of the situation; if they don't, a follow-up 'I don't think so, do you?' should make your position quite clear.

'I'm genuinely interested: why did you think it was OK to ask me to do this for you?'
For all your most annoying one-favour-too-far situations.

'Nice offer. But on reflection: No.'

Good in a sex scenario.

'I'm flattered; but no.'

Ditto.

'I think it's a bit ... I would say "soon", but I suppose what I actually mean is "... unappealing".'

As above. OK, OK, I'm showing off. But you know. Maybe.

'I'm too old, too rich and too well-dressed for that shit.'

The dream. The end goal. The No-iest, most nuclear motherlode of all possible Nos.

24

Everything Else You Ever Wanted To Know About Hot Feminism, But Were Too Afraid To Ask

Twerking

Not with *my* knees, sadly.

And as a bigger point, should you find yourself raging against the super-sexual imagery that permeates pop music – for which twerking became the byword, circa 2013 – against the discrepancy which dictates that Miley Cyrus (arch twerker) must sexualise herself, but Kanye West need not – direct it at the broader cultural moment, never, ever at the young women who comply.

Taylor Swift

Genius. Poet. Instinctive feminist, whose music empowers, and whose tendency to destroy her ex-boyfriends in her lyrics teaches her fans much about their capacity to unleash hell on any man who crosses them. Also, she's really surprisingly tall. Also: I just love her, OK?

Taking Your Husband's Surname

I wouldn't do it. I'm a writer, my name is my professional currency. Plus it scans nicely, don't you think (dah-dah DAH-dah)? Plus I wouldn't get married in the first place. I've always seen it as admitting defeat. But enough about me: if changing your surname isn't the purest of feminist acts (which it isn't; so much admin to declare your allegiance to some bloke), nor is it one of the things that matters. It's hardly going to derail the feminist process if you go all Mrs. So take your husband's name if you want to, my sweets; you'll get no beef from me. (I gotta say, I struggle harder with the custom of automatically giving children their father's surname. Surely the byline, the main credit for the planet's legions of screaming, highly breakable puke-makers belongs to the individuals who suffered significant agonies, and were nearly rent in two, during the process of giving the little flesh dollies life, i.e. their mothers?)

Topless Sunbathing

Yes, yes, fine; just use SPF 30 or higher, will you?

Swearing

Fucking brilliant.

Women's Magazines

Women's mags get a bad rap from feminist quarters. They're broadly viewed as enslaved to advertisers; sex- and/or celebrity- and/or fashion-obsessed, generally reductive about a woman's position in the world, lightweight and bitchy.

For pretty much the entirety of my career, I've worked on both women's magazines and broadsheet newspapers. I flip between writing for the two – sometimes on the same day, sometimes within the same hour – constantly. I do not dumb down for the women's mags, nor do I compromise my politics (feminist and otherwise).

Newspapers are wonderful places. From a professional perspective, they're the love of my life. However, they are also incredibly male environments. They are still largely run by men, which skews their content towards men – and which means that for a woman they are tough places to work. You walk into a newspaper as a woman, and you are a bit Other. Probably outnumbered, often outranked; on quiet days in the newsroom, the TV will be turned to a football match, groups of men will assemble beneath the screens to watch, and to jingle the change in their pocket as they semi-silently commune – and who gives a fuck if you, woman employee, happen to be on deadline and could do without the raucous crowd? As a female journalist working at a women's mag, you know absolutely that your gender is not an issue, because the vast majority of your colleagues are female, and because your audience is female.

In terms of women's magazine content – it's not perfect, from a feminist perspective, not at all, but nor is any kind of media. Papers, TV, and so on and so forth . . . We are all of us impacted by commercial and sales concerns, and by straightforward blind prejudice. But we are all also trying. We work within the parameters that we have, we slip our messages and our beliefs through, under the wire – and increasingly, over the wire – quietly and consistently and in any way we can. That is part of the skill, and part of the fun. We also know that our readership is not stupid, or vulnerable, or necessarily looking for anything other than a quick, joyful, diversionary flick on a lunchtime. That the readers of a women's mag also read newspapers and blogs and watch *Newsnight*, same as anyone else. To assume they treat women's mags as some sort of solemn bible on How To Live And What To Know, and that therefore women's mags need to honour their responsibility as The One True Guider Of Women, is a bit silly.

Selfies

A hideously bad idea. The voluntary decanting of all our currency and power and sense of our selves into a series of digitally manipulated, carefully filtered, precisely angled head shots which we know are at best semi-representative of what we actually look like (never mind, who we actually are), and which we then post online in the vague hope that a bunch of people we don't know terribly well, whose opinion of us is neither here nor there, will be moved to tell us we look all pretty. Bonko. Batshit. Daft. It's also, if you ask me, a new ground zero of our communal burgeoning body image issues. All those unrealistic, beautiful images of celebrities and models so often identified as ground zero on the mass body hating – none of them would be nearly so affecting if we weren't feeling the pressure to constantly publish image of ourselves, too; if we weren't feeling increasingly like we can and should look good in digital Facebook images, as well as in the flesh. Unlike the beautiful celebs – we don't have to do this. It is our immense privilege and good fortune that we don't have to invite judgement of photographic images of ourselves. So why on earth would we give that up? Hot Feminists, hear me: we will lose this battle, unless we stop taking multiple, carefully curated pictures of ourselves, and posting them online. Only sadness and madness can possibly result from our selfie habit.

Twitter
Fools heed the trolls, arseholes retweet the praise.

FOMO
The easiest way of addressing FOMO – the social networking perpetuated anxiety that everyone else in the world is having a better time than you are, going to better parties or on better holidays, wearing better clothes and in the company of better people – is to gently remind yourself that if you're not there, doing whatever it is they're doing: well! How much fun can they *really* be having? (Also: no one who is having the time of their lives, also has time to tweet.)

It Bags

Overrated, overpriced, tricky to store. I prefer a mid-range, mid-priced bag no one else has got yet.

Drugs

No one ever took cocaine with a view to making herself more interesting (and being more interesting = the ultimate end goal).

Sexy Back-Up Dancers

It will be to my eternal chagrin that I never was one.

Sexist Hip Hop Lyrics

Silly little boys.

Niqabs and Burkas

Oh, I struggle with this! My instinct tells me: no woman should hide herself from the world because her religion dictates it, and on the grounds that her husband will enjoy her more if he can revel in the knowledge that she is generally unlooked upon, his special treat to lust over in private. But then, I don't believe in any god so what do I know about any act of religious faith? Nothing. And how can I possibly defend a woman's right to wear anything she likes – to wear as little as she likes, or as many hats as she likes, or as much skintight body-con as she likes, regardless of her age – while simultaneously decrying this specific clothing choice? I just *can't*.

And yet, and yet, and yet . . .

The Onward Rumbling 'Where Are All The Decent Female Role Models?' Debate

Utter tosh! Partly because the entry point for 'good female role model' is so much higher than it is for men, of whom we just don't expect all that much in the first place. They play sport, you say? Gosh! They are good role models, aren't they? They haven't left their wife yet? Bow down before their moral grandeur!

On top of which, the expression 'bad female role model' has become a useful non-specific sort of an insult at the disposal of anyone hoping to take a specific woman down a peg or two, without having to define precisely what it is she's done wrong because basically: they aren't really sure. They just don't approve of her very much. Often, the coded meaning of 'bad female role model' is 'blatantly sexual individual' or, if you'd rather, 'slut'; see Miley Cyrus (arch-twerker) and Kim Kardashian, to whom the 'bad role model' label is often applied, for further deets.

When we say 'Oh, how I wish there were more good female role models knocking about!' what we actually mean is 'Oh, I wish celebrity women would be a bit better behaved, a bit less inclined to get quasi-naked and make sex tapes which get leaked by the dastardly ex-boyfriends they should totally have known better than to date in the first place, the little idiots . . . Even though, yeah, I'll admit it, I dated my fair share of raging dickheads at their age, it's just that I wasn't famous, so nobody cared . . .' Which isn't that reasonable a position to maintain, when you think about it. And PS: it is not a pop star's job to be a good role model. It is a pop star's job to be a good pop star, which – if you're doing it right – mainly involves debauchery and extremely small clothes and drunkenness and generally acting pretty much the exact opposite of 'good female role model'.

Abs

The most feminist of all erogenous zones, the consequence of hard work and dedication, the physical expression of core strength. A structural, physical integrity which (in an ideal world) hints at an interior sort of integrity.

Kate Moss

She's never openly declared herself a feminist, but no worries. A woman doesn't have to to be empowering nonetheless, and there's something thrilling about the way Moss – a bloody woman, let's not forget – has steadily and consciously accumulated huge power and mountains of dosh; and there's something even more thrilling about the way she – again, a woman – lives exactly the way she wants, with no pretence of apology or attempt at explanation.

Victoria Beckham

Like Moss, I've never heard VB declare herself a feminist, yet there's something so definitive about the way this woman lives her life, something self-determined, something I find entirely empowering by example. Beckham is a self-made woman in a new and very female sense of the expression, she's the ultimate consequence of nothing more than her own endless, tireless hard work; and heaven knows, I love a grafter.

Madonna

If the Youngsters of Now learn about sex from free porn, I learned about it from Madonna; from her lyrics, her visuals, her videos and her conical bras, which taught me how I could and should think about sex, about how fine it is for a woman to be predatory and unashamed. Madonna made me feel great about sex at a time it really mattered – when I was just about to start having it. I owe her a big fat debt for that. I find the chorus of sniggering, the finger pointing, the 'C-RINGE' commentary directed her way as she gets older pretty shoddy. It's quite as if we think age is some punishment she deserves, but for what, precisely? For teaching a million teenage girls to like sex?

TV's Apparently Insatiable Hunger For Crime Dramas Which Revolve Around The Abduction, Imprisonment, Defilement And Murder Of Scores Of Pretty Young Women

Boring. And also, unrealistic. Those sorts of fetishistic serial killings almost never happen. And *also* also: this is what we consider a jolly evening's entertainment? Because we find endlessly revisited variations on and depictions of women's fear, violation, lurid death, et cetera, to be ... *diverting*?

Because we just really dig the notion of women as perpetual victims? And while we're on the subject:

The Victimification Of Women

Duff. So very duff! Stuff is not brilliant for women, there's a shitload of work still to be done, but it needs to be approached from a position of strength and possibility, not from a place of: oh, poor us! We *are* victims of some stuff, of some situations, and certainly of a general injustice; but we must not define ourselves as victims. We are winning some battles, reformatting some wars. We are also: badly behaved, contradictory, naughty, funny, silly, messy, and more than capable of making a victim of someone else – all of which is preferable to, and more powerful than, occupying a perennial victim role. Part of the struggle for increased equality is the struggle to be allowed to just be bad, some times.

Staying Up All Night

It all just goes onto repeat after 3 a.m. Truth.

Banter

The precise point at which teasing flirtation tips into something more aggressive, and infinitely less agreeable. It's also a deeply annoying word.

Gendered Words

Adjectives almost uniquely applied to women, which carry with them stigma. Bossy, shrew, whore, bitch, gossip, witch, nag, et cetera. By far the simplest way to deffuse and de-gender this lot is to apply them to men at least as often as you apply them to women, if not more; heaven knows, they're as relevant when directed menwards.

Diet Coke

Nectar. One of the main feminist food groups. A thrill, a treat; a carbonated, beautifully-branded, singularly eloquent love song to the modern female condition.

Unflagging And Unquestioning Allegiance To The Sisterhood

The central feminist principle that we favour and embrace and support and admire and even *love*, all other women, at all times . . . which is clearly highly unrealistic. Sometimes, other women will annoy you. Sometimes, you will hate another woman's fucking guts. Sometimes, they will do you a wrong so unforgivable they become your biggest nemesis and you swear vengeance upon their souls and I WILL NOT REST, BTW, UNTIL I HAVE SET THE WRONG YOU DID ME RIGHT AND YOU KNOW WHO YOU ARE, DON'T YOU? *DON'T YOU?* YEAH YOU DO . . .

Sorry.

Got a little lost there.

Anyway.

The notion of sisterhood is gorgeous in theory, but unworkable in practice. I wouldn't believe you for a heartbeat if you said you loved all women. Far too many of us are

356

vile, or not playing by the same rules, and that's without taking into account the very real issue of how violently our personalities can clash, on account of there being so very many of us, every last one of whom is perilously different to the rest. The American politician and diplomat Madeleine Albright once said: 'There is a special place in hell for women who don't help other women,' and while I commend her intentions, I also think she hasn't met some of the women I've met, the kind who'll view another woman's willingness to help them as a readily exploited sign of weakness, because, of course, being a woman doesn't predispose you to being a good person. In addition to which: no one ever expected a man to go out of his way to help another man. No bloke ever stopped to think: am I being nice enough to the new guy in the office? Am I being adequately supportive? Maybe I should give him a little smile next time I see him, ask if he'd like a cup of tea, that sort of thing . . .

No.

They did not.

The myth of the sisterhood is a chink in feminism's armour, it means that any sort of woman-on-woman aggro can be perceived as proof that feminism is a lie, or a joke, or a façade; when women-on-women aggro is often entirely legitimate, an inevitable consequence of our burgeoning ambition, or our increasing desire to assert ourselves, or Twitter.

However, I do believe we are all somewhat capable of

instinctive animosity towards another woman based on a regrettable, generalised, conditioned, subconscious and entirely faux notion we're in competition with each other to get our hands on some man's sperm. I did it, only last month: two friends and I went to Paris for a weekend, ended up in a jovial bar at about 1 a.m., into which walked three staggeringly gorgeous, tall and glamorous women, whom my friends and I instantly decided were probably prostitutes, on the grounds that they were too pretty by half and we were too drunk.

Not hot.

It's important to check the origins of your rage against any other chick. Is it rational? Do you know her in some meaningful way? Did the consequences of her actions do you some quantifiable damage? That sort of thing. Always reserve hating another woman's fucking guts for when she does you up like a kipper, in a real and measurable way. You don't want to be wasting that sort of emotional energy on the bikini-friendly contestant on this season's *I'm A Celebrity . . . Get Me Out Of Here!*, or that journalist lady you hate reading so much, only you just don't seem to be able to stop . . .

Kindness

Proceed with it; but never confuse it with meekness, subservience, self-defeating acts of people pleasing, or softness.

Actually, scratch that last one

A little softness is just fine.

Acknowledgements

With enormous thanks to

Hannah Black, Veronique Norton and Elizabeth Caraffi at
Hodder & Stoughton; my agents Gordon Wise at Curtis
Brown, and Josh Varney and Mady Niel at 42. Nicola Jeal
(for making me the best journalist I could be) and Jane
Bruton and Marianne Jones (for giving me time off the day
job to book-write). Robert Lee for checking out the contracts; Michelle Kane, Emily Dean, Elizabeth Day and
Vicky Harper for cheerleading and early reading. Everyone
whose thoughts and theories I have quoted, misquoted,
bastardised and borrowed without asking.

And The Man I Keep In My Flat, who never told me not to
write anything I wanted to.